Islamic Art

Islamic Art

N Farukh

MD Publications Pvt Ltd
New Delhi
www.mdppl.com

Published by :

MD Publications Pvt Ltd
"MD House", 11, Darya Ganj,
New Delhi - 110 002
Phone : +91-11- 45355555
E-mail : contact@mdppl.com
Website: www.mdppl.com

ISBN : 978-81-7533-307-9

Published and Printed by Mr. Pranav Gupta on behalf of **MD Publications Pvt Ltd** at Repro India Limited.

Preface

Islamic art is perhaps the most accessible expression of a complex civilization that often seems enigmatic to outsiders. Through its brilliant use of color and its superb balance between design and form, Islamic art creates an immediate visual impact. Its strong aesthetic appeal transcends distances in time and space, as well as differences in language, culture, and creed. Islamic art not only invites a closer look but also beckons the viewer to learn more.

The term Islamic art may be confusing to some. It not only describes the art created specifically in the service of Islam, but it also characterizes secular art produced in lands under Islamic rule or influence, whatever the artist's or the patron's religious affiliation. The term suggests an art unified in style and purpose, and indeed there are certain common features that distinguish the arts of all Islamic lands. Although this is a highly dynamic art, which is often marked by strong regional characteristics as well as by significant influences from other cultures, it retains an overall coherence that is remarkable given its vast geographic and temporal boundaries.

Calligraphy is the most important and pervasive element in Islamic art. It has always been considered the noblest form of art because of its association with the Qur'an, the Muslim holy book, which is written in Arabic. This preoccupation with beautiful writing extended to all arts - including secular manuscripts; inscriptions on palaces; and those applied to metalwork, pottery, stone, glass, wood, and textiles - and to non-Arabic-speaking peoples within the Islamic commonwealth whose languages - such as Persian, Turkish, and Urdu - were written in the Arabic script.

Another characteristic of Islamic art is a preference for covering surfaces with patterns composed of geometric or vegetal elements. Complex geometric designs, as well as intricate patterns of vegetal ornament (such as the arabesque), create the impression of unending repetition, which is believed by some to be an inducement to contemplate the infinite nature of God. This type of nonrepresentational decoration may have been developed to such a high degree in Islamic art because of the absence of figural imagery, at least within a religious context.

Royal patronage played an important role in the making of Islamic art, as it has in the arts of other cultures. The construction of mosques and other religious buildings, including their decoration and furnishings, was the responsibility of the ruler and the prerogative of high court officials. Such monuments not only provided for the spiritual needs of the Muslim community but often served educational and charitable functions as well. Royal patronage of secular art was also a standard feature of Islamic sovereignty, one that enabled the ruler to demonstrate the splendor of his court and, by extension, the superiority of his state.

I am very grateful to Mr. Pranav Gupta, Director of MD Publications Pvt Ltd, New Delhi, for his kind cooperation and support for this book.

N Farukh

Contents

1

Islamic Art
An Introduction

The term 'Islamic art' not only describes the art created specifically in the service of the Muslim faith (for example, a mosque and its furnishings) but also characterizes the art and architecture historically produced in the lands ruled by Muslims, produced for Muslim patrons, or created by Muslim artists. As it is not only a religion but a way of life, Islam fostered the development of a distinctive culture with its own unique artistic language that is reflected in art and architecture throughout the Muslim world.

The lands newly conquered by the Muslims had their own pre-existing artistic traditions and, at least initially, those artists who had worked under Byzantine or Sasanian patronage continued to work in their own indigenous styles but for Muslim patrons. The first examples of Islamic art, therefore, rely on earlier techniques, styles, and forms reflecting this blending of classical and Iranian decorative themes and motifs.

Even religious monuments erected under Umayyad patronage that have a clearly Islamic function and meaning, such as the Dome of the Rock in Jerusalem, demonstrate this amalgam of Greco-Roman, Byzantine, and Sasanian elements. Only gradually, under the impact of the Muslim faith and nascent Islamic state, did a uniquely Islamic art emerge. The rule of the Umayyad Aliphate (661–750) is often considered to be the formative period in Islamic art. One method of classifying the Islamic art, used in Islamic galleries at the Metropolitan Museum, is according to the dynasty reigning when the work of art was produced. This type of periodization follows the general precepts of Islamic history, which is divided into and punctuated by the rule of various dynasties, beginning with the Umayyad and Abbasid dynasties that governed a vast and unified Islamic state, and concluding with the more regional, though powerful, dynasties such as the Safavids, Ottomans, and Mughals.

With the spread of its geography and long history, Islamic art was inevitably subject to a wide range of regional and even national styles and influences as well as changes within the various periods of its development. It is then all the more remarkable that even under these circumstances Islamic art has always retained its intrinsic quality and unique identity. Just as the religion of Islam embodies a way of life and serves as a cohesive force among ethnically and culturally diverse people, the art produced by and for Muslim societies has basic identifying and unifying characteristics. Perhaps the most salient of these is the predilection for all-over surface decoration. The four basic components of Islamic ornament are calligraphy, vegetal patterns, geometric patterns, and figural representation.

Calligraphy

Calligraphy is the highly regarded and the most fundamental element of Islamic art. It is significant that the Qur'an, the book of God's revelations to Prophet Muhammad, was transmitted in Arabic, and that the inherent within the Arabic script is the potential for developing a variety of ornamental forms. The employment of calligraphy as ornament had not only definite aesthetic appeal but also often included an underlying talismanic component. While most works of art had legible inscrip-tions, not all Muslims would have been able to read them. However, one should always keep in mind that calligraphy is principally a means to transmit a text, albeit in a decorative form.

Objects from different periods and regions vary in the use of calligraphy in their overall designs, demonstrating the creative possibilities of calligraphy as ornament. In some cases, calligraphy is the dominant element in the decoration. In these examples, the artist exploits the inherent possibilities of the Arabic script to create writing as an ornament. An entire work may give the impression of random brushstrokes, or a single letter may develop into a decorative knot. In other cases, highly esteemed calligraphic works on paper are themselves ornamented and enhanced by their decorative frames or backgrounds. Calligraphy can also become part of an overall ornamental program, clearly separated from the rest of the decoration. In some cases, calligraphy may be combined with vegetal scrolls on the same surface, though often on different levels, creating interplay of decorative elements.

Vegetal Patterns

Vegetal patterns employed alone or in combination with the other major types of ornament—calligraphy, geometric pattern, and figural representation—adorn a vast number of buildings, manuscripts, objects, and textiles, produced throughout the Islamic world. Unlike calligraphy, of which an increasingly popular use as ornament in the early Islamic Arab lands represented a new development, vegetal patterns and the motifs they incorporate were drawn from existing traditions of Byzantine culture in the eastern Mediterranean and Sasanian Iran.

The early centuries of the Islamic era saw the initial adoption of seminaturalistic pre-Islamic motifs and patterns, followed by widespread and highly diverse experimentation adapting these forms to suit the aesthetic interests and tastes of the new Muslim patrons. It was not until the medieval period (tenth–twelfth centuries) that a highly abstract and fully developed Islamic style emerged, featuring the most original and ubiquitous pattern often known as "arabesque." This term was coined in the early nineteenth century following Napoleon's famed expedition in Egypt, which contributed so much to the phenomenon of Orientalism in Europe and later in the United States. Arabesque simply means 'in the Arab fashion' in French and few scholars of Islamic art use it today.

With the Mongol invasion of western Asia in the thirteenth century and the establishment of a Mongol court in Iran in the thirteenth and fourteenth centuries, numerous Chinese motifs and patterns were adopted, though sometimes in markedly revised form. This period saw many transformations in the decorative language of Islamic art that would endure for centuries. In sixteenth-century Europe, first in Italy and then in the North, Islamic-style vegetal patterns were developed. In the sixteenth- and seventeenth-centuries, Empires of the Ottomans, Safavids, and Mughals (present-day Turkey, Iran, and India), complicated versions of established patterns were utilized, sometimes incorporating a new interest in naturalistic-looking flowers or blossoms. With the exception of the garden and its usual reference to paradise, vegetal motifs and patterns in Islamic art are largely devoid of symbolic meaning.

Geometric Patterns

Geometric patterns make up one of the three nonfigural types of decoration in Islamic art which also include calligraphy and vegetal patterns. Whether isolated or used in combination with nonfigural ornamentation or figural representation, geometric patterns are popularly associated with Islamic art, largely due to their aniconic quality. These abstract designs not only adorn the surfaces of monumental Islamic architecture but also function as the major decorative element on a vast array of objects of all types. While geometric ornamentation may have reached a pinnacle in the Islamic world, the sources for both the shapes and the intricate patterns already existed in late antiquity among the Greeks, Romans, and Sasanians in Iran. Islamic artists appropriated key elements from the classical tradition and then, complicated and elaborated upon them in order to invent a new form of decoration that stressed the importance of unity and order. The significant intellectual contributions of Islamic mathematicians, astronomers, and scientists were essential to the creation of this unique new style.

Consisting of or generated from such simple forms as the circle and the square, geometric patterns were combined, duplicated, interlaced, and arranged in intricate combinations and, thus, becoming one of the most distinguishing features of Islamic art. However, these complex patterns seem to embody a refusal to adhere strictly to the rules of geometry. As a matter of fact, geometric ornamentation in Islamic art suggests a remarkable amount of freedom; in its repetition and complexity, it offers the possibility of infinite growth and can accommodate the incorporation of other types of ornamentation as well. In terms of their abstractness, repetitive motifs, and symmetry, geometric patterns have much in common with the so-called arabesque style seen in many vegetal designs. Calligraphic ornamentation also appears in conjunction with geometric patterns.

The four basic shapes, or "repeat units," from which the more complicated patterns are constructed are: circles and interlaced circles, squares or four-sided polygons, the ubiquitous star pattern ultimately derived from squares and triangles inscribed in a circle and, multisided polygons. It is clear, however, that the complex patterns found on many objects include a number of different shapes and arrangements, allowing them to fit into more than one category.

Figural Representation

With the spread of Islam outside the Arabian Peninsula in the seventh century, the figurative artistic traditions of the newly conquered lands profoundly influenced the development of Islamic art. Ornamentation in Islamic art came to include figural representations in its decorative vocabulary, drawn from a variety of sources. Although the often cited opposition in Islam to the depiction of human and animal forms holds true for religious art and architecture, in the secular sphere such representations have flourished in nearly all Islamic cultures.

The Islamic resistance to the representation of living beings ultimately stems from the belief that the creation of living forms is unique to God and, it is for this reason that the role of images and image makers has been controversial. The strongest statements on the subject of figural depiction are made in the Hadith (Traditions of the Prophet), where painters are challenged to "breathe life" into their creations and threatened with punishment on the Day of Judgment. The Qur'an is less specific but condemns idolatry and uses the Arabic term musawwir ("maker of forms," or artist) as an epithet for God. Partially, as a result of this religious sentiment, figures in painting were often stylized and, in some cases, the destruction of figurative art-works occurred. Iconoclasm was previously known in the Byzantine period and aniconicism was a feature of the Judaic world, thus, placing the Islamic objection to figurative representations within a larger context. As ornament, however, figures were largely devoid of any larger significance and perhaps, therefore, posed less challenge.

As with other forms of Islamic ornamentation, artists freely adapted and stylized basic human and animal forms, giving rise to a great variety of figural-based designs. Figural motifs are found on the surface decoration of objects or architecture, as part of the woven or applied patterns of textiles, and, most rarely, in sculptural form. In some cases, decorative images are closely related to the narrative painting tradition, where text illustrations provided sources for ornamental themes and motifs. As for manuscript illustration, miniature paintings were integral parts of these works of art as visual aids to the text, therefore no restrictions were imposed. A further category of fantastic figures, from which ornamental patterns were generated, also existed. Some fantastic motifs, such as harpies (female-headed birds) and griffins (winged felines), were drawn from pre-Islamic mythological sources, whereas others were created through the visual manipulation of figural forms by artists.

New Visual Language Transmitted Across Asia

In the creation of luxury textiles and objects for the Mongol elite, Chinese artists developed a visual language that was an effective means of establishing their rule and consolidating their presence throughout the vast Empire. A number of motifs that were part of the existing artistic repertoire were adopted as imperial symbols of power and dominance—the dragon and the phoenix, for example, two mythical beasts that integrated the ideas of cosmic force, earthly strength, superior wisdom, and eternal life. The Mongol versions of the creatures are the highly decorative sinuous dragon with legs, horns, and beard and the large bird with a spectacular feathered tail floating in the air (12.49.4). In Iran, these motifs were often paired and became so popular with the Ilkhanids that they eventually lost their original meaning, becoming part of the common artistic repertoire in the first half of the fourteenth century.

Other motifs of this period that were familiar throughout the Asian continent are the peony, the lotus flower (91.1.559), and the lyrical image of the recumbent deer, or djeiran, gazing at the moon. The flowers, often seen in combination and viewed from both the side and top, provided ideal patterns for textiles and for filling dense backgrounds on all kinds of portable objects. The djeiran became widespread in the decorative arts because of the well-established association of similar quadrupeds with hunting scenes.

For the semi-nomadic Mongols, portable textiles and clothing were the best means of demonstrating their acquired wealth and power, so it is reasonable to assume that the main mode of transmission of motifs such as the dragon and peony was through luxury textiles. The most prominent clothing accessories were belts of precious metal (gold belt plaques, The Nasser D. Khalili Collection of Islamic Art). Many of the textiles illustrated here prove transmission from east to west, yet in some instances, exemplified by the Chinese silk with addorsed griffins (cloth of gold: winged lions and griffins, The Cleveland Museum of Art), the origin of the image is clearly Central or western Asia. The Mongol period is unique in art history because it permitted the cross-fertilization of artistic motifs via the movement of craftsmen and artists throughout a politically unified continent.

The Age of Süleyman "the Magnificent" (r. 1520–1566)

Under Süleyman, popularly known as "the Magnificent" or "the Lawmaker," the Ottoman Empire reached the apogee of its military and political power. Süleyman's armies conquered Hungary, over which the Ottomans maintained control for over 150 years, and they advanced as far west as Vienna, threatening the Habsburgs. To the east, the Ottoman forces wrested control of Iraq from the Safavids of Iran. In the Mediterranean, their navy captured all the principal North African ports, and for a time the Ottoman fleet completely dominated the sea. By the end of Süleyman's reign, Ottoman hegemony extended over a great portion of Europe, Asia, and Africa.

Along with geographic expansion, trade, economic growth, and tremendous cultural and artistic activity helped define the reign of Süleyman as a "Golden Age."

Developments occurred in every field of the arts; however, those in calligraphy, manuscript painting, textiles, and ceramics were particularly significant. Artists renowned by name include calligrapher Ahmad Karahisari as well as painters Shahquli and Kara Memi.

In architecture, the most outstanding achievements of this period were the public buildings designed by Sinan (1539–1588), chief of the Corps of Royal Architects. While Sinan is often remembered for his two major commissions, the mosque complexes of Süleymaniye in Istanbul (1550–57) and of the later Selimiye in Edirne (1568–74), he designed hundreds of buildings across the Ottoman Empire and contributed to the dissemination of Ottoman culture. Apart from mosques and other pious foundations—including schools, hospices, and soup kitchens, supported by shops, markets, baths, and caravanserais—Süleyman also commissioned repairs and additions to major historical monuments. The tile revetment of the Dome of the Rock in Jerusalem, as well as several additions to sites in Mecca and Medina, the two Holy Cities of Islam date from this period.

Art and Nationalism in Twentieth-Century Turkey

With the dissolution of the Ottoman sultanate and the establishment of the Republic of Turkey in 1923, artists and politicians alike called for a new kind of art to represent the fledgling nation. While there was a general agreement on the rejection of the last flowering of Ottoman art, no single, all-encompassing style emerged to replace it. The early years of the Republic saw the rise of dozens of new schools of art and the energetic organization of many young artists.

Representative of this period was the simultaneous existence of the Association of Independent Painters and Sculptors, founded in 1928, and the D Group, started in 1933. Members of the former preferred folkloric scenes, as reflected in the work of Cevat Dereli or Turgut Zaim, while the latter was a more heterogeneous collection of artists.

Some members such as Nurullah Berk worked in a painterly mix of European and Turkish styles; others, like Çemal Tollu, took on the more abstract influences of Cubism and Constructivism, or worked in an abstract manner with a political bent, like Abidin Dino.

Alongside this work undertaken by the artists themselves was an official exploration of the nation's arts. Mustafa Kemal Atatürk, first president of the Republic (1923–38), sought to revise a number of aspects of Turkish culture and to stress the ancient heritage and village life of the country. Thus it was thought important to remove all Arabic and Persian cultural influences, including use of the Arabic alphabet and easternized forms of dress. To revitalize the countryside, hundreds of "People's Houses" were opened. These were in one way community centers, where theater productions were staged and films screened. They also functioned as preservation societies, where work by local artists was exhibited, and songs by local musicians recorded. Following in this vein, Atatürk's successor Ismet Inönü (1938–50) instituted the Provincial Tours for Painters, which, between 1938 and 1944, sent ten artists each year to live and work in different parts of the country. During this period, large numbers of lifesize portraits and statues of Atatürk were commissioned, such as the portrait by Nazmi Ziya Güran. His image functioned as a symbol of modernity and thus was displayed publicly, a practice that continues today. Images of Atatürk are seen everywhere in Turkey and contemporary artists such as Nese Erdok continue to celebrate his legacy in a contemporary idiom.

Simultaneous to this Turkicizing movement, Europe continued to inform the education and aesthetics of Turkish artists. Government grants allowed students to study abroad, and foreign artists were hired to teach in the Turkish academies. Sculpture was introduced at this time, and Rudolf Belling of Germany came to head the department at the Academy of Fine Arts in 1937. Realizing the propagandizing potential of this medium, the government commissioned a number of public works to commemorate the War for Independence and the role Atatürk played in it.

Architecture also took a page from the European scene. The new capital of Ankara was to be a symbol of Turkey's modern future and a strong contrast to the country's ancient past, epitomized by Istanbul. Thus the city's development represented a vastly different approach from later Ottoman works such the Dolmabahçe Palace. The German urban planner Hermann Jansen won the competition for the city's master plan in 1927, and the new governmental center was deliberately located across town from the ancient citadel.

This was designed by the Austrian Clemens Holzmeister as a triangular complex with the Grand National Assembly at its apex. While some feel that the Ankara architecture was not truly in the International Style it was meant to be, the difference from the Ottoman period was obvious; it sufficed that these stark concrete buildings with no ornament were clearly not of the old school.

Soon after the influx of European architects and their integration into the education system, Turkey began to produce its own modernist architects. Sevki Balmumcu designed the 1933–34 Ankara Exhibition Hall, and Aptullah Ziya constructed the Ministry of Foreign Affairs Residence in the same year. Atatürk's mausoleum (completed in 1955), designed by Emin Onat and Orhan Arda, is an austere building combining the Turkish tradition of the türbe and the Anatolian tradition of the mausoleum in a new, modern manner. The involved participation of Turkish architects is reflected in the writings of the journal Mimar (founded in 1931, later called Arkitekt).

In the realm of painting, the government arranged a number of important shows, including the Exhibition of Paintings of the Revolution, held on the tenth anniversary of the declaration of the Republic, and the State Exhibition of Painting and Sculpture, which was held annually for a number of years. While showcasing the work of young artists, these exhibits also represented the first attempts at ordering, preserving, and classifying modern painting. Particularly notable in this regard was Fifty Years of Turkish Art, the show that opened the museum at the Dolmabahçe Palace in 1937.

While in general Atatürk's achievements were lauded, literature of the early Republican period also recorded the angst of the Turkish people who were caught between reform and tradition, and the sudden changes forced upon them. Reaction against the adoption of European modernism in architecture was allowed fuller expression after the death of Atatürk in 1938. Thus the building of the Turkish Historical Society by Turgut Cansever and Ertur Yener (Ankara, 1966), which won the Aga Khan Award for architecture, utilizes the basic form of the Turkish house with a plain facade and protected interior court together with modern building materials. The return to Turkish roots was reflected in the cinema of these years as well. Certain directors claimed that their aesthetics came from Turkish painting and their pacing from traditional storytelling styles.

Since the 1940s, Turkish art has followed Western trends while retaining a link to local idioms. Artists such as Adnan Turani and Burhan Dogançay, both members of the calligraphic movement, used the forms of Islamic calligraphy as a point of reference. Their work was a response to Atatürk's abandonment of the Arabic in favor of the Latin script.

The Art of Nishapur (Mid 9th–Early 12th Century)

Nishapur began to assume major influence from the mid-ninth century A.D., becoming in the tenth through twelfth centuries one of the great political, commercial, and cultural centers in medieval Iran and the Islamic world. The richest oasis and chief city of the eastern Iranian province of Khorasan, Nishapur was well situated along the Silk Road across which goods were exchanged between the Far and Near East. Excavations were undertaken by the Iranian Expedition of the Metropolitan Museum from 1935 to 1940, with a final season in 1947. The excavations were spread over several different mounds, or tepes, that revealed the residential quarters as well as a palace or a governmental building. The material unearthed at Nishapur, of high artistic as well as documentary importance, was produced locally and traded, paralleling the city's political and commercial prominence.

Special mention should be made of the advanced development of the underglaze-painting technique seen in Nishapur's ceramic wares. It was presumably in eastern Iran or the immediately adjacent part of Central Asia that slip painting under a transparent lead-fluxed glaze was first put to use (in the ninth century), and it was in these regions that this technique reached perhaps its highest peak of refinement. In the eleventh and twelfth centuries, a new type of pottery began to take precedence; one which featured white bodies made of ground and compounded silicaceous materials.

Nishapur was also an important center for the manufacture of glass, metal, and stone vessels as well as textiles. None of the latter was found in the excavations, no doubt, due to their highly perishable nature. However, beautifully decorated spindle-whorls were excavated by the hundreds. Smaller items such as toys, game pieces, musical instruments, and beads help to throw light on everyday activities in Nishapur and give us a better understanding of its ongoing life.

Architecture and architectural decoration were also highly developed at Nishapur. A refined tradition of wall painting, revealed by the excavations, shows links with Buddhist Central Asia and Sasanian tradition as well as with ninth-century painting of Aliphal Iraq. Carved stucco decoration, perennially important in Iranian architecture, is most notably represented by the reconstruction of a small iwan, or hall, of the tenth century (from the mound called Sabz Pushan), whose dadoes must have given an even more sumptuous visual effect before the loss of their polychrome painting.

The Art of the Abbasid Period (750–1258)

Under the Abbasid Aliphate (750–1258), which succeeded the Umayyads (661–750) in 750, the focal point of Islamic political and cultural life shifted eastward from Syria to Iraq, where, in 762, Baghdad, the circular City of Peace (madinat al-salam), was founded as the new capital. The Abbasids later also established another city north of Baghdad, called Samarra' (an abbreviation of the sentence "He who sees it rejoices"), which replaced the capital for a brief period (836–83). The first three centuries of Abbasid rule were a golden age in which Baghdad and Samarra' functioned as the cultural and commercial capitals of the Islamic world. During this period, a distinctive style emerged and new techniques were developed that spread throughout the Muslim realm and greatly influenced Islamic art and architecture.

Since the style set by the capital was used throughout the Muslim world, Baghdad and Samarra' became associated with the new artistic and architectural trend. As virtually nothing remains from Abbasid Baghdad today, the site of Samarra' is particularly significant for understanding the art and architecture of the Abbasid period. In Samarra', a new way of carving surfaces, the so-called beveled style, as well as a repetition of abstract geometric or pseudo-vegetal forms, later to be known in the West as "arabesque," were widely used as wall decoration and became popular in other media such as wood, metalwork, and pottery. In pottery, Samarra' also witnessed an extensive use of color in decoration and, possibly, the introduction of the technique of luster painting over a white glaze. Admired for its glittering effect reminiscent of precious metal, luster painting, the most notable technical achievement at the time, spread in the following centuries from Iraq to Egypt, Syria, Iran, and Spain and eventually also contributed to the development of ceramic decoration in the Western world. In terms of architecture, along with the palace of Jawsaq al-Khaqani (ca. 836 onward), the mosques of al-Mutawakkil (848–52) and Abu Dulaf (859–61) in Samarra' were important in setting the style that was emulated in regions as far as Egypt or Central Asia, where it was adapted to need and taste.

In the tenth century, Abbasid political unity weakened and independent or semi-autonomous local dynasties were established in Egypt, Iran, and other parts of the realm. Following the capture of Baghdad by the Buyids (932–1062) and Seljuqs (1040–1194) in 945 and 1055, Abbasid Aliphs retained little more than moral and spiritual influence as the heads of Orthodox Sunni Islam. The Abbasid realm witnessed a brief revival under Aliphs al-Nasir (r. 1180–1225) and al-Mustansir (r. 1226–42), when Baghdad once again became the greatest center for the arts of the book in the Islamic world and the Mustansiriyya Madrasa (1228–33), the first college for the four canonical schools of Sunni law, was built. However, this burst of artistic vitality came to a temporary halt with the sack of Baghdad by the Ilkhanid branch of the Mongols in 1258. Though surviving Abbasids fled to Mamluk Egypt, these Aliphs would only have nominal influence. The end of the Abbasid Aliphate thus marked the end of the universal Arab-Muslim Empire.

The Art of the Almoravid and Almohad Periods (ca. 1062–1269)

The Almoravid dynasty (al-Murabitun, ca. 1062–1150), a newly emerged Islamic power in North Africa, ethnically more Berber than Arab, conquered Morocco and founded Marrakesh as its capital in 1062. Led by Yusuf ibn Tashufin, the Almoravids entered al-Andalus (Islamic Spain) after the fall of Toledo in 1085 in response to the Ta'ifa leaders' pleas for help in repelling the Christian armies of northern Spain. They assumed control of al-Andalus in 1090, while maintaining their primary seat of government in Marrakesh. In this way, the Almoravids came to rule parts of the Sahara, Morocco, Algeria, and Spain and controlled important ports as well as trans-Saharan trade.

Repudiating the lack of piety and what they considered to be the decadence of the Ta'ifa kings, and following the conservative Malikiyya school of Islamic law, the Almoravids disdained as well the opulent arts of the Spanish Muslims. Although they began by sponsoring austere programs of architectural decoration, their later monuments and textile manufactory in Almería indicate that the Almoravids eventually succumbed to the luxury culture of al-Andalus. Especially spectacular from this period is the minbar from the Kutubiyya Mosque, Marrakesh, commissioned in 1137 by the last Almoravid sultan, Ali ibn Yusuf (r. 1106–42), for his congregational mosque. In North Africa, the mosques of Algiers (ca. 1097), Tlemcen (1136), and Qarawiyin in Fez (1135) are important architectural examples from this period.

In the mid-twelfth century, the Almoravids were replaced by the Almohads (al-Muwahhidun, 1150–1269), a new Berber dynasty from North Africa. By 1150, the Almohads had taken Morocco as well as Sevilla, Cordoba, Badajoz, and Almería in the Iberian Peninsula. The Almohads made Sevilla their capital in al-Andalus, while retaining Marrakesh as their center of power in North Africa. Following the Almohad defeat by the combined armies of Aragon and Castile at the Battle of Las Navas de Tolosa in 1212, a turning point in the peninsula's history, al-Andalus once again fractured into tribute-paying principalities, vulnerable to the depredations of Christian kingdoms. These principalities, except for Nasrid-ruled Granada, soon lost their sovereignty.

As religious reformation was integral to the Almohad establishment, their courts in Marrakesh and Sevilla became centers of Islamic learning. In Almohad arts, a rigorous style saw the increasing schematization of ornament and the continued use of geometric design. The Great Mosque and the minaret called La Giralda, which they built in Sevilla, are paradigms of Almohad style. In North Africa, architectural developments included the walls of Fez, Rabat, and Marrakesh and the mosques of Taza (1142), the Kutubiyya (Marrakesh, 1147–58), Tinmal (1153–54), the Qasba (Marrakesh, 1195), and Hasan (Rabat, 1199; unfinished).

The Art of the Ayyubid Period (ca. 1171–1260)

The Ayyubid dynasty came to power under the leadership of the Kurdish Zengid general Salah al-Din (r. 1169–93), known in Europe as Saladin. After repulsing a Crusader army that had reached the gates of Fatimid Cairo and occupying Egypt on behalf of the Zengids (1160s), Salah al-Din declared the Fatimid Aliphate to be at its end, and established the Ayyubid sultanate (1171). Soon thereafter, Salah al-Din also gained control over Yemen (1174) and Syria (1180s). The conflict with the Crusaders continued throughout the Ayyubid period; Jerusalem was captured by the Muslims in 1187, then, following a failed treaty, ceded until 1244, when the city was retaken for good. The sultanate depended on mamluks (slave soldiers) for its military organization, yet the end of the dynasty in 1250 was largely caused by Turkic mamluks themselves, who overthrew the last Ayyubid sultan in Egypt, al-Malik al-Ashraf (r. 1249–50) and founded the Mamluk sultanate (1250–1517).

In the arts, the Ayyubids are known especially for their works in inlaid metalwork and ceramics, particularly luster- and underglaze-painted wares. Some objects from this period, including a group of inlaid metalwork pieces, also have Christian scenes. Signatures of artists on refined and prized brass works inlaid with silver seem to indicate that the craftsmen were from Mosul (in present-day Iraq) and had fled from the approaching Mongol armies. In the case of ceramics produced in Syria, the influence of Seljuq Iran is prevalent. Among other arts, enameled glass rose to excellence in this period and carved wood was also esteemed by Ayyubid patrons. Techniques established and developed during this time formed the foundation of the arts in the Mamluk period.

The Ayyubids were also vigorous builders. Their generous patronage led to tremendous architectural activity in Egypt and especially in Syria, and their local courts revived the cities of Damascus and Aleppo. The outstanding secular architecture from this period includes the fortified citadels of Cairo (1187) and Aleppo (early thirteenth century). Meanwhile, the establishment of madrasas, higher institutions for religious learning, such as the Zahiriya (1219) in Aleppo and that of Salih Najm al-Din Ayyub (1243) in Cairo, exemplify the Ayyubid interest in Sunni education after the Shici interlude in the region under the Fatimids. Furthermore, the Madrasa al-Sahiba in Damascus (1233), built by Salah al-Din's sister Rabia Khatun, as well as the Mausoleum of Salih Najm al-Din Ayyub (1250), commissioned by his wife Shajarat al-Durr, reflects the importance of women as patrons of architecture under the Ayyubids. In terms of commemorative buildings and pious architectural initiatives, the Mausoleum of Imam al-Shafici (1211) and the Tomb of the Abbasid Aliphs (1242–43) in Cairo are especially noteworthy.

The Art of the Fatimid Period (909–1171)

In the tenth to twelfth centuries, an area including present-day Algeria, Tunisia, Sicily, Egypt, and Syria came under the rule of the Fatimid dynasty (909–1171), an offshoot of a Shici sect from North Africa. The Fatimid rulers traced descent from Muhammad's daughter Fatima (hence Fatimid) via Ismacil, the seventh Shici imam, and thus presented a threat to the political and religious authority of the orthodox Sunni Abbasid Aliph. The circular design of the city of al-Mansuriya, one of their first capitals, founded in 947, can be interpreted as a deliberate challenge to the round city of Abbasid Baghdad, the "city of peace" (madinat al-salam). This opposition became more significant following the Fatimid conquest of Egypt in 969. At this time, the Fatimids founded the city of Cairo (al-Qahira, "the triumphant") and established it as their new capital (973). While Egypt came to enjoy enormous prosperity primarily due to its intermediary role in the lucrative trade between the Mediterranean and India, Cairo soon rivaled the Abbasid capital of Baghdad.

The opulence of the Fatimid court fueled a renaissance in the decorative arts, which made Cairo the most important cultural center in the Islamic world. Nearby, Old Cairo, known as al-Fustat, became a major center for the production of pottery, glass, and metalwork, and rock-crystal, ivory, and wood carving; textile factories run by government officials created tiraz fabrics in the name of the Aliph elsewhere in the Egyptian region, especially the Nile Delta. A novel, more refined style developed in pottery; bands with small animals and inscriptions now formed the major decoration in textiles; and rock-crystal carvers demonstrated great skill in works created for and treasured by the Aliphs themselves.

The artwork from this period exemplifies the creativity and ingenuity of Fatimid craftsmen. The technique of lusterware on ceramic, developed originally in Iraq, was revived in Egypt and Syria. Some lusterware pieces from this period are signed by their makers, an indication of the esteem in which the craftsmen were held. Wood carving and jewelry were executed with equal skill and inventiveness. Fatimid artists created new decorative motifs and made greater use of figural forms, both human and animal. Figures were stylized but lively, while traditional vegetal and geometric decorations maintained their abstract quality.

In architecture, the Fatimids followed Tulunid techniques and used similar materials, but also developed those of their own. In Cairo, their first congregational mosque was al-Azhar ("the splendid") founded along with the city (969–73), which, together with its adjacent institution of higher learning (al-Azhar University), became the spiritual center for Ismacili Shici.

The Mosque of al-Hakim (r. 996–1013), an important example of Fatimid architecture and architectural decoration, played a critical role in Fatimid ceremonial and procession, which emphasized the religious and political role of the Fatimid Aliph. Besides elaborate funerary monuments, other surviving Fatimid structures include the Mosque of al-Aqmar (1125) as well as the monumental gates for Cairo's city walls commissioned by the powerful Fatimid emir and vizier Badr al-Jamali (r. 1073–94).

The Art of the Ilkhanid Period (1256–1353)

The Mongol invasions of the Islamic world began in 1221 with the conquest of eastern Iran. A more devastating wave of conquest, however, came with Genghis Khan's grandson Hülegü, when Mongol forces subjugated all of Iran and by 1258 had also taken Baghdad, thus bringing to an end the Abbasid Aliphate (750–1258).

Establishing rule over most of West Asia, including Iraq, Iran, Khorasan, the Caucasus, and parts of Asia Minor, Hülegü (r. 1256–65) assumed the title of "Il-Khan," meaning lesser Khan, subordinate to the Great Khan ruling in China. This branch of the Mongol dynasty, which became known as the Ilkhanids (1256–1353), centered its power in northwest Iran.

Although Mongol conquests initially brought devastation and affected the balance of artistic production, in a short period of time, the control of most of Asia by the Mongols—the so-called Pax Mongolica—created an environment of tremendous cultural exchange. Following the conversion to Islam of the Il-Khan Ghazan (r. 1295–1304) in 1295 and the establishment of his active cultural policy in support of his new religion, Islamic art flourished once again. East Asian elements absorbed into the existing Perso-Islamic repertoire created a new artistic vocabulary, one that was emulated from Anatolia to India, profoundly affecting artistic production.

During the Ilkhanid period, the decorative arts—textiles, pottery, metalwork, jewelry, and manuscript illumination and illustration—continued along and further developed established lines. The arts of the book, however, including illuminated and illustrated manuscripts of religious and secular texts, became a major focus of artistic production. Baghdad became an important center once again. In illustration, new ideas and motifs were introduced into the repertoire of the Muslim artist, including an altered and more Chinese depiction of pictorial space, as well as motifs such as lotuses and peonies, cloud bands, and dragons and phoenixes. Popular subjects, also sponsored by the court, included well-known stories such as the Shahnama (Book of Kings), the famous Persian epic. Furthermore, the widespread use of paper and textiles also enabled new designs to be readily transferred from one medium to another.

Along with their renown in the arts, the Ilkhanids were also great builders. The lavishly decorated Ilkhanid summer palace at Takht-i Sulayman (ca. 1275), a site with pre-Islamic Iranian resonances, is an important example of secular architecture. The outstanding Tomb of Uljaytu (built 1307–13; r. 1304–16) in Sultaniyya, however, is the architectural masterpiece of the period. Following their conversion to Islam, the Ilkhanids built numerous mosques and Sufi shrines in cities across Iran such as Ardabil, Isfahan, Natanz, Tabriz, Varamin, and Yazd (ca. 1300–1350). After the death of the last Ilkhanid ruler of the united dynasty in 1335, the Empire disintegrated and a number of local dynasties came to power in Iraq and Iran, each emulating the style set by the Ilkhanids.

The Art of the Mamluk Period (1250–1517)

The Mamluk sultanate (1250–1517) emerged from the weakening of the Ayyubid realm in Egypt and Syria (1250–60). Ayyubid sultans depended on slave (Arabic: mamluk, literally "owned," or slave) soldiers for military organization, yet mamluks of Qipchaq Turkic origin eventually overthrew the last Ayyubid sultan in Egypt, al-Malik al-Ashraf (r. 1249–50) and established their own rule. Their unusual political system did not rely entirely on family succession to the throne—slaves were also recruited into the governing class and hence the name of the sultanate later given by historians. Following the defeat of Mongol armies at the Battle of cAyn Jalut (1260), the Mamluks inherited the last Ayyubid strongholds in the eastern Mediterranean. Within a short period of time, the Mamluks created the greatest Islamic Empire of the later middle Ages, which included control of the holy cities Mecca and Medina.The Mamluk capital, Cairo, became the economic, cultural, and artistic center of the Arab Islamic world.

Mamluk history is divided into two periods based on different dynastic lines: the Bahri Mamluks (1250–1382) of Qipchaq Turkic origin from southern Russia, named after the location of their barracks on the Nile (al-bahr, literally "the sea," a name given to this great river), and the Burji Mamluks (1382–1517) of Caucasian Circassian origin, who were quartered in the citadel (al-burj, literally "the tower"). After receiving instruction in Arabic, the fundamentals of Islam, and the art of warfare, slaves in the royal barracks were manumitted and given responsibilities in the Mamluk hierarchy.

Art and Architecture under the Bahri Mamluks (1250–1382)

The Bahri reign defined the art and architecture of the entire Mamluk period. Prosperity generated by the east-west trade in silks and spices supported the Mamluks' generous patronage.

Despite periods of internal struggle, there was tremendous artistic and architectural activity, developing techniques established by the Ayyubids and integrating influences from different parts of the Islamic world. Refugees from east and west contributed to the momentum. Mamluk decorative arts—especially enameled and gilded glass, inlaid metalwork, woodwork, and textiles—were prized around the Mediterranean as well as in Europe, where they had a profound impact on local production. The influence of Mamluk glassware on the Venetian glass industry is only one such example.

The reign of Baybars's ally and successor, Qala'un (r. 1280–90), initiated the patronage of public and pious foundations that included madrasas, mausolea, minarets, and hospitals. Such endowed complexes not only ensured the survival of the patron's wealth but also perpetuated his name, both of which were endangered by legal problems relating to inheritance and confiscation of family fortunes. Besides Qala'un's complex, other important commissions by Bahri Mamluk sultans include those of al-Nasir Muhammad (1295–1304) as well as the immense and splendid complex of Hasan (begun 1356). These structures were emulated by high-ranking officials and influential emirs who built similar foundations, such as the complex of Salar and Sanjar al-Jawli (begun 1303) and that of the emir Shaykhu (1350–55).

Art and Architecture under the Burji Mamluks (1382–1517)

The Burji Mamluk sultans followed the artistic traditions established by their Bahri predecessors.

Although the state was faced with its greatest external and internal threats in the early fifteenth century, including the devastation of the eastern Mediterranean provinces by the Central Asian conqueror Timur (Tamerlane; r. 1370–1405), as well as famine, plague, and civil strife in Egypt, patronage of art and architecture resumed. Mamluk textiles and carpets were prized in international trade. In architecture, endowed public and pious foundations continued to be favored. Major commissions in the early Burji period in Egypt included the complexes built by Barquq (r. 1382–99), Faraj (r. 1399–1412), Mu'ayyad Shaykh (r. 1412–21), and Barsbay (r. 1422–38).

In the eastern Mediterranean provinces, the lucrative trade in textiles between Iran and Europe helped revive the economy. Also significant was the commercial activity of pilgrims en route to Mecca and Medina. Large warehouses, such as the Khan al-Qadi (1441), were erected to satisfy the surge in trade. Other public foundations in the region included the mosques of Aqbugha al-Utrush (Aleppo, 1399–1410) and Sabun (Damascus, 1464) as well as the Madrasa Jaqmaqiyya (Damascus, 1421).

In the second half of the fifteenth century, the arts thrived under the patronage of Qa'itbay (r. 1468–96), the greatest of the later Mamluk sultans. During his reign, the shrines of Mecca and Medina were extensively restored. Major cities were endowed with commercial buildings, religious foundations, and bridges. In Cairo, the complex of Qa'itbay in the Northern Cemetery (1472–74) is the best known and admired structure of this period. Apart from his own patronage, Qa'itbay encouraged high-ranking officials and influential emirs to build as well. Building continued under the last Mamluk sultan, Qansuh al-Ghawri (r. 1501–17), who commissioned his own complex (1503–5); however, construction methods reflected the finances of the state. At this time, the Portuguese were gaining control of the Indian Ocean and barring the Mamluks from trade, their richest source of revenue. Though the Mamluk realm was soon incorporated into the Ottoman Empire (1517), Mamluk visual culture continued to inspire Ottoman and other Islamic artistic traditions.

The Art of the Mughals after 1600

After the death of Akbar, architect of the Mughal Empire and active patron of the arts, his son Jahangir (r. 1605–27) ascended to the throne. As a prince, Jahangir had established his own atelier in Allahabad and had strong artistic tastes, preferring a single painter to work on an image rather than the collaborative method of Akbar's time. He also encouraged careful plant and animal studies, and prized realistic portraiture and Europeanized subjects. The books Jahangir commissioned ranged from literary works such as the Razmnama (a Persian translation of the Hindu epic, the Mahabharata) to historical texts, including an illustrated version of the memoirs of his reign, the Tuzuki Jahangiri. But more common from his era are lavishly finished albums containing paintings and calligraphy samples mounted onto pages with decorative borders and then bound with covers of stamped and gilded or painted and lacquered leather. If he could not obtain a work he wanted, he had it copied, and at one time dispatched an artist to Iran to paint a likeness of ShahAbbas.

Jahangir's claim that he could instantly recognize any painter's work is a reflection of the rise of the individual artist. Many signatures are preserved on works from this period, with such masters as Bishan Das, Manohar, Abu'l-Hasan, Govardhan, and Daulat emerging as recognizable artistic personalities.

Jahangir's successor Shah Jahan (r. 1628–58) is most celebrated for his architectural achievements, the Taj Mahal being his (and perhaps the country's) best known monument. He commissioned this tomb for his wife after her death in 1631 and it took sixteen years to complete.

The building is set on the bank of the Jumna River in Agra with a formal eightfold garden and reflecting pools in front, its elevation of inlaid white marble striking against the red sandstone of the other buildings in the complex. After moving the capital from Agra to Delhi in 1648, Shah Jahan built a new city there, called Shahjahanabad, and a congregational mosque (1650–56), the largest in all of India. Paintings from his reign were characterized by formal portraits and courtly scenes, replacing the more wide-ranging and personal subject matter under Jahangir. The major commission of his reign was a history called the Padshahnama, illustrated through the 1640s.

Shah Jahan's rule was forcibly terminated by his son in 1658. Aurangzeb (r. 1658–1707) held increasingly orthodox Sunni beliefs, and his reign saw the decline of Mughal patronage of the arts. Early portraits of him do exist, and he commissioned some notable architectural projects such as the Pearl Mosque (in the Red Fort at Delhi), but in 1680 he banned music and painting from his court. The emperors who followed him were too weak and the state too poor to support the production of sumptuous paintings and books as before; under Bahadur Shah (r. 1707–12) and Muhammad Shah (r. 1719–48), there was a slight resurgence in the arts, but the 1739 raid of Delhi by Nadir Shah caused much of the city's population to flee and the artistic community to be permanently dispersed. By the 1800s, the Mughals were nominally still emperors of India, but under the protection of the British.

The reduction of artists in the Mughal painting workshops by Jahangir, Shah Jahan, and Aurangzeb meant that a number of artists had to find new work, and many regional courts benefited greatly from the influx of former imperial employees. Painting at the Hindu Rajasthani courts such as Bikaner, Bundi, and Kota, and at the provincial Muslim courts of Lucknow, Murshidabad, Faizabad, and Farrukhabad, were all transformed as Mughal artists provided fresh inspiration. Among the important subimperial patrons of the early period was Abd al-Rahim Muhammad Khan-i Khanan (1561–1626/7), commander-in-chief of the Mughal armies under both Akbar and Jahangir. A copy of the epic Ramayana (1597–1605)—with 130 illustrations—and six other manuscripts can be attributed to his atelier.

The late Mughal era was also a fruitful period for the provincial and regional patronage of architecture. The maharaja Jai Singh founded the city of Jaipur, known for its palaces and astronomical observatory built in 1734, and Safdarjang, the nawab of Oudh, erected a tomb in Delhi based on that of Humayun (1753–4).

The Art of the Mughals before 1600

The dynasty founded by Babur, the Mughal dynasty, ruled over the greatest Islamic state of the Indian subcontinent. As a youth, Babur, a prince of the house of Timur, was unable to maintain his sovereignty over the small Central Asian state bequeathed to him by his father. Instead, he turned his attention to the southeast, where he occupied Kabul in 1504, and almost immediately thereafter embarked on his conquest of India. By 1527, Babur had defeated both the forces of the Lodi sultan and those of the Hindu confederacy. However, at the time of his death, in 1530, he had not yet transformed his territorial acquisitions into an Empire. This task was left to Humayun, Babur's son and successor, who unfortunately lacked the military genius of his father and soon forfeited the Mughal foothold in India. Only through Persian military intervention did he manage to regain the capital cities of Agra and Delhi in 1555. Yet it is Humayun's son Akbar who can be credited with the real foundation of the Mughal Empire.

During his reign, which lasted nearly fifty years (1556–1605), Akbar established dominion over northern and central India, as far east as Bengal. He secured the northwestern frontier, gateway to India for so many previous invasions, through his control of Kabul. Akbar's most important territorial gain was the sultanate of Gujarat, in the west, which provided the Mughal Empire with enormous wealth from its commercial centers, as well as access to the Arabian Sea and hence opportunity for lucrative trade with both the Europeans and the Ottoman Empire. Unlike his grandfather, Akbar succeeded in consolidating the Empire and establishing a strong administrative system. He was deeply interested in spiritual and religious issues, and in 1582 formulated a new code of religious behavior. Weekly discussions at court included not only representatives of various Muslim religious communities but also non-Muslim theologians including Hindus, Jains, Christians, Jews, and Zoroastrians.

Akbar was also the first great Mughal patron of the arts. Of his various building projects, the most ambitious was the new capital city of Fatehpur Sikri, near Agra. Built mostly between 1571 and 1585, when Akbar adopted Lahore as his principal residence, the palace buildings at Fatehpur Sikri reflect a synthesis of Timurid traditions of Iran and Central Asia with indigenous traditions of Hindu and Muslim India.

Although he is said to have been illiterate, Akbar assembled a royal atelier, first at Fatehpur Sikri, then at Lahore, from which he commissioned numerous illustrated manuscripts that incorporate Persian, Indian, and even European elements. In fact, the artists who worked for Akbar, the first great Mughal patron of the arts of the book, included Persians as well as Indian Muslims and Hindus. This collaborative process helped to foster the development of a specifically Mughal style, which was initiated under Akbar and is demonstrated by pages from diverse late-sixteenth-century manuscripts. This style of painting was further developed and refined during the reigns of Jahangir and Shah Jahan during the seventeenth century.

The Art of the Nasrid Period (1232–1492)

Founded by Muhammad I al-Ghalib of Arjona (r. 1232–73), the Nasrid dynasty ruled Granada and neighboring Jaén, Almería, and Málaga in the southern Iberian Peninsula. The early period of Nasrid rule was characterized by insistent pressure from Christian armies from the north, which successfully conquered Valencia, Játiva, and Jaén and made the Nasrids tribute-paying vassals in 1243. The Nasrids formed tentative alliances with the Marinids of the Maghrib and kept uneasy peace with their Christian overlords. Despite its precarious political situation, for over two and a half centuries Granada served as a great cultural center of the Muslim West, attracting leading scholars and literati of the day. Severe political crises in the Maghrib in the fifteenth century, combined with the union of the Christian kingdoms of Castile and Aragon through the marriage in 1469 of Ferdinand and Isabella, whose avowed mission was the expulsion of the Muslims from the Iberian Peninsula, proved to be the downfall of the Nasrids. The last Nasrid ruler, Muhammad XII (called Boabdil by Spanish historians), was exiled to the Maghrib on January 2, 1492. The termination of Nasrid rule also brought to an end almost 800 years of an Islamic presence on the Iberian Peninsula.

During the fourteenth century, the Nasrid sultans dedicated themselves to the decoration of their splendid palaces. Their most singular artistic achievement was the famous Alhambra (al-qalca al-hamra), or the red castle, so-called perhaps because of the color of the walls and towers that surround the citadel. Situated on a hill overlooking Granada, the Alhambra was conceived as more than a well-fortified palace—it was a royal city. The creation of a succession of Nasrid rulers, in particular Ismacil I (r. 1314–25), Yusuf I (r. 1333–54), and Muhammad V (r. 1354–59, 1362–91), the Alhambra was a powerful image for a waning monarchy, a vast stage set for the diminishing power of the last Muslim rule on the peninsula. Work on the palace-city continued for nearly two centuries; the resulting architectural complex, with its intricate succession of rooms and courts, its rich interior facades, and its numerous gardens, fountains, and watercourses, is one of the most magnificent examples of Islamic architecture.

Nasrid arts grew from Almohad traditions but displayed far more variety and splendor than their precursors. Textiles recall the rich interior settings of the Alhambra. Also important are ceramics overglaze-decorated in luster, a technique dating back to ninth-century Iraq and dispersed to many parts of the Islamic world. Initially lusterware was manufactured in Málaga, Murcia, Almería, and possibly Granada, but by the fifteenth century, Manises, near Valencia, supplanted Málaga as the main center of luster production. These Spanish luster-painted wares, whether produced under Muslim or Christian patronage, had an important impact on the ceramic industry of Italy, where they gave rise to the development of maiolica. The finest military arts that survive from al-Andalus are also from this period; the Nasrid's luxury arms, which were probably never used in battle, offer examples of a rich craft used to support a public image.

The Art of the Ottomans after 1600

In the early seventeenth century, both Ottoman book production and architecture remained traditional. The court scriptorium continued to produce its established series of texts—biographies, travel accounts, genealogies, and geographies—many of which were illustrated or illuminated. The Mosque of Ahmed I in Istanbul (1609–16), also known as the "Blue Mosque" because of the interior tile scheme, continues in the vocabulary of the great architect Sinan (1539–1588).

Later in the century, a weakening Ottoman economy began to affect the arts. An influx of gold and silver from the New World caused inflation and the treasury shrunk without military victories and booty to refill the coffers. The sultans were forced to reduce the number of artists they employed in the nakkaºhane (royal scriptorium) to ten from the high of over 120 in the time of Süleyman the Magnificent (r. 1520–66), and for many years did not increase the set prices they paid for ceramics, paintings, and carpets. It became more profitable for artists to produce items for the open market than to be tied to the workshops of the low-paying court, and sultans had to pass edicts forcing them to finish imperial commissions. One of the few arts that maintained a high level of quality was calligraphy. Hafiz Osman (1642–1698) was the master of this era, teacher to Sultan Mustafa II (r. 1695–1703) and his son, Sultan Ahmed III (r. 1703–30).

Under Ahmed III the arts revived. He built a new library at the Topkapi Palace and commissioned the Surnama (Book of Festivals, ca. 1720, Topkapi A.3593), which documents the circumcision of his four sons as recorded by the poet Vehbi. The paintings detail the festivities and processions through the streets of Istanbul, and were completed under the direction of the artist Levni (d. 1732), whose work is also known from a set of portraits collected in a Murakka (Topkapi H.2164). While his style was traditional, other artists of his time were greatly affected by the European prints and engravings that began to circulate in Ottoman lands.

Ahmed's reign is also known as the Tulip Period. The popularity of this flower is reflected in a new style of floral decoration that replaced the saz style of ornament with serrated leaves and cloud bands that had characterized Ottoman art for many years, and is found in textiles, illumination, and architectural ornament. The architecture of this period is exemplified in the monumental fountain constructed by Ahmed III outside the gate to the Topkapi Palace. Ambassadors dispatched to Paris and Vienna sparked further changes with their descriptions of the

Baroque architecture of Versailles and Fontainebleau, but many of the Baroque-inspired palaces built during Ahmed's reign were destroyed in the revolt that forced him to abdicate in 1730. The earliest building to survive is the Nuru Osmaniye Mosque (1748–55), begun by Mahmud I and finished by Osman III. Its flamboyant decoration, ornate moldings, and vegetal carvings are the hallmark of the style that continued into the nineteenth century.

The Art of the Ottomans before 1600

At the time of its foundation in the early fourteenth century, the Osmanli or Ottoman state was one among many small principalities that emerged as a result of the disintegration of the Seljuq sultanate in Anatolia and subsequent instability caused by Mongol rule. This embryonic Ottoman state, located on the frontiers of the Islamic world, gradually absorbed former Byzantine territories in Anatolia and the Balkans. In 1453, this expansion culminated in the Ottoman capture of Constantinople, the great capital of Eastern Christendom. With the conquest of the Mamluk Empire in 1517, the Ottomans ruled over the most powerful state in the Islamic world. By the middle of the sixteenth century, continued military success in an area extending from Central Europe to the Indian Ocean gave the Ottomans the status of a world power.

In the arts, there is a paucity of extant objects from the early Ottoman period, but it is apparent from surviving buildings that Byzantine, Mamluk, and Persian traditions were integrated to form a distinctly Ottoman artistic vocabulary. Significant changes came about with the establishment of the new capital in former Byzantine Constantinople. After the conquest, Hagia Sophia, the great Byzantine church, was transformed into an imperial mosque and became a source of inspiration for Ottoman architects. Mehmed II ("the Conqueror," r. 1444–46, 1451–81) envisaged the city as the center of his growing world Empire and began an ambitious rebuilding program. He commissioned two palaces (the Old and the New, later Topkapi, palaces) as well as a mosque complex (the Mehmediye, later Fatih complex), which combined religious, educational, social, and commercial functions. In his commissions, Mehmed drew from Turkic, Perso-Islamic, and Byzantine artistic repertoires. He was also interested in developments in Western Europe. Ottoman, Iranian, and European artists and scholars flocked to Mehmed's court, making him one of the greatest Renaissance patrons of his time.

Under Mehmed's successors, his eclectic style, reflective of the mixed heritage of the Ottomans, was gradually integrated into a uniquely Ottoman artistic vocabulary. Further geographic expansion brought additions to this vocabulary. Most significantly, the victory against the Safavids at a battle in eastern Anatolia (1514) and the addition of Mamluk Syria, Egypt, and the Holy Cities of Islam (Mecca and Medina) to the Ottoman realm under Selim I ("the Grim," r. 1512–20), led to the increased presence of Iranian and Arab artists and intellectuals at the Ottoman court.

The reign of Süleyman (popularly known as "the Magnificent" or "the Lawmaker"), often regarded as a "Golden Age," was defined by geographic expansion, trade, and economic growth, as well as cultural and artistic activity. The age of Süleyman (r. 1520–66) witnessed the zenith of Ottoman art and culture. Among the most outstanding achievements of this period were the mosques and religious complexes built by Sinan (1539–1588), one of the most celebrated Islamic architects. Hundreds of public buildings were designed and constructed throughout the Ottoman Empire, contributing to the dissemination of Ottoman culture. In the period following Süleyman's death, architectural and artistic activity was resumed under patrons from the imperial family and the ruling elite.

Commissions continued outside the imperial capital, with many pious foundations established across the realm.

During the late fifteenth and sixteenth centuries, developments occurred in every artistic field, with those in architecture, calligraphy, manuscript painting, textiles, and ceramics being particularly significant. Apart from Istanbul, various cities in the provinces were also recognized as major artistic and commercial centers: Iznik was renowned for ceramics, Bursa for silks and textiles, Cairo for the production of carpets, and Baghdad for the arts of the book. Ottoman visual culture had an impact in the different regions it ruled. Despite local variations, the legacy of the sixteenth-century Ottoman artistic tradition can still be seen in monuments from the Balkans to the Caucasus, from Algeria to Baghdad, and from Crimea to Yemen, that incorporate signature elements such as hemispherical domes, slender pencil-shaped minarets, and enclosed courts with domed porticoes.

The Art of the Safavids before 1600

In the early sixteenth century, Iran was united under the rule of the Safavid dynasty (1501–1722), the greatest dynasty to emerge from Iran in the Islamic period. The Safavids descended from a long line of Sufi shaikhs who maintained their headquarters at Ardabil, in northwestern Iran. In their rise to power, they were supported by Turkman tribesmen known as the Qizilbash, or red heads, on account of their distinctive red caps. By 1501, Ismacil Safavi and his Qizilbash warriors wrested control of Azerbaijan from the Aq Quyunlu, and in the same year Ismacil was crowned in Tabriz as the first Safavid shah (r. 1501–24). Upon his accession, Shici Islam became the official religion of the new Safavid state, which as yet consisted only of Azerbaijan. But within ten years, all of Iran was brought under Safavid dominion. However, throughout the sixteenth century, two powerful neighbors, the Shaibanids to the east and the

Ottomans to the west (both orthodox Sunni states), threatened the Safavid Empire.

In the arts, manuscript illustration was prominent in royal patronage. Ismacil's son, Tahmasp (r. 1524–76), who had been trained in painting at an early age, was an active patron of the arts of the book. Artists from the Qara Quyunlu, Aq Quyunlu, and Timurid court studios were brought together and their work helped form a new Safavid style of painting. One of the most renowned manuscripts from the period is a now-dispersed copy of the Shahnama epic (1970.301.2). Drawing inspiration from designs generated in the royal painting workshop, textiles and carpets were manufactured of luxury materials as furnishings for the court. In architecture, the Safavids commissioned mosques, mausolea, and palace complexes, restored major shrines, and contributed to sites of veneration and pilgrimage, though Shah Ismail is known to have built throughout his Empire, only the modest buildings of his reign survive. Text references and scattered remains indicate that Shah Tahmasp also sponsored numerous building projects, particularly at Qazvin, his capital after 1555, but little survives.

The most distinguished of Safavid rulers and the greatest patron of the arts was Shah Abbas (r. 1587–1629). His reign was recognized as a period of military and political reform as well as of cultural florescence. It was in large measure due to Abbas' reforms that the Safavid forces were able finally to defeat the Ottoman army in the early seventeenth century. Reorganisation of the state and the ultimate elimination of the powerful Qizilbash group that continued to threaten the authority of the throne brought stability to the Empire. In 1597–98, Shah Abbas transferred his capital to Isfahan, in southern Iran, where he built a new city alongside the old one. The centerpiece of his capital was the new Maidan-i Shah (Royal Square), which was conceived and constructed initially for state ceremonies and sports. Over the next several decades, major monuments would be erected on three sides of the Royal Square by Abbas and his successors. Shah Abbas encouraged trade with Europe, silk being Iran's main export. Carpets and textiles were also important export items, and these were produced in workshops set up under state patronage in Isfahan and other cities. The art of painting continued to flourish, with single-page paintings and drawings becoming more popular than manuscript illustration. Artistic and architectural developments under Shah Abbas continued into the early seventeenth century.

The Art of the Seljuq Period in Anatolia (1081–1307)

Following their conquest of Baghdad in 1055, the Seljuq dynasty, descendants of the Central Asian Turkic Oghuz tribe, soon established hegemony over most of West Asia, including present-day Iran, Iraq, and Syria. Raids on the Byzantine frontier eventually led to the Battle of Manzikert (modern Malazgirt in eastern Turkey) in 1071 and the resulting Seljuq victory opened Anatolia to Turkic settlement. A branch of the Seljuqs assumed rule from Nicaea (Iznik) in northwestern Anatolia (1078–81) and became known as the Seljuqs of Rum ("Rome"), referring to the Roman Byzantine past of the Seljuq territories.

Notwithstanding the advance of Crusader armies, battles against the Byzantines, and conflicts with neighboring rival Turkic principalities, the Seljuqs were able to establish uncontested authority following the Latin conquest of Constantinople during the Fourth Crusade (1204). The first half of the thirteenth century corresponds to the zenith of Seljuq power in Anatolia until they were defeated by the Ilkhanids, the Mongol dynasty ruling in Iran, at the Battle of Köse Dagh (1243), after which the Seljuqs became Mongol vassals. Especially during the reign of Ala' al-Din Kay-Qubadh (r. 1220–37), the Seljuq realm witnessed tremendous commercial, artistic, and cultural activity, the heart of which was the new Seljuq capital, Konya.

Apart from an earlier brief period of Arab rule in the east, Anatolia was new to Islam, and the Seljuqs were thus among the first to cultivate Islamic art and architecture in these lands. As heirs to the Great Seljuqs of Iran, the sultans of Rum adopted Perso-Islamic traditions and, for the most part, maintained established designs, materials, and techniques in their congregational mosques, madrasas (theological schools), mausolea, caravanserais, and palaces. The Ala' al-Din Mosque (1156–1220), the Karatay (1252) and Ince Minareli (1258) madrasas in Konya, the Sifahiye (1217–18) and Gök madrasas (1271) in Sivas, the Great Mosque and Hospital in Divrigi (1228–29), the Khuand Khatun complex in Kayseri (1237–38), and the Cifte Minareli Madrasa in Erzurum (1253) are among the important surviving examples of monumental Anatolian Seljuq architecture. In the arts, continued use of luster- and overglaze-painted tiles, as well as creations in wood and metal, are especially noteworthy.

Along with Perso-Islamic traditions, however, Anatolia had a strong Byzantine and Armenian Christian heritage, which now intermingled with Central Asian Turkic nomadic, northern Mesopotamian, and Crusader cultures. The exchange and synthesis of these different traditions is vividly reflected in Seljuq architecture and art. For instance, Gök Madrasa features carved stone, typical of Armenian architecture, alongside brick, a common material in Iran and Central Asia.

The Art of the Seljuqs of Iran (ca. 1040–1157)

The Seljuqs, a Turkic dynasty of Central Asian nomadic origins, became the new rulers of the eastern Islamic lands following their defeat of the powerful Ghaznavids at the Battle of Dandanakan (1040). By 1055, the Seljuqs had reached and taken over Baghdad, which put an end to

Buyid rule, and established themselves as the new protectors of the Abbasid Aliphate and Sunni Islam. Within fifty years, the Seljuqs created a vast though relatively short-lived Empire, encompassing all of Iran, Iraq, and much of Anatolia. By the close of the eleventh century, as the Seljuq realm became troubled due to internal conflicts and the division of the realm among heirs, the Empire dissolved into separate territories governed by different branches of the dynasty. The main branch of the Seljuq house, the so-called Great Seljuqs, maintained control over Iran. Under the Seljuq sultanate, Iran enjoyed a period of material and cultural prosperity, and the ingenuity in architecture and the arts during this period had a notable impact on later artistic developments.

The Seljuq cultural and artistic efflorescence continued well beyond the sultanate's political influence. In fact, as there are few surviving dated examples of Iranian art from the Seljuq period proper, works of art dating to the late twelfth and early thirteenth centuries are frequently labeled "Seljuq" even though they might have been produced under the patronage of one of several local dynasties. Turkic Seljuq rulers adopted and supported local Perso-Islamic traditions, and Seljuq art is recognized for weaving together Persian, Islamic, and Central Asian–Turkic elements. During this period, the arts of Iran gained distinction in the Islamic world.

Important developments and innovations contributed to the renown of Seljuq art. Beginning in the second half of the twelfth century, the art of inlaying bronze or brass objects with precious metals such as copper, silver, and gold became prominent in the eastern Iranian province of Khorasan. Such objects were often decorated with Arabic inscriptions written in the "animated" script, developed during this period, in which the letters were transformed into human and animal figures. The same shapes known in metalwork were also produced in contemporary pottery. These ceramic wares demonstrate the advancement of new techniques or the further refinement of existing ones. Especially notable were the works produced in Kashan, in the luster and mina'i techniques. Also significant, though little known today due to few surviving examples, were the arts of the book.

The Seljuqs were also great patrons of architecture. An unprecedented number of madrasas (institutions of higher learning) were erected throughout the Seljuq realm. Most notable, however, was the Madrasa Nizamiya, founded in Baghdad by the great Seljuq vizier Nizam al-Mulk (r. 1063–92) to support Orthodox Sunni education (1067). In mosque architecture, the courtyard with four vaulted halls (iwans) on each side became prevalent. The transformed congregational mosque in Isfahan whose additions were commissioned by Nizam al-Mulk and Taj al-Mulk, two Seljuq administrators, for Sultan Malikshah (r. 1073–92) and his wife Terkan Khatun, was the most celebrated and influential Seljuq monument. Also important during this period were funerary monuments, the most prominent being the immense Mausoleum of Sultan Sanjar in Merv (r. ca. 1096–1157), in modern Turkmenistan.

The Art of the Timurid Period (ca. 1370–1507)

The Timurids were the final great dynasty to emerge from the Central Asian steppe. In 1370, the eponymous founder, Timur (Tamerlane), who belonged to a Turko-Mongol tribe settled in Transoxiana, became master of this province and established Samarqand as his capital.

Within thirty-five years, he subjugated all of Central Asia, greater Iran, and Iraq, as well as parts of southern Russia and the Indian subcontinent. To the west, Timurid forces defeated the Mamluk army in Syria and that of the Ottomans at Ankara (1400–2). In 1405, while preparing to invade China, Timur died. The vast Empire he carved proved to be difficult to keep; his son and successor, Shahrukh (r. 1405–47), barely managed to maintain the

Empire's boundaries, and subsequent Timurid princes sought to establish their own kingdoms, weakening the Empire with internal strife. Eventually only Khorasan and Transoxiana remained Timurid, and during the remaining years of the dynasty, these were ruled by separate branches of the Timurid family.

By bringing craftsmen from different conquered lands to his capital in Samarqand, Timur initiated one of the most brilliant periods in Islamic art. Timurid art and architecture provided inspiration to lands stretching from Anatolia to India. Though Timur's extensive Empire itself was relatively short-lived, his descendants continued to rule over Transoxiana as leading patrons of Islamic art. Through their patronage, the eastern Islamic world became a prominent cultural center, with Herat, the new Timurid capital, as its focal point. Timurid rulers were sympathetic to Persian culture and lured artists, architects, and men of letters who would contribute to their high court culture. Some of these rulers were also great patrons of the arts of the book, commissioning manuscripts that were copied, compiled, and illustrated in their libraries. Due to the flourishing of manuscript illumination and illustration, the Herat school is often regarded as the apogee of Persian painting. The Timurid period saw great achievements in other luxury arts, such as metalwork and jade carving. This cultural efflorescence found its ultimate expression at the court of Sultan Husain Baiqara (r. 1470–1506), the last effective Timurid ruler.

Many Timurid princes were also prodigious builders—religious institutions and foundations such as mosques, madrasas, khanqahs (convents), and Sufi shrines were the main beneficiaries of their building programs. Major architectural commissions from Timur's lifetime include the Aq Saray palace (Shahr-i Sabz, ca. 1379–96); the shrine of Ahmad Yasavi (Turkestan City, ca. 1397); Timur's congregational mosque (Samarqand, ca. 1398–1405), popularly known as the mosque of Bibi Khanum after his wife, who built a madrasa next to it; and the Gur-i Amir (Samarqand, ca. 1400 – 1404), Timur's burial place. Trademarks of the Timurid style were monumental scale, multiple minarets, polychromy tilework, and large bulbous double domes. The Timurid period also witnessed women as active patrons of architecture. Along with their immediate successors, the Shaibanids, the Timurid cultural tradition was also partly carried on by the Ottoman, Safavid, and Mughal Empires.

The Art of the Umayyad Period (661–750)

After the death of Muhammad in 632, a series of four Aliphs (Arabic: khalifa, "successor"), known as the Rightly Guided, succeeded. Under their command, the Arab armies carried the new faith from Arabia to the shores of the Mediterranean and to the eastern reaches of Iran. However, following the assassination of Ali ibn Abi Talib—Muhammad's cousin, son-in-law, and fourth Aliph (r. 656–61)—in 661, Mucawiya, the governor of Syria under the Rightly Guided Aliphs, seized power and established the Umayyad Aliphate, the first Islamic dynasty (661–750). During Mucawiya's reign (661–80), the seat of Islamic power was transferred from the Arabian Peninsula to Syria. Under Mucawiya's successors, the important historic city of Damascus was transformed into the capital of an Empire that extended from the Atlantic Ocean to the Indus River.

The Umayyad period is often considered the formative period in Islamic art. At first, even though Arabic became the official language and Islam the principal religion of the diverse lands unified under Umayyad rule, artists continued to work in their established manner. The main artistic influence came from the late antique classical naturalistic tradition, which had been prevalent on the eastern shores of the Mediterranean. This was also supplemented by the more formal modes developed by the Byzantines and

Sasanians, a factor that especially affected metalwork, textiles, and the depiction of animal, vegetal, and figural motifs. With time, however, artists developed new techniques, forms, and decorative conventions that distinguished their works from earlier ones. Thus, through a process of adoption, adaptation, and creation, a new sense of artistic expression emerged that became distinctly Islamic in character shortly after the demise of the Umayyad dynasty.

As with the arts, the Umayyad period was also critical in the development of Islamic architecture. While earlier architectural traditions continued, the requirements of the new religion and customs of the new Arab rulers necessitated a different usage of space. In the case of religious buildings, the Umayyads often constructed their monuments on sites of historical or symbolic significance. The Dome of the Rock in Jerusalem (691), the first major Umayyad architectural undertaking completed under the patronage of the Aliph Abd al-Malik (r. 685–705), was built on a prominent site formerly occupied by Solomon's Temple and later associated with Muhammad's ascent to heaven. Other renowned religious buildings from the Umayyad period date from the reign of al-Walid (r. 705–15) and include the enlarged mosque in Medina (706–10), the former house of Muhammad. Also significant are the mosques of Damascus (706), where the site of the former Roman temple and fourth-century Byzantine church dedicated to Saint John the Baptist was transformed into the congregational mosque of the Umayyad capital, and of Jerusalem (709–15). In terms of secular architecture, Umayyad desert palaces such as Mshatta, Qasr cAmra (Jordan), cAnjar (Lebanon), Khirbat al-Mafjar (Palestine), and Qasr al-Hayr East and West (Syria) (all ca. 700–750), are a testimony to the wealth of their patrons and the creativity of Umayyad architects.

The Art of the Umayyad Period in Spain (711–1031)

On July 19, 711, an army of Arabs and Berbers unified under the aegis of the Islamic Umayyad Aliphate landed on the Iberian Peninsula. Over the next seven years, through diplomacy and warfare, they brought the entire peninsula except for Galicia and Asturias in the far north under Islamic control; however, frontiers with the Christian north were constantly in flux. The new Islamic territories, referred to as al-Andalus by Muslims, were administered by a provincial government established in the name of the Umayyad Aliphate in Damascus and centered in Cordoba. Of works of art and other material culture only coins and scant ceramic fragments remain from this early period of the Umayyad governors (711–56).

When the Umayyad Aliphate of Damascus was overthrown by the Abbasids in 750, the last surviving member of the Umayyad dynasty fled to Spain, establishing himself as Emir Abd al-Rahman I and thus initiating the Umayyad emirate (756–929). Abd al-Rahman I (r. 756–88) made Cordoba his capital and unified al-Andalus under his rule with a firm hand, while establishing diplomatic ties with the northern Christian kingdoms, North Africa, and the Byzantine Empire and maintaining cultural contact with the Abbasids in Baghdad. The initial construction of the Great Mosque of Cordoba under his patronage was the crowning achievement of this formative period of Hispano-Islamic art and architecture.

The Umayyads reclaimed their right to the Aliphate during the reign of Abd al-Rahman III (r. 912–61), who became the first Spanish Umayyad emir to declare himself Aliph (929). Under the Umayyad Aliphate (929–1031), Cordoba became perhaps the greatest intellectual center of Europe, with celebrated libraries and schools. Hispano-Umayyad art reached its apogee during the lengthy reign of Abd al-Rahman III and his son al-Hakam II (r. 961–76) and the regency of the powerful cAmirids, particularly al-Mansur (978–1002), chamberlain to the nominal ruler, the child-prince Hisham II (r. 976–1013 with interruption). Despite their open rejection of Abbasid political authority, the Umayyads of Cordoba emulated the opulent palatial arts of the centers of Abbasid power, Baghdad and Samarra'. There was also influence from the Fatimid rulers, who had established an independent Shici Aliphate in North Africa in 909 and occupied Egypt in 969.

Perhaps in response to these eastern Mediterranean cultural impulses, which coexisted with a strong indigenous artistic component, there began to appear in Cordoba a revival of the Umayyad period, almost nostalgia for the time when the Umayyads ruled the Islamic world from Damascus. Art patronage as a sign of kingship and authority is a theme that emerged from these creative appropriations from abroad and the past. Luxurious objects such as boxes of carved ivory and gilt silver, bronze animal statuary, and richly figured silks were commissioned for palaces decorated with ornate marble capitals, stucco wall panels, and marble fountains. Abd al-Rahman III's palace city at Madinat al-Zahra' set the standard for artistic taste in the Aliphate, and al-Hakam II's addition to the Great Mosque of Cordoba marked the imposition of a palatial level of luxury and hierarchy on this religious monument.

The Arts of Iran, 1600–1800

The Safavids continued to be important patrons of the arts under Shah Abbas (r. 1587–1629). Among the artists of his time was Riza Abbasi (ca. 1565–1635), son of the court painter Ali Asghar and pupil of the well-known Mucin. Although he was heir to a very traditional form of painting, Riza introduced a new set of subjects to the Persian oeuvre (50.164). Semi-nude women, languid youths, and lovers soon came to replace the heroes of the Shahnama and the Khamsa in many an artist's repertoire. These fashionable figures were also copied in textiles, figural tile panels, and other media. It is not, however, simply the subject matter of his paintings, but Riza's gift for capturing the inner emotions of his sitter and his famed calligraphic line that have earned him admiration. His work set the tone for much of the seventeenth century, as his students used it as a springboard for developing their own styles (1974.290.43).

The role of Iran as a major participant in a larger economy created by the European commercial expansion of the sixteenth century was another influence in the arts of this era. The production of artistic goods became hugely profitable and Abbas had a large hand in encouraging the growth of local crafts. In pottery, imitations of ceramics from Iznik in Turkey and of blue-and-white ware from China were especially popular, and the native technique of lusterware was revived (30.95.158).

Carpet weaving was transformed from a craft practiced by nomads and peasants into a national industry, with designs drafted by professional artists in the court workshops (50.190.1). Many Persian carpets can be found in collections throughout Europe as they became status symbols. Fabrics were another major industry; travelers Jean Chardin and Jean-Baptiste Tavernier both described silk-weaving factories in the cities of Yazd and Kashan, and the production of velvet increased as it became highly fashionable (59.58).

In the seventeenth century, adventurous traders and ambassadors sent by foreign kings came to Iran bearing works of art as presents to Persian high officials. The many prints, illustrated books, and oil paintings they brought provided new inspiration for artists in Iran. In some instances, these works were copied directly, such as lovers from a Dutch print that appear as a fresco, or a biblical scene reworked as a book-binding (34.23). In other cases, the European works provided new technical devices, which local artists combined with elements of traditional Persian painting. Modeling, foreshortening, spatial recession, and the medium of oil painting were all adopted by Persian artists but were employed in depictions of familiar subjects or in combination with traditional conventions.

Another effect of the economic boom was the creation of a new class of patrons. The urban rich, Armenian merchants, foreign travelers, and artists interested in each other's works could now all afford to purchase art. As a result, single-page paintings, less costly than fully illustrated manuscripts, became popular. In addition, artists were no longer dependent on the royal workshop for employment.

After Abbas I, the Safavids continued as patrons, but on a reduced scale. Abbas II (r. 1642–66) added the Chihil Sutun, a pavilion with large-scale wall paintings of historical and literary subjects, to the royal complex in Isfahan. Sulayman (r. 1666—94) commissioned two further palaces, the Hasht Bihisht and the Talar-i Ashraf. The great days of Safavid art were over, however, and Iran was heading in new directions.

Under the Afsharids (1736–96), Zands (1750–94), and Qajars (1779–1924), lifesize oil painting became the new medium for expressing royal identity. Portraits of Nadir Shah of the Afsharid dynasty have strong military overtones. He was often depicted on horseback (a European convention), or with ships amassed in the background, a reference to the navy he was attempting to build. The Zand royal image was more relaxed, the iconic image being Karim Khan smoking a huqqa pipe. His reign marked the start of Mirza Baba's career, but this artist was more active in the following Qajar era. Heavy modeling, atmospheric lighting, and static poses mark Qajar portraits. The canvases were often shaped to fit into niches, and formed an integral part of architectural decoration.

Architecturally, the contributions of the Zands lie mainly in Shiraz, which Karim Khan redeveloped along the lines of Isfahan with a large public square as the central organizational unit. Under the Qajars, the capital was moved to Tehran and the city was much developed in the years after 1800.

2

The Arts of the Book in the Islamic World, 1600-1800

The technical aspects of calligraphy, painting, and bookbinding are important facets of the study of Islamic art. Treatises by sixteenth-century Persian authors Qazi Ahmed and Sadiqi Beq are the major sources on the working methods of artisans in the Islamic world. Further information on the organization of manuscript workshops and the division of labor within them is recorded in court annals and payrolls.

The production of illustrated books was concentrated in royal workshops because of the large expense involved. Many rulers were connoisseurs who collected books and paintings by famous artists. Books were also financial investments, donated toward the endowment of charitable foundations, and status symbols, presented as gifts between heads of state.

Workshops supported by rulers and members of their extended family produced copies of famous literary works, histories, and Qur'ans. Once a patron decided on a project, the director of the workshop saw it through to its conclusion. He laid out the pages, decided which parts of the text to illustrate, and chose scribes and artists based on the particular project.

The first step in creating a book was to make the paper. In the Islamic world, paper was made from rags of linen and hemp, not tree pulp. The rags were cut into strips and softened in limewater, then pounded into a pulp and soaked in a vat. To form a sheet of paper, a rectangular mold was placed into the vat and then left to dry. The water seeped out and the page hardened in the mold. Decorative touches were often added to the paper: some were tinted, some were sprinkled with gold, and others were marbled. Marbled papers were created by dispensing drops of colorant onto the surface of a water bath and running combs through the drops to create a pattern; a sheet of paper was then laid on the surface of the bath to absorb the colors. After drying, the paper was prepared to receive ink and paint with the application of a starchy solution that rendered the surface smooth and nonporous.

A scribe then prepared his ink (made of carbon boiled with gallnuts), made his pens, and pressed guidelines into the paper. He then copied the text, leaving spaces for illustrations where the director of the workshop had indicated.

After the text was completed, the pages passed to the painters. Most manuscripts were the work of a number of artists, each chosen to illustrate a particular scene; some artists, for instance, were known for their portraits, others for their battle scenes. A single page might also represent a collaborative effort, as junior artists were called upon to fill in backgrounds and landscapes. Before starting to paint, the artist laid out the composition with a very fine brush. Some elements might be copied from preexisting sketches by means of a device called a pounce. To create a pounce, the artist laid a piece of transparent paper or animal skin over the sketch to be copied and pricked holes into the top sheet around the outlines of the image below. To transfer the image to his new painting, he laid the pounce on top of the fresh sheet of paper and dusted it with charcoal powder from a cloth bag.

To create his pigments, the artist turned to nature. Mineral sources were gold, silver, lapis lazuli, ground cinnabar (for vermilion), orpiment (for yellow), and malachite (for green). These materials were expensive and substitutes were often used. Indigo was a common source of dark blue and azurite was used for a lighter blue. Verdigris produced green, and lead or a combination of mercury and sulfur created red. (Because a number of these materials are unstable or corrosive, the colors of many illustrated manuscripts have faded or tarnished, and some paints have eaten through the paper.) The pigment had to be suspended in a medium that allowed it to be brushed on to the page. Originally this was albumen or glue, which gave a glossy sheen to the paintings; after the sixteenth century, gum arabic, with a more matte finish, was used instead.

After the paintings were completed, illuminators and gilders added flourishes to the text, such as chapter headings, colored frames, and rulings. They also created frontispieces and end pages. Finally, each sheet was burnished with a hard stone or glass.

At this stage, the leaves of the book were ready to be sewn and bound. The covers were joined to a spine and a fore-edge flap that folded over the ends of the pages and tucked under the top cover. Bindings were decorated with simply tooled geometric or vegetal patterns, until the fifteenth-century Persian development of a design with a central oval medallion, pendants, and corner pieces created by the use of a mold. Half the binding was stamped and then the mold was reversed, forming a mirror image of the design in the other half. Surrounding the central medallion were arranged rich floral motifs, arabesques, and cloud bands. This style soon spread to India and Turkey. Through the sixteenth century, designs became more elaborate, with the addition of miniature figures and landscapes, and the doublures (interior covers) also came to be decorated. Patterns for these were created in cut-out leather, colored papers, and gilding. In the nineteenth century, lacquered bindings with painted designs replaced these elaborate leather works.

Birth of Islam

Born in Mecca, in western Arabia, Muhammad (ca. 570–632), last in the line of Judeo-Christian prophets, received his first revelation in 610. Muslims believe that the word of God was revealed to him by the archangel Gabriel in Arabic, who said, "Recite in the name of thy Lord …" (Sura 96). These revelations were subsequently collected and codified as the Qur'an (literally "recitation" in Arabic), the Muslim holy book. As the source of Muslim faith and practice, the Qur'an describes the relationship between an almighty and all-knowing God and his creations. The Qur'an also maintains that all individuals are responsible for their actions, for which they will be judged by God, and so it provides guidelines for proper behavior within the framework of a just and equitable society.

At this time, Mecca was a prosperous city whose wealth and influence were based on the caravan trade and on the Kacba, a shrine and a place of pilgrimage housing the pagan deities then being worshipped by the Arabs. Muhammad's message, heralding a new socio-religious order based on allegiance to one god—Allah—was unpopular among the leaders of Mecca, and they forced Muhammad and his followers to emigrate north to the oasis town Yathrib (Medina). This occurred in 622, the year of the hijra, or "emigration," which marks the beginning of the Muslim calendar. In Medina, Muhammad continued to attract followers and, within a few years, Mecca had also largely embraced Islam. Upon his return to Mecca, one of the Prophet's first acts was to cleanse the Kacba of its idols and rededicate the shrine to Allah.

Although Muhammad died in 632, his followers, led by a series of four Aliphs (Arabic: khalifa, "successor") known as the Rightly Guided, continued to spread the message of Islam. Under their command, the Arab armies carried the new faith and leadership from the Arabian Peninsula to the shores of the Mediterranean and to the eastern reaches of Iran. The Arabs conquered Syria, Palestine, and Egypt from the Byzantine Empire, while Iraq and Iran, the heart of the Sasanian Empire, succumbed to their forces. Here in these lands, Islam fostered the development of a religious, political, and cultural commonwealth and the creation of a global Empire.

While the full formation of a distinctive Islamic artistic language took several centuries, the seeds were sown during the Prophet's time. Because it is through writing that the Qur'an is transmitted, the Arabic script was first transformed and beautified in order that it might be worthy of divine revelation. Thus, calligraphy started to gain prominence, becoming essential also to Islamic ornament. In architecture, following the hijra, Muhammad's house in Medina developed into a center for the Muslim community and became the prototype for the mosque, the Muslim sanctuary for God. The early structure, known as the hypostyle mosque, included a columned hall oriented toward Mecca and an adjacent courtyard surrounded by a colonnade. The call to prayer was given from a rooftop (later the minaret was developed for this purpose). Essential elements of the mosque were a minbar (pulpit) for the Friday sermon and a mihrab (prayer niche) set in the wall oriented toward Mecca.

Byzantine Art under Islam

The Byzantine Empire's interaction with Islamic culture had a profound effect on its art. Islam's rise and military success were the greatest threat to the stability of the Empire and its territories. Mirroring the political climate, art became a medium of confrontation and cooperation between the two sides. The exchange and adaptation of motifs and genres became a common expression of power and individuality in the face of constantly changing relations between the two groups.

Islamic leaders were impressed by Byzantine mosaics and invited mosaicists to work on the Dome of the Rock in Jerusalem. Islamic artists used Christian models for iconography. Meanwhile, Byzantine artists adapted Islamic motifs for their own use. The First Church of the Monastery of Hosios Loukas, in Phokis, Greece, is decorated with patterns based on the Arab Kufic script. The words do not mean anything, they are purely aesthetic, but they are clearly a nod to Islamic art. The batrashil (14.137), a silk liturgical vestment, shows an understanding of Syriac and Arabic, this time in its legible form—the artist even used Arabic to sign her name. The writing is embroidered onto the garment. A processional cross (1999.103) from Ethiopia is a fusion of wood sculpture and metalwork clearly inspired by Islamic shapes and patterns, which were most likely learned from textiles, ceramic vessels and tiles, and glass developed in the Muslim world. The illuminated gospel (1998.66) from Ethiopia also employs a design inspired by Islamic ornamentation known as harag, which means the tendril of a climbing plant.

Calligraphy in Islamic Art

Calligraphy is the most highly regarded and most fundamental element of Islamic art. It is significant that the Qur'an, the book of God's revelations to the Prophet Muhammad, was transmitted in Arabic, and that inherent within the Arabic script is the potential for developing a variety of ornamental forms. The employment of calligraphy as ornament had a definite aesthetic appeal but often also included an underlying talismanic component. While most works of art had legible inscriptions, not all Muslims would have been able to read them. One should always keep in mind; however, that calligraphy is principally a means to transmit a text, albeit in a decorative form.

Objects from different periods and regions vary in the use of calligraphy in their overall design, demonstrating the creative possibilities of calligraphy as ornament. In some cases, calligraphy is the dominant element in the decoration. In these examples, the artist exploits the inherent possibilities of the Arabic script to create writing as ornament. An entire word can give the impression of random brushstrokes, or a single letter can develop into a decorative knot. In other cases, highly esteemed calligraphic works on paper are themselves ornamented and enhanced by their decorative frames or backgrounds. Calligraphy can also become part of an overall ornamental program, clearly separated from the rest of the decoration. In some examples, calligraphy can be combined with vegetal scrolls on the same surface though often on different levels, creating interplay of decorative elements.

Commercial Exchange, Diplomacy, and Religious Difference between Venice and the Islamic world

Venetian Traders in the Islamic World

Marco Polo's (1254–1324) intrepid twenty-five-year journey took him from Venice to China, where he met the Great Khan of the Mongol Empire, Kublai Khan. Though his experience was exceptional for its duration and for the illustrious people whom he encountered, Polo is simply the most famous of the thousands of Venetian merchants who sought to make a fortune by acquiring luxury goods, spices, and raw materials in the East and selling them for a high return on Venetian markets. For Venetians, Levantine emporia became synonymous with profit, and visiting them was a crucial part of a young nobleman's education. Their most frequent ports of call included Istanbul, Damascus,

Cairo, Aleppo, Tripoli, and Alexandria. Handbooks and travel diaries, often written in Venetian dialect, offered these merchants advice about tariffs, prices, weights, and measures in these cities, while astrolabes and portolans aided them in overseas travel. In many Near Eastern cities, Venice had established trading colonies where its traveling merchants could find lodging, food, a public bath, and a church upon arrival. Multilingual interpreters, known as dragomans, were often readily available for hire, though many Venetian merchants did learn Arabic and Persian so that they could have firsthand interactions with Muslim traders and custom officials. Arabic words in particular infiltrated the Venetian dialect as a result.

In recognition of the importance of Near Eastern trade to its economy, the Venetian Republic assumed control of the local shipbuilding industry at an early date. By the fourteenth century, Venetians had developed a special type of large cargo ship, the cog or round ship, which they armed with crossbowmen to protect against pirate attacks while at sea. Both state convoys and private ships regularly shuttled Venetian merchants back and forth from Near Eastern ports, often even in the winter. By contrast, and contrary to the nineteenth-century myth, Islamic merchants only rarely traveled to Venice. As a result, Venetians were able to maintain their status as middlemen for the sale of oriental goods to mainland Europe for centuries, and to grow rich from its profits. Venice's status as a world emporium served a crucial role in the city's self-definition.

Diplomatic Relations between Venice and the Islamic World

Venetians gained the advantage in Near Eastern trade over other Europeans thanks to their skilled diplomatic efforts, which had a two-pronged approach. At the highest level, Venetian doges engaged Muslim sultans and other officials in trade negotiations, a process facilitated by ambassadors. Reports of their diplomatic visits highlight the importance of display, ritual, and gift exchange. For example, in 1502 the Venetian envoy Benedetto Sanudo ceremonially presented an emir in Alexandria with fine cloth and Parmesan cheese (a favorite diplomatic gift). In Cairo, Sanudo's official gifts to the sultan included luxury textiles, furs, and yet more cheese, and in return he received chickens, sweetmeats, and watermelons. At the climax of his visit, he was ceremonially robed in a gown of silk woven with gold thread and lined with ermine. The gifts from the sultan to the doge included twenty pieces of Chinese porcelain of various sizes.

At a lower, but still important level, Venice engaged consuls, known as baili, to serve two-year terms at the trading colonies in the Near East. Elected by the Venetian Senate from the ranks of the nobility, the consuls paid tribute to sultans and local admirals and arbitrated in the event of a trading dispute while in residence.

In at least one important instance, a Venetian artist served as an emissary to an Islamic power. In 1479, Gentile Bellini, official painter to the Venetian Republic, traveled to the court of Mehmet II (r. 1444–46; 1451–1481) in Istanbul as a diplomatic favor. During his nearly two-year stay, Bellini created painted and bronze medals of the sultan similar to those he and other Venetian artists made of Venice's own ruler, the doge. In addition, a courtier recorded that "Gentile made several beautiful pictures, and most of all things of luxury, some beautiful in style, of which there were a large number in the [sultan's new] palace." Prior to his departure from Istanbul in January 1481, Mehmet II honored Bellini with the titles of golden knight and palace companion and gave him a gift of a gold chain with a medallion. Few of the works of art created by Bellini during his Ottoman sojourn survive, but the episode lives on as one of the high points in artistic and cultural exchange between Venice and its Islamic neighbors.

Christian Venice and the Islamic Near East

Venice's worldview was intimately bound to its relation to its Near Eastern neighbors, as is perhaps nowhere better illustrated than in the story of how it acquired its patron, Saint Mark. The Egyptian city of Alexandria, where in the first century A.D. the evangelist had died and was interred, came under Muslim control in the seventh century. In 828, two Venetian merchants restored the saint to Christian soil by surreptitiously carrying his relic home with them to Venice. The doge triumphantly received the miracle-working relic and enshrined it in a new church, the Basilica San Marco. In this way, Venetians deftly combined their identity as traders in the Muslim world with that of defenders of the Christian faith.

The papacy often sought to prohibit trade between the Christians of Western Europe and the Muslims of the Near East with trade embargos.

However, their livelihood depended so much on east-west trade, Venetians in particular fought to have such bans lifted and, on occasion, even defied the pope. During the Crusades, the Venetians compromised their position with the papacy by acting opportunistically to maintain their good trade relations with the Muslim world.

Figural Representation in Islamic Art

With the spread of Islam outward from the Arabian Peninsula in the seventh century, the figurative artistic traditions of the newly conquered lands profoundly influenced the development of Islamic art. Ornamentation in Islamic art came to include figural representations in its decorative vocabulary, drawn from a variety of sources. Although the often cited opposition in Islam to the depiction of human and animal forms holds true for religious art and architecture, in the secular sphere, such representations have flourished in nearly all Islamic cultures.

The Islamic resistance to the representation of living beings ultimately stems from the belief that the creation of living forms is unique to God, and it is for this reason that the role of images and image makers has been controversial. The strongest statements on the subject of figural depiction are made in the Hadith (Traditions of the Prophet), where painters are challenged to "breathe life" into their creations and threatened with punishment on the Day of Judgment. The Qur'an is less specific but condemns idolatry and uses the Arabic term musawwir ("maker of forms," or artist) as an epithet for God.

Partially as a result of this religious sentiment, figures in painting were often stylized and, in some cases, the destruction of figurative artworks occurred. Iconoclasm was previously known in the Byzantine period and aniconicism was a feature of the Judaic world, thus placing the Islamic objection to figurative representations within a larger context. As ornament, however, figures were largely devoid of any larger significance and perhaps therefore posed less challenge.

As with other forms of Islamic ornamentation, artists freely adapted and stylized basic human and animal forms, giving rise to a great variety of figural-based designs. Figural motifs are found on the surface decoration of objects or architecture, as part of the woven or applied patterns of textiles, and, most rarely, in sculptural form. In some cases, decorative images are closely related to the narrative painting tradition, where text illustrations provided sources for ornamental themes and motifs.

As for manuscript illustration, miniature paintings were integral parts of these works of art as visual aids to the text, therefore no restrictions were imposed. A further category of fantastic figures, from which ornamental patterns were generated, also existed. Some fantastic motifs, such as harpies (female-headed birds) and griffins (winged felines), were drawn from pre-Islamic mythological sources, whereas others were created through the visual manipulation of figural forms by artists.

Geometric Patterns in Islamic Art

Geometric patterns make up one of the three nonfigural types of decoration in Islamic art, which also include calligraphy and vegetal patterns. Whether isolated or used in combination with nonfigural ornamentation or figural representation, geometric patterns are popularly associated with Islamic art, largely due to their aniconic quality. These abstract designs not only adorn the surfaces of monumental Islamic architecture but also function as the major decorative element on a vast array of objects of all types. While geometric ornamentation may have reached a pinnacle in the Islamic world, the sources for both the shapes and the intricate patterns already existed in late antiquity among the Greeks, Romans, and Sasanians in Iran. Islamic artists appropriated key elements from the classical tradition, then complicated and elaborated upon them in order to invent a new form of decoration that stressed the importance of unity and order. The significant intellectual contributions of Islamic mathematicians, astronomers, and scientists were essential to the creation of this unique new style.

Consisting of, or generated from, such simple forms as the circle and the square, geometric patterns were combined, duplicated, interlaced, and arranged in intricate combinations, thus becoming one of the most distinguishing features of Islamic art. However, these complex patterns seem to embody a refusal to adhere strictly to the rules of geometry. As a matter of fact, geometric ornamentation in Islamic art suggests a remarkable amount of freedom; in its repetition and complexity, it offers the possibility of infinite growth and can accommodate the incorporation of other types of ornamentation as well. In terms of their abstractness, repetitive motifs, and symmetry, geometric patterns have much in common with the so-called arabesque style seen in many vegetal designs. Calligraphic ornamentation also appears in conjunction with geometric patterns.

The four basic shapes, or "repeat units," from which the more complicated patterns are constructed are: circles and interlaced circles; squares or four-sided polygons; the ubiquitous star pattern, ultimately derived from squares and triangles inscribed in a circle; and multisided polygons. It is clear, however, that the complex patterns found on many objects include a number of different shapes and arrangements, allowing them to fit into more than one category.

Glass from Islamic Lands

At the time of the Arab conquest in the seventh century A.D., glassmaking had flourished in Egypt and western Asia for more than two millennia and glassmakers in those regions went about their business despite the momentous political, social, and religious changes taking place around them. Glassmakers inherited many of the techniques of their forebears in the Byzantine and Sasanian Empires, including glassblowing, the use of molds, the manipulation of molten glass with tools, and the decorative application of molten glass. Islamic glass production from the seventh through the fourteenth century was also greatly innovative and witnessed glorious phases—such as those of superb relief-cut glass and spectacular gilded and enameled objects—that established its supremacy in glassmaking manufacture throughout the world.

While many of the objects may not have been made under a ruler's patronage, they certainly are "fit for a sultan." Islamic glass can be better studied according to the techniques of its manipulation—from undecorated blown vessels to mosaic glass to mold-blown, hot-worked, cut and engraved, and painted objects, though vessels produced after the seventeenth century and greatly influenced by the European trade may be studied in a proper historical context.

In the field of Islamic art, glass is a craft that often rose to excellence but has been largely overlooked by art historians. Thousands of anonymous glassmakers, from Cairo to Delhi, proudly transmitted their knowledge from one generation to the next, experimenting with the colors, shapes, techniques, and surface decoration of this extraordinarily versatile material. Their most outstanding results, from public and private collections worldwide, encourage a widespread appreciation of the artistic forms of Islamic glass—a fitting legacy for this ancient craft.

Tools of the Glassmakers

Since the invention of glassblowing in the first century B.C., glassmakers have been using the same tools to model, manipulate, and decorate molten glass. Two molds from the medieval Islamic world are the only ones to survive, but the basic technology of nonindustrial glassmaking and the tools employed have not changed.

The blowpipe is an iron or steel tube, usually about five feet long, for blowing a parison, or gather, of molten glass. Molds are used to impress decorative patterns on the parison. Dip molds have the typical form of a conical beaker, but two- or three-part hinged molds were also used in the Islamic world. The pontil, a solid metal rod that is applied to the base of a vessel to hold it after it is cut off from the blowpipe, became a common tool in the early Islamic period (7th–8th century). The pontil leaves an irregular ring-shaped mark on the base that is commonly known as a "pontil mark." Wooden blocks, jacks, and shears are used to shape an object. Blocks are used to form the gather into a sphere prior to inflation; jacks, to shape the mouth of an open vessel; and shears, to trim excess hot glass during production. A marver—a smooth flat stone or metal surface over which softened glass is rolled—is also an essential tool of the glassmaker. Of course, no tool would be of much use without a glassmaker's dexterity and talent.

Archaeological Excavations

Scientific excavations are extremely valuable for a better understanding of the history, art, architecture, urban planning, and everyday life of a specific site. In terms of material culture, glass objects and fragments are second in quantity only to pottery at most Islamic sites, offering a wide variety of shapes, colors, and decoration for analysis.

There are, however, a number of problems related to the study of excavated Islamic glass. Only in exceptional cases do glass objects bear informative inscriptions providing names and dates. Both as luxury goods that were traded and exchanged and as simple containers for oils, perfumes, and liquids of all kinds, Islamic glass circulated throughout the Islamic world and as far as southeastern Asia, northern China, and Europe. Glass was also shipped in large quantities as cullet (glass lumps and discarded broken vessels), suitable for remelting and making new glass inexpensively. Thus, the glass of a bottle created in Egypt, for example, may have been recycled as far as Central Asia; a new object may have been made that had a chemical composition usually attributed to Egyptian vessels but a shape and decoration that suggested a different origin. While it clearly is problematic for scholars to determine their place or date of production, excavated objects may be of great help in better understanding the chronology and origin of Islamic glass. The three most prolific excavated sites that have yielded glass in the Islamic world are Fustat (Old Cairo) in Egypt, Samarra' in Iraq, and Nishapur in northeastern Iran.

Islamic Arms and Armor

Since its emergence in seventh-century Arabia, the religion of Islam spread rapidly, by swift military conquest and by conversion, throughout the Middle East and North Africa. During the eighth century, large parts of India were Islamized, while Muslim armies also began the occupation of Spain, portions of which remained Islamic until the end of the fifteenth century. By the seventeenth century, areas under Islamic religious and political control stretched from the southern Philippines across southern Asia and the Middle East through Turkey and into central Europe. Inevitably, due to Islam's wide geographic dissemination and long history, Islamic arms and armor reflect a wide range of regional and national styles as well as technical, social, and artistic changes during the various phases of their history.

The expression "Islamic arms and armor" is a term often somewhat restrictively applied to arms and armor of the Mamluk period (1250–1517) in Egypt and Syria, the Ottoman Empire (ca. 1299–1922), the Near East, especially Persia, and those areas of India under Mughal rule (1526–1858). One of the main characteristics of Islamic armor is that, compared to its European counterparts, it is often relatively lighter and less extensive.

This fact owes as much to a strategic and tactical preference of most Muslim armies for speed over heavy protection, as to the usually hot climate of regions under Islamic rule. An example is the extensive and continued use of mail armor until well into the nineteenth century, while in Western Europe this type of defense had been largely relegated to a secondary position with the development of plate armor at the beginning of the fifteenth century. In Islamic armor, the use of plate was usually confined to helmet, short vambraces (arm defenses) and greaves (lower leg defenses), and, to some extent, reinforcement of the mail shirt.

Apart from shirts made entirely of mail, one of the most typically "Islamic" forms of body defense is a shirt composed of steel plates joined by areas of mail, which appears to have been developed first in Iran or Anatolia during the early fifteenth century. Variations with plates of different sizes and configurations were being worn in many parts of the

Ottoman Empire by the sixteenth century, whence it was probably introduced into India early in the Mughal period due to the Ottoman influence on Mughal military practices.

The most familiar characteristic of Islamic armor is perhaps the distinctive conical-shape helmets, which, with some variation, are found in most European and Near Eastern areas under Islamic rule. One variation is known as a "turban helmet." Its prototype can be found in the pre-Islamic Sasanian tradition (224–336) of Persia, but its sweeping outline, reminiscent of the domes of mosques, has contributed to this type of helmet being recognized today as decidedly Islamic. Many of the early surviving examples date from the fifteenth century and seem to have been made in Iran and Turkey.

Additional protection was afforded by shields, usually of round shape, and constructed—unlike the majority of their European counterparts—of metal. The weapon most readily associated by today's audiences with Muslim warriors of bygone times is probably the scimitar or saber, having a long, slightly curved blade with a single cutting edge. Other arms included javelins (throwing spears), battle axes, maces, and recurve bows (so called because the ends of the arms/limbs in their relaxed state curve forward, adding additional momentum to the arrow when the bow is strung). Although the above weapons were certainly also used by foot soldiers, all were essentially suited for use by cavalry.

Firearms had been introduced to the Islamic world by trade and armed conflict in both the East and West, and the manufacture of cannon and handheld firearms became a highly regarded craft in many regions under Islamic rule. What are today commonly referred to as "Islamic firearms" are weapons from various regions, which were derived from seventeenth-century European prototypes in the construction of their locks and in the shape of their butts. Many were fitted either with European locks, acquired by trade or as booty, or with locks that were manufactured in Islamic regions but were in fact copies of European types. Some types, such as the matchlock, remained popular in some areas under Islamic rule until long after they had become obsolete in Western Europe.

Many examples of Islamic arms and armor are especially noteworthy for their opulent decoration, a fact for which they were already renowned in the middle Ages. Sword blades of "Damascus steel" or "watered steel" refer to blades that had been given a wavy or "watered" pattern, produced in the steel prior to forging using specific smelting and crucible techniques.

Although this technique was practiced in the Islamic Middle East at least since the Middle Ages, in Western Europe such blades were believed to originate from Damascus (Syria), hence the name. Along similar lines, the inlay of metal surfaces such as those of a breastplate or a sword blade with gold or silver was known as "damascening," a term again alluding to the city of Damascus and the apparent Eastern origins of this technique.

Islamic arms and armor were decorated using a variety of techniques such as damascening, gilding, inlay, gold and silver encrusting, as well as setting with jewels and enameling. On some ceremonial items, the decoration could achieve such sumptuous and spectacular effects that the final appearance of the object has more in common with an item of jewelry than a weapon.

Indeed, the splendor of the Mughal Empire was such that even today the term "mogul" is synonymous with enormous wealth and power, a notion easily verified by Mughal arms and armor.

Apart from floral and animal motifs, a dominant part of Islamic iconography on arms and armor is confined to calligraphy. Although the representation of (sacred) figures is not strictly forbidden in the Qur'an, images as objects of devotion were avoided in Islamic art from its very beginning. Islamic artists relied instead on the words of the Prophet Muhammad to inspire and to give literal shape to their designs.

As a result, calligraphy in Islamic lands developed into a fine art, becoming in the process the principal form of religious ornament. Thus, Islamic arms and armor were often decorated with a wide variety of Qur'anic passages and pious invocations, which functioned as expressions of piety, as powerful defenses in the form of talismans, or simply as visually pleasing ornament.

3

Islamic Art and Culture
The Venetian Perspective

Islamic Philosophy and Science in Venice

Precisely because Venice remained so open to foreign cultures, all kinds of philosophical, scientific, religious, and literary texts circulated in the city throughout the medieval and Renaissance periods. Mostly interested in Greek and Latin works, Venetian literati, however, understood that transmission occurred through Arabic texts.

After printing presses were established in Europe in 1469, Venice's prolific publishing shops quickly multiplied the number of copies of Arab texts in Latin translation. Venetian publishers issued Ptolemy's astronomical work Almagest, Averroes' philosophical Destructio destructionis, and many other related texts. In the most luxurious editions, Venetian illuminators enhanced the text with images of learned turbaned men, who often wield astrolabes (Islamic decorative arts, such as mosque lamps, ceramics, and blazons.

What is perhaps most remarkable is the Venetian painters' intimate knowledge of Near Eastern costume. During his visit to Constantinople in 1479–81, Gentile Bellini made portraits of Sultan Mehmet II and figure studies of local men and women from different social groups, including soldiers and scribes; in each instance, he painstakingly described their costumes. He and his pupils later drew on his studies in their paintings, which accounts for their strikingly detailed representations of Ottoman turbans and dress. Later, the Bellini protégés Vittore Carpaccio and Giovanni Mansueti became veritable experts in Mamluk dress and its decorum, most likely as a direct result of increased Mamluk-Venetian diplomatic relations at the end of the fifteenth and beginning of the sixteenth century. For Venetian Renaissance painters, stock drawings, or simili, of Muslim figures became prized possessions, passed down from one generation to another and circulated among workshops for reuse.

By 1525, the last canvases painted in the Oriental mode for the Venetian confraternities were in place, many of the city's most important Orientalist painters had died, and the Ottomans had conquered the Mamluk Empire. The Venetian tradition of setting large narrative scenes in the Islamic world had no followers in the late sixteenth century, when portraits of Muslims, most often Ottoman sultans, or the inclusion of a single Muslim figure in a religious scene were more characteristic.

During the second half of the sixteenth century, costume books emerged as a popular new genre and reflect a greater curiosity about foreign cultures derived from travels and new discoveries. Venice and the Veneto, where at least nine examples were published between 1540 and 1610, played a leading role in the costume book's early development. The most famous and important example is Cesare Vecellio's Degli abiti antichi et moderni di diverse parti del mondo of 1590, which became a model of the genre. It includes more than 500 illustrations and pays special attention to Venetian and Ottoman dress.

By the sixteenth century, Venice's relations with her Muslim neighbors became increasingly complex. Venetian merchants continued trading in the eastern Mediterranean, but Turkey's aggressive navy made travel more precarious.

As a result, Venetians began representing Muslim subjects in less sympathetic ways. Turbaned men were frequently stereotyped as aggressive warriors or ridiculed as acrobats in Venetian paintings, drawings, prints, and even in wooden ship decorations.

Even in the changed political environment, the Islamic Near East continued to occupy a place in the collective imagination of Venetians. Wealthy patrons commissioned paintings with Muslim subjects, such as Turkish women relaxing in the sultan's harem, to decorate their private palaces. These scenes serve as an important prologue to the new Orientalism, a pan-European phenomenon, of the nineteenth century.

Collecting Islamic Art in Venice

The presence of Islamic art in Venice can be documented from the middle Ages until today. The earliest objects to arrive in the city—such as the luxurious relief-cut glass and rock crystal vessels from Fatimid Egypt in the Treasury of San Marco—can perhaps best be interpreted as spolia, or booty, rather than as a sign of an appreciation of Islamic art per se. Over the centuries, however, Venetian merchants and diplomats definitely developed a taste for Islamic ceramics, textiles, arms and armor, metalwork, and manuscripts and displayed them in their homes as works of art alongside objects from other periods and places. Perhaps no greater testament to the esteem of Islamic artifacts in Venice can be found than the portraits of Venetian patrician families with one of their most prized possessions, an oriental carpet.

By the eighteenth and nineteenth centuries, so much Islamic art had accumulated in Venice's palaces and churches that the city became an important destination for collectors of Islamic art, such as Wilhelm von Bode of Germany, wanting to make new acquisitions. Provenance research reveals that many Islamic art objects now in

Western European collections passed through Venice first. Major examples still remain in the city today, however, and the number of Venetian museums and churches with works of Islamic art is truly impressive; they include the Biblioteca Nazionale Marciana, the Basilica and Treasury of San Marco, the Museo Civico Correr, the Fondazione Giorgio Cini, and the Museo Franchetti alla Ca' d'Oro.

Carpets from the Islamic World, 1600–1800

Under the Ottoman, Safavid, and Mughal dynasties, carpet weaving was transformed from a minor craft based on patterns passed down from generation to generation into a statewide industry with patterns created in court workshops. In this period, carpets were fabricated in greater quantity than ever before. They were traded to Europe and the Far East where, too precious to be placed on the ground, they were used to cover furniture or hung on walls. Within the Islamic world, especially fine specimens were collected in royal households.

In Iran, the carpet and textile industries formed part of Shah Abbas' (r. 1587–1629) program for restructuring the economy and attracting European merchants to the country. He transferred silk merchants and weavers to the new capital of Isfahan and signed trade treaties with Spain, England, and France. Of the scores of carpets exported abroad at this time, the "Polonaise" type (50.190.1) was the most popular; over 300 of them are in foreign collections, and many bear the coat of arms of the family that commissioned them. Vase and garden carpets were among the other common types. In each of these, vegetal motifs replace the figural ones of the previous century.

In Ottoman Turkey, weaving patterns and techniques changed in the early sixteenth century after conquests in Persia and Egypt. Anatolia had been known for carpets with stylized animal and geometric designs, but with these new cultural contacts, carpets designed around a central medallion and with flowing saz-style vegetation came into vogue. Similar motifs also appeared on book covers, textiles, and in manuscript borders. The style of these Ottoman court rugs, first produced in Istanbul, then spread to other weaving centers in Cairo and Ushak (58.63; 1984.69), but never fully overtook the various regional carpet traditions. Caucasian and Armenian carpets retained their customary geometric patterns, and kilims (or flat-weaves) remained popular (62.156).

Before the time of Akbar (r. 1556–1605), it seems that few carpets were produced in India—perhaps because of the climate—but his court historians record royal workshops in the capitals of Fatehpur Sikri, Lahore, and Agra. Early Mughal rugs closely resemble those from contemporary Persia, and in particular those produced in Herat. Later in the seventeenth century, patterns changed as European engravings and illustrated books circulated at the court, and a Mughal idiom, distinct from the Persian manner of depicting flora, developed. With the work of European traders, Indian carpets traveled to the West and as far-East as China and Japan, and were avidly collected in England and Portugal.

Many carpets now have no record of date or place of origin. Early scholars devised one dating system based on carpets that appeared in Italian and Flemish paintings, and some rugs are now known by the name of the artist in whose paintings they appear, such as Lotto and Holbein. More recent studies focus on the technical aspects of carpet production, such as material, dyes, and weaving structure, finding these to be important clues in determining where a particular carpet was made. While patterns were popular over wide geographical areas or were sent from court workshops to provincial production centers, each region had a characteristic style of weaving that remained the same over time. In Persia, for instance, an asymmetrical knot was most often used, and in Turkey a symmetrical one. Egyptian carpets are always fully woollen, and Indian ones are recognized by their distinctive red hue.

Islamic Art of the Deccan

The "Deccan" (derived from Dakshina) is a geographical term that refers to the plateau in south central India still ruled by Hindu kings when the first Muslim sultanates of India were established in Delhi. The Khaljis (1290–1320) and the Tughluqs (1320–1414) after them both tried to conquer the Deccan but were ultimately unsuccessful. The officers of Muhammad ibn Tughluq rebelled against him and an independent sultanate was declared under the leadership of the general Zafar Khan. His descendants, known as the Bahmanids (1347–1528), ruled from a capital located first in Gulbarga and later in Bidar.

In the late fifteenth century, the provinces of the Bahmanid dynasty broke off into separate states, each with a vibrant and distinct culture flourishing mainly in the late sixteenth and early seventeenth centuries. The art, poetry, and music of the Deccani courts were marked by an affinity for Persia; many rulers of this area were of Persian descent or were Shici and thus felt stronger ties to the west than to the Sunni rulers in northern India. These courts, namely Bijapur, Golconda, Ahmadnagar, Bidar, and Berar, were known for their unique techniques of casting metal, carving stone, and painting. Each respective capital was developed with the addition of citadels and tombs and a distinctive style of architecture evolved as well.

Bijapur was ruled by the cAdil Shahis from 1489 to 1686. Sultan Ibrahim cAdil Shah II (r. 1580–1627), a poet, calligrapher, and musician himself, was the dynasty's greatest patron of the arts. He attracted artisans, writers, and thinkers from all over the Islamic world to his court, and during his reign the city became the most important center of painting in the Deccan. Bijapur-style paintings are characterized by subject matter deriving largely from

Mughal painting, but distinctively treated with a vivid palette and somewhat fantastic backgrounds. Rulers are portrayed in intimate moments, strolling through gardens or relaxing with a lover. Painting continued to flourish under Ibrahim's successor Muhammad cAdil Shah (r. 1627–56), but this ruler's greatest commission was architectural. Known as Gol Gumbad, his tomb has a dome 43.9 meters in diameter, at the time of its construction the largest space covered by a single dome.

The Qutb Shahis (1496–1687) of Golconda had very close ties to the Safavids of Iran, who exported many artists to this court. The close working relationship of the Persian and Indian artists can be seen in the unique painting style of such manuscripts as the Kulliyat, a collection of verses in Urdu penned by Muhammad Quli Qutb Shah (r. 1580–1612), a contemporary of Ibrahim cAdil Shah and, like him, a poet, statesman, and important patron of the arts.

The Nizam Shahis were based in Ahmadnagar from 1490 to 1636, but after 1600 ruled under the Mughals. Their brief moment of patronage produced an illustrated history, the Tarif-i Husain Shahi, celebrating the king who led the victory over the Hindu Vijayanagar state, and various royal portraits.

After the fall of the Bahmanids, their viziers the Baridis (1504–1619) continued to rule in the city of Bidar, famed for a metalworking technique invented there. So-called bidri ware is cast from an alloy of zinc mixed with copper, tin, and lead and inlaid with silver or brass. It is then covered with a mud paste containing sal ammoniac, which turns the base metal black, highlighting the color and sheen of the inlaid metal.

It was only after a Mughal military presence was established in Ahmadnagar in 1600 that the imperial Mughal aesthetic exerted an influence on painting of the Deccan. After this time there grew a greater interest in accurate portraiture and hieratic court scenes, and colors became more restrained. The typical portraits of sultans and court members against plain backgrounds, darbar scenes, and wedding processions were all produced at workshops in the Deccan. Such changes were made by artists at Hindu courts under the aegis of the Mughals at this time as well.

The Mughals conquered the last of the Deccani sultanates in 1686, but were only able to control the area until 1724, when the Asaf Jahis asserted their independence. They continued to rule in the former Qutb Shahi capital of Hyderabad until India itself gained its independence, and their court carried Persianate culture of the Deccan well into the twentieth century.

The Magic of Signs and Patterns in North African Art

North Africa, or the Maghrib, comprises Morocco, Algeria, Tunisia, and Libya. Art of the Maghrib is distinguished by a mystical quality drawing on the region's symbols and signs that originate in pre-Islamic Berber motifs and a rich Islamic heritage introduced to the region by Arabs in the seventh century. From the Fezzan and Tassili petroglyphs in Libya and Algeria to the Neolithic paintings of Morocco, North African artists have a large reservoir of art that continues to influence their work. One example of such influence is found in the engravings of Tunisian artist Gouider Triki (born 1949) with suggestions of the supernatural found in ancient rock paintings.

Artists also make use of traditional signs and symbols as a metaphor for colonial policies that imposed foreign languages and cultures and the subsequent curtailment of liberties in the postcolonial era. An imaginative discourse of signs often undercuts, disrupts, and subverts the rational dictum of language that has become a forbidden medium for free expression. For example, letters take on new meaning in the work of Algerian artist Rachid Koraïchi (born 1947), who draws on poetry in an illegible Arabic script using reverse mirror imagery; having fled persecution in his native Algeria, Koraïchi turns the alphabet into a symbol of protest. Koraïchi and other North African artists explore the formal dimension of signs, symbols, and the Berber alphabet, invoking their aesthetic qualities, using them in structural compositions or expanding on their mystical properties by synthesizing new symbols from old forms.

Traditionally, symbols and signs are found in pottery, textiles, carved or painted wood, leather works, jewelry, amulets, and tattoos. Algeria's Kabyle women paint with their fingers on pottery and upon the walls of their village homes; many of their shapes and symbols have a marked resemblance to Neolithic pottery found in the region. Believed to carry healing qualities or to embody magical attributes that guard against misfortune and the evil eye, these signs and symbols assume new forms and meanings in contemporary art. By combining signs with magical numbers or stylizing traditional symbols, contemporary artists tap the unconscious to create abstract work that references the past and present. On several visits to North Africa, German artist Paul Klee was inspired by these mystical shapes and incorporated signs, number, and letters into his work; his interpretation of line and color would in turn influence several Maghribi artists.

Islamic art and architecture flourished in the Maghrib, where some of the earliest examples are found in Fez, Qairouan, Meknas, and Algiers. With the exception of Morocco, and to a lesser extent Tunisia and Algeria, by the mid-sixteenth century Islamic art centers were concentrated in non-Arab countries. In the twentieth century, Moroccan artisans continued to preserve traditional crafts with distinctive Andalusian influences. The Moroccan craftsman is referred to respectfully as mu'alim, or master artisan; his skills are valued by modern artists who borrow freely from traditional crafts, reformulating old techniques and incorporating them into their work. Farid Belkahia (born

1934) represents a movement in Moroccan art that questions modern artistic references. He relies exclusively on local materials, replacing chemical paints with natural dyes, and using surfaces other than canvas such as copper, pottery, wood, handmade paper, and lamb skins. The stretched irregular or shaped surfaces of skin form the background to gargantuan drawings of signs and symbols of an archaic language. In particular, Belkahia uses magical numbers such as five or khmasa, representing the hand of Fatima (the Prophet Muhammad's daughter), a protective symbol against the evil eye. Other commonly used signs and symbols are lozenges, crescents, stars, diamonds, triangles, dots, and odd numbers or their multiple.

Ahmed Cherkaoui (1934–1967), one of the foremost abstract artists in Morocco, combines the repetitive Islamic style with abstract signs and symbols, and uses bright colors of greens, red, blue, and yellow to contrast with the white background. Similar brilliant colors are used by many self-taught artists of the Maghrib, now considered to have produced the most accomplished naive art in the twentieth century. For example, Algerian artist Baya Mahieddine (1931–1999), whose dreamlike imagery is based on mysticism and magic, used stylized fish and grapes to celebrate a cycle of life in which women live with imaginary animals. The art of North Africa's self-taught artists is neither strictly traditional nor Western in style; rather, there is a fusion of elements transcending time and place.

The dense repetitive geometric patterns typical of North African ceramics is infused with new significance in the installation Four Generations of Women by French-born Algerian artist Zineb Sedira (born 1963). Representing a generation of North African artists born in France and living in the West, Sedira examines the shifting of identities and questions preconceived notions of East and West by challenging both Western and Islamic perceptions of gender and Islamic art. Within what might initially be construed as mundane repetition of Islamic geometric designs are faces of women entrapped in a pattern that forms a matrilineal chain incorporating human figures within a predominantly nonfigurative Islamic aesthetic.

Glossary

Berber: Generic name given to the indigenous tribes of North Africa by the Greeks, who referred to all North Africans as "barbarians" or foreigners. The diverse indigenous people of North Africa refer to themselves as Amazigh (pl. Imazighen), meaning "noble ones." Ethnically Caucasian, they are close to the Semites. Their language, Tamazigh, of the Afro-Asiatic group, uses Arabic, Hebrew, Latin, or Tamazigh letters. The Berbers live in ten North African countries, including the Maghrib nations and Egypt. Most Berbers converted to Islam and adopted Arab/Islamic traditions. The majority of Berbers live in Morocco and Algeria in the regions of the Atlas Mountains and the Sahara Desert.

Kabyle: A Berber tribe originating in the rugged northeastern mountain region of Algeria. They speak the Kabyle Berber dialect.

Modern Art in West and East Pakistan

Pakistan became an independent state in 1947. Artists created works of art to promote the establishment of Pakistan as a modern country. This joyous occasion, however, was tempered by looming difficulties. The nation was located in two geographically distinct units separated by a thousand miles. The form of its government seemed uncertain—its founders had envisioned a democratic state in which all religions, including Islam, could be worshipped freely. However, because Pakistan was created as the homeland for South Asia's Muslim population, there was pressure to govern with Islamic law. In this tense political climate, writers critiqued and questioned the founding of the nation in stories, novels, and poems.

Modern Painting in West Pakistan

New on the world stage, Pakistani artists aimed to present themselves as modern according to international standards. They adopted styles prevalent in Europe and the United States, but they also experimented with indigenous traditions to see how these could fit into the modern world.

The first artist in Pakistan to have an exhibition of modern paintings was a woman—Zubeida Agha (1922–1997). Trained in both Pakistan and Europe, Agha developed an approach to painting that reflected her education and experience. Her images of landscapes and people are simplified forms made with a variety of vibrant colors reminiscent of both Fauvism and Rajput miniatures.

In the 1950s, Shakir Ali (1916–1975), fresh from Europe, taught and later became principal of the National College of Arts. He brought back with him knowledge about Cézanne and Cubism, which offered new ways of interpreting the natural world in art. Ali's simplified and heavily outlined images of people, animals, and objects reflect a familiarity with Primitivism, a style developed in Europe yet influenced by Eastern art. Anna Molka Ahmed (1917–1994), coming from London to Lahore with her husband, also experienced the art world in both Pakistan and Europe. Her paintings are suggestive of French Impressionism in her use of thick, impasto brushstrokes to present life in Pakistan.

Shakir Ali, along with Gulgee (born 1926) and Sadequain (1930–1987; 1980.3.2), was also interested in local practices, in particular Islamic calligraphy. These artists experimented with calligraphy in paintings that placed centuries-old texts into modern formats. Gulgee's calligraphy paintings are abstract and gestural interpretations of Arabic and Urdu letters. His sweeping layers of paint explore the formal qualities of oil paint while they make references to Islamic design elements. Ranging in styles, Sadequain's representations of calligraphy include anthropomorphic letters that are angular and sharp, similar to his figurative works of the poor and downtrodden. In other calligraphic images, Sadequain transformed text into objects.

Modern Painting in East Pakistan

Zainul Abedin (1914–1976) is considered the pioneer of modernism in East Pakistan. Formally, in paintings and drawings, he relied on the Kalighat folk art made in Bengal as well as the art of earlier Indian painters, including Jamini Roy (1887–1972) and Abanindranath Tagore (1871–1951). But in his choice of topics such as famine and working-class life, his subject matter is more socially aware than the work of these earlier artists.

4

Orientalism in Nineteenth-Century Art

The Orient—including present-day Turkey, Greece, the Middle East, and North Africa—exerted its allure on the Western artist's imagination centuries prior to the turn of the nineteenth century. Figures in Middle Eastern dress appear in Renaissance and Baroque works by such artists as Bellini, Veronese, and Rembrandt, and the opulent eroticism of harem scenes appealed to the French Rococo aesthetic. Until this point, however, Europeans had minimal contact with the East, usually through trade and intermittent military campaigns.

In 1798, a French army led by General Napoleon Bonaparte invaded Egypt and occupied the country until 1801. The European presence in Egypt attracted Western travelers to the near and Middle East, many of whom captured their impressions in paint or print. In 1809, the French government published the first installment of the twenty-four-volume Description de l'Égypte (1809–22), illustrating the topography, architecture, monuments, natural life, and population of Egypt. The Description de l'Égypte was the most influential of many works that aimed to document the culture of this region, and it had a profound effect on French architecture and decorative arts of the period, as evidenced in the dominance of Egyptian motifs in the Empire style.

Some of the first nineteenth-century Orientalist paintings were intended as propaganda in support of French imperialism, depicting the East as a place of backwardness, lawlessness, or barbarism enlightened and tamed by French rule. Antoine-Jean Gros (1771–1835)—a pupil of Jacques-Louis David and a history painter in Napoleon's employ who never traveled to the Near East himself—conveys this idea in Napoleon in the Plague House at Jaffa(1804; Musée du Louvre, Paris), featuring an Eastern architectural setting and figures in exotic dress.

A propagandizing work, it depicts the then-general's visit to plague-afflicted prisoners during the siege of Jaffa. Recalling both Christian imagery and the divine touch of kings, Gros depicts Napoleon touching an inmate, who gestures in incredulity. Proponents of the Romantic Movement, such as Eugène Delacroix (1798–1863), also avidly took up themes of violence and cruelty in Oriental subjects. Delacroix's Massacre at Chios (1824) and Death of Sardanapalus (1827–28; both Louvre) embody in images of war and destruction the Romantic themes of human pathos, uncontrollable force, and emotional extremes. The emphasis on military brutality in many Oriental subjects by Western artists reflects ongoing conflicts throughout the century: the Greek War of Independence (1821–30), the conquest of Algeria by the French in the 1830s, and the Crimean War (1853–56).

While many Europeans relied on published travelogues and officially sanctioned literature like the Description de l'Égypte for their impressions of the Near East, many artists, including Delacroix, Jean-Léon Gérôme (1824–1904), Théodore Chassériau (1819–1856), Alexandre- Gabriel Decamps (1803–1860), and William Holman Hunt (1827–1910), made one or more journeys to the region. Genre painting, the prevalent form of Orientalist art in the nineteenth century, was greatly influenced by artists' direct experience of everyday life in Near Eastern cities and settlements. Gérôme popularized the theme of the bashi-bazouk, or Turkish mercenary soldier, often depicted in routine activities (05.13.4) or at leisure, as in a canvas by Charles Bargue (1825/26–1883). For Decamps, whose late career was shaped by the year he spent in Asia Minor (1828–29), depictions of military life (87.15.93) elevated genre subjects to the grandeur of history painting. These artists and their contemporaries also produced scenes of quiet domesticity, maternity—as in Chassériau's Scene in the Jewish Quarter of Constantine (1996.285)—and religious piety, seen in Gérôme's Prayer in the Mosque (87.15.130).

Occasionally, the Near Eastern setting provided a backdrop for religious works with Christian themes. This approach appealed particularly to British artists, as the explicitness of detail encouraged in the Orientalist style upheld the Protestant necessity for iconographic clarity and fidelity to nature in religious art. From his sojourn in Palestine in the 1850s, William Holman Hunt produced paintings such as The Finding of Christ in the Temple (1860; Birmingham Museum & Art Gallery), which uses an Orientalist setting, and The Scapegoat (1854–55; Lady Lever Art Gallery, Port Sunlight), a Christian allegory set in the Palestinian landscape.

Some of the most popular Orientalist genre scenes—and the ones most influential in shaping Western aesthetics—depict harems. Probably denied entrance to authentic seraglios, male artists relied largely on hearsay and imagination, populating opulently decorated interiors with luxuriant odalisques, or female slaves or concubines (many with Western features), reclining in the nude or in Oriental dress. Jean-Auguste-Dominique Ingres (1780–1867) never traveled to the East, but used the harem setting to conjure an erotic ideal in his voluptuous odalisques. Beyond their implicit eroticism, harem scenes evoked a sense of cultivated beauty and pampered isolation to which many Westerners aspired. The taste for Orientalism further manifested itself in Eastern architectural motifs, furniture, decorative arts, and textiles, which were increasingly sought after by a European elite. Proponents of the Aesthetic movement in Great Britain (1860s–80s), who collectively advocated an aesthetic of beauty for its own sake and valued form over content in art, took particular inspiration from Oriental interiors. This taste is exemplified in the Arab Hall (1877–79) in the London home of artist Frederic Leighton (1830–1896): glittering with mosaic tiles collected from Leighton's journeys to the East, it served as a gathering place for like-minded aesthetes.

The potency of Orientalist images remained undiminished for many artists into the twentieth century, including Auguste Renoir, Henri Matisse, Paul Klee, Wassily Kandinsky, August Macke, and Oskar Kokoschka, all of whom took up Orientalist themes.

Shah Abbas and the Arts of Isfahan

In 1597–98, Isfahan became the new capital of Iran when Shah Abbas I (r. 1587–1629) moved the Safavid government there as part of his larger plan to lift the country from the slump into which it had fallen. In order to revive the national economy, Abbas courted foreign traders and made commercial agreements with several European nations. He increased carpet and textile production in state workshops and settled 300 Chinese potters and their families in Iran to capitalize on the vogue for Chinese ceramics. He then relocated the Armenians from the city of Julfa, who controlled much of the Persian end of a bustling international silk trade, to a neighborhood in Isfahan called New Julfa and gave them the monopoly on silk exports. Abbas also created a new standing army which halted the encroachments of the Mughals and the Ottomans and restabilized the country's territories.

Abbas reinforced the image of the Safavid polity with the architecture of his new capital. From the old Seljuq city center he built a two-kilometer-long bazaar to a new town square called the Maidan-i Shah, located to the south near the Zaianda River. Four commanding structures were ranged on the sides of this square: an entrance to the bazaar painted with murals depicting Abbas' victories over the Uzbeks on the north, the Shah Mosque (1611–66) on the south, the Mosque of Shaykh Lutfallah (1603–19) on the east, and the Ali Qapu, a two-story audience hall, on the west. The four bases of the Safavid state—religion, trade, military, and the royal family itself—were thus united in one monumental visual statement.

Jean Chardin, a French jeweler who traveled throughout Iran in 1664–70 and again in 1671–77, exclaimed that Isfahan was "the greatest and most beautiful town in the whole Orient."

He described the city's population as a mix of Christians, Jews, fire-worshippers, Muslims, and merchants from all over the world. He counted 162 mosques, 48 colleges, 1,802 caravanserais, 273 baths, and 12 cemeteries, indicating Abbas' extensive architectural work in the city. Among the most scenic quarters was the area behind the Ali Qapu, where a series of gardens extended to the Chahar Bagh, a long boulevard lined with parks, the residences of nobles, and the palaces of the royal family. Tile panels and frescoes from the pavilions of the Chahar Bagh in the Museum's collection are examples of the lavish decoration of these structures.

Shah Abbas was also an active patron of painting and book production. His commission of a Shahnama reestablished the royal painting atelier that had shrunk during the reigns of his two predecessors. He also had the fifteenth-century Timurid manuscript Mantiq al-tair (The Language of the Birds) refurbished; four paintings were added and the manuscript presented to the shrine at Ardabil in 1609. His reign witnessed the careers of such artists as Riza, Sadiqi, Ali Riza Tabrizi, and Mir Imad.

After Abbas' death in 1629, both the Safavid state and its capital suffered. His successors were ill-prepared to rule and cities such as Shiraz rose to prominence as regional rulers became more powerful. The glory days of Isfahan came to an end in 1722 when the city was besieged by one of the Afghan tribes then in rebellion against the Safavids, and the dynasty, for all intents and purposes, ceased to rule.

The Shahnama

With its 50,000 rhyming couplets the Shahnama, or "Book of Kings," is one of the most voluminous epics of world literature. The poem narrates the history of the ancient kings of Iran from the mythical beginnings to the Arab conquest in 651 A.D. It was completed around 1010 A.D. by Abu'l Qasim Firdausi Tusi (935–1020), and was dedicated to the Ghaznavid ruler Mahmud of Ghazna (r. 998–1030), who had succeeded in gaining power over eastern Iran and modern-day Afghanistan by the end of the tenth century. In the eyes of the poet, this king appeared as the long-awaited ruler who could end dynastic strife and reunify the region. Thus, he seemed the ideal dedicatee for a work meant to celebrate Iran's past glory. Unfortunately, the ruler's response was not as enthusiastic and generous as expected. According to some sources, before dying, the poor and sick Firdausi voiced his disappointment for the little compensation received in a harsh satire against the sultan.

The history of Iran recounted in the Shahnama unfolds in fifty kingdoms, which are divided into three successive dynasties: the Pishdadiyan (1970.301.13)—the early legendary shahs, who established civilization (1970.301.2) and fought against the forces of evil (1970.301.3); the Kayanids—the principal protagonists of the enmity with Turan, the first and foremost antagonist of Iran (1970.301.36); and the Sasanians—the last glorious dynasty to rule a unified Iran before the advent of Islam (1970.301.62). The last section of the poem is considered to be the more historical one, and was occasionally referred to by medieval Islamic historiographers. Yet, the poem also revives pre-Islamic traditions, folklore, and oral literature. Kings and heroes are engaged in battles against foreign monstrous enemies (1970.301.4) and supernatural creatures (1970.301.51; 1970.301.3) that threaten their lives and the survival of their reigns. At the same time, the poem meditates on more profound human experiences and narrates the moral struggles, romantic interludes, and deaths of its many protagonists (1970.301.35).

With its interplay of lore and history (1970.301.73), the Shahnama offers models of conduct and rulership that inspired numerous generations of rulers. In addition to being a great work of literature, in fact, the poem can also be considered a successful example of "mirror for princes," a popular genre in the medieval and early modern Islamic world intended for the education and edification of rulers. The teachings and moral exempla offered by the virtuous kings and paladins of the Shahnama are among the aspects that explain its great success throughout history. All kings who ruled Iran, both local and foreign, continued to commission the production of new copies of the epic, which were often lavishly illustrated and illuminated.

By appropriating this cultural treasure and assimilating its ideas and values, many foreign rulers also used it as an ideological tool, one that allowed them to establish their legitimate succession to the kings of the past. Prestigious manuscripts such as the so-called Great Mongol Shahnama (ca. 1330), also in the Metropolitan Museum's collection, the Baysunghur Mirza Shahnama (1430), and the Shah Tahmasp Shahnama (1520–40) (see below)—sponsored, respectively, by the Ilkhanid (1256–1353), Timurid (1389–1501), and Safavid dynasties (1501–1736)—survive as evidence of this practice, and as testaments to the cultural and artistic importance of this literary masterpiece through the centuries.

The Shahnama of Shah Tahmasp

The Shahnama of Shah Tahmasp (r. 1524–76), also known as the Shahnama-yi Shahi, is arguably the most luxuriously illustrated copy of Firdausi's epic ever produced in the history of Persian painting (1970.301.21). Its pages, with outstanding measurements for an illustrated book (approximately 48 x 32 cm), are made of fine paper enriched with large gold-sprinkled borders and lavish illuminations. Accompanying the 759 folios of text, written in superb nasta'liq script, are 258 paintings of exquisite quality and artistic originality.

This project was realized at the royal atelier in Tabriz, the first capital of the Safavid dynasty (1501–1736), and involved two generations of the most renowned artists of the time. Among them were Sultan Muhammad, Mir Musavvir, and Aqa Mirak, who succeeded each other as directors of the project through the years. Scholars still disagree about the actual dates of execution of the manuscript. It was begun around the early 1520s, probably under Shah Isma'il (r. 1501–24), the founder of the dynasty, and carried out for at least another twenty years under Shah Tahmasp, the manuscript's dedicatee and principal sponsor.

The artistic importance of this manuscript cannot be overestimated. It is considered one of the highest achievements in the arts of the book for its superb calligraphy, painting, and illumination. From a pictorial point of view, it also marks the synthesis of the two most important phases of the Persian tradition—the Turkman style, which developed in Tabriz and Shiraz, and the Timurid style, associated with Herat. These two strains were absorbed into the new artistic idiom of the early Safavids. Thus, the lively treatment and bright colors of landscape (1970.301.2; 1970.301.21) and surfaces (architecture: 1970.301.13; 1970.301.35; textiles: 1970.301.2; 1970.301.51) inspired by the Turkman school, coexist with the more sober palette and balanced compositional layout (1970.301.62) of the Herat school, whose impact is particularly evident in some of the later paintings (1970.301.73).

Not long after its completion, the manuscript left Iran and was sent as a gift on the occasion of the accession of the Ottoman sultan Selim II (r. 1566–74). Contemporary Ottoman and European sources document the arrival of the Iranian embassy in Edirne on February 21, 1568, and even record the thirty-four camels bearing luxurious gifts that accompanied it. The Shahnama-yi Shahi is explicitly identified in one account as a lavish copy of the Shahnama in the name of Shah Tahmasp with 259 (sic) miniatures, and listed along with the Holy Qur'an, oriental porcelains, precious textiles, brocades, and silk carpets, also part of the gift. Until the early twentieth century, the manuscript remained in the library of the Topkapi Palace, Istanbul, where it continued to entertain generations of rulers. The inserts with commentaries and descriptions of the paintings in Ottoman Turkish, which were added sometimes around 1800, bear witness to the artistic curiosity and intellectual inspiration this work provided many centuries after its production. Today the manuscript is dispersed among private and public collections. The Metropolitan Museum has seventy-eight of the pages with paintings in its collection.

Trade and the Spread of Islam in Africa

Multiple Trajectories of Islam in Africa

Islam had already spread into northern Africa by the mid-seventh century A.D., only a few decades after the Prophet Muhammad moved with his followers from Mecca to Medina on the neighboring Arabian Peninsula (622 A.D./ 1 A.H.). The Arab conquest of Spain and the push of Arab armies as far as the Indus River culminated in an Empire that stretched over three continents, a mere hundred years after the Prophet's death. Between the eighth and ninth centuries, Arab traders and travelers, then African clerics, began to spread the religion along the eastern coast of Africa and to the western and central Sudan (literally, "Land of Black people"), stimulating the development of urban communities. Given its negotiated, practical approach to different cultural situations, it is perhaps more appropriate to consider Islam in Africa in terms of its multiple histories rather then as a unified movement.

The first converts were the Sudanese merchants, followed by a few rulers and courtiers (Ghana in the eleventh century and Mali in the thirteenth century). The masses of rural peasants, however, remained little touched. In the eleventh century, the Almoravid intervention, led by a group of Berber nomads who were strict observers of Islamic law, gave the conversion process a new momentum in the Ghana Empire and beyond. The spread of Islam throughout the African continent was neither simultaneous nor uniform, but followed a gradual and adaptive path. However, the only written documents at our disposal for the period under consideration derive from Arab sources (see, for instance, accounts by geographers' al-Bakri and Ibn Battuta).

Islamic Influence on African Societies

Islamic political and aesthetic influences on African societies remain difficult to assess. In some capital cities, such as Ghana and Gao, the presence of Muslim merchants resulted in the establishment of mosques. The Malian king Mansa Musa (r. 1312–37) brought back from a pilgrimage to Mecca the architect al-Sahili, who is often credited with the creation of the Sudano-Sahelian building style. Musa's brother, Mansa Suleyman, followed his path and encouraged the building of mosques, as well as the development of Islamic learning. Islam brought to Africa the art of writing and new techniques of weighting. The city of Timbuktu, for instance, flourished as a commercial and intellectual center, seemingly undisturbed by various upheavals. Timbuktu began as a Tuareg settlement, was soon integrated into the Mali Empire, then reclaimed by the Tuareg, and finally incorporated into the Songhai Empire. In the sixteenth century, the majority of Muslim scholars in Timbuktu were of Sudanese origin. On the continent's eastern coast, Arabic vocabulary was absorbed into the Bantu languages to form the Swahili language. On the other hand, in many cases conversion for sub-Saharan Africans was probably a way to protect themselves against being sold into slavery, a flourishing trade between Lake Chad and the Mediterranean. For their rulers, who were not active proselytizers, conversion remained somewhat formal, a gesture perhaps aimed at gaining political support from the Arabs and facilitating commercial relationships. The strongest resistance to Islam seems to have emanated from the Mossi and the Bamana, with the development of the Segu kingdom. Eventually, sub-Saharan Africans developed their own brand of Islam, often referred to as "African Islam," with specific brotherhoods and practices.

Local Mixes of Islamic and African Aesthetics

Because of its resistance to the representation of people and animals, the nature of Islam's interaction with the visual arts in Africa was one in which Islamic forms were accommodated and adapted. Muslim clerics' literacy and esoteric powers drew scores of converts to Islam. Sub-Saharan Muslim clerics known as marabouts began fabricating amulets with Qur'anic verses, which came to displace indigenous talismans and medicinal packets. These amulets are featured in the design of many traditional African artifacts.

Islam also reinforced the African fondness for geometric design and the repetition of patterns in decorating the surface of textiles and crafted objects. Local weaving may have been transformed with the importation of North

African weaving techniques. Islam has also often existed side by side with representational traditions such as masquerading. Such practices have often been viewed as supplemental rather than oppositional to Islam, particularly when they are seen as effective or operating outside of the central concerns of the faith.

An early example of this was noted by Ibn Battuta, the Maghribi scholar who visited Mali in 1352–53 and witnessed a masquerade performance at the royal court of its Muslim king. In many areas of Africa, the coexistence of Islam with representational art forms continues today. But although Islam has influenced a wide range of artistic practices in Africa since its introduction, monumental architecture is the best-preserved legacy of its early history on the continent. Mosques are the most important architectural examples of the tremendous aesthetic diversity generated by the interaction between African peoples and Islamic faith.

5

Venice and the Islamic World, 828–1797

Founded in the seventh century and built upon more than 100 islets in a lagoon off the northeast coast of the Italian peninsula, Venice grew to be one of the largest cities in Europe and the capital of a great trading Empire whose reach extended far into the eastern Mediterranean. Venice initially had strong political ties to Byzantium, and in the tenth and eleventh centuries Venetian merchants obtained the trading privileges from the Byzantine emperors that gave them a distinct advantage over their rivals from other Western European cities. The fact that Venetian gold ducat had currency throughout the Near East is an indication of the ubiquity and importance of Venetian merchants there. As Byzantium gradually gave way to Islamic Aliphates from the eighth century onward, meeting its ultimate demise in 1453 at the hands of the Ottoman sultan Mehmet II, Venetians increasingly came into contact with Muslims and their ideas, culture, and way of life. As a result, Venice became Christian Europe's most important interface with the Muslim civilizations of the Near East.

The artistic consequences of the dynamic relationship that Venice forged with its Islamic trading partners, especially the Mamluks of Egypt and Syria, the Ottomans of Turkey, and the Safavids of Iran, were felt over nearly a thousand-year period. The same merchant galleys that carried spices, soap, cotton, and industrial supplies from the bazaars of the Islamic Near East to the markets of Venice also brought with them luxurious carpets, velvets, silks, glass, porcelain, gilded bookbindings, illustrated manuscripts, and inlaid metalwork. Not surprisingly, these and other portable works of Islamic art, which were often superior in quality to what was available in Europe, made an indelible impression upon artistic taste and production in Venice. From the medieval to the Baroque eras, Venetians acquired Islamic art and adapted and imitated its techniques. In turn, albeit to a lesser extent, the arts of Venice became of interest to the Islamic world.

The chronological framework of these essays is provided by the year 828, when two Venetian merchants stole Saint Mark's relics from Alexandria (then part of the Muslim world) and brought them to their home city, and the year 1797, when the Venetian Republic fell to the French conqueror Napoleon Bonaparte.

The Venetian Perspective

Islamic Philosophy and Science in Venice

Precisely because Venice remained so open to foreign cultures, all kinds of philosophical, scientific, religious, and literary texts circulated in the city throughout the medieval and Renaissance periods. Mostly interested in Greek and Latin works, Venetian literati, however, understood that transmission occurred through Arabic texts.

After printing presses were established in Europe in 1469, Venice's prolific publishing shops quickly multiplied the number of copies of Arab texts in Latin translation. Venetian publishers issued Ptolemy's astronomical work Almagest, Averroes' philosophical Destructio destructionis, and many other related texts. In the most luxurious editions, Venetian illuminators enhanced the text with images of learned turbaned men, who often wield astrolabes (Islamic decorative arts, such as mosque lamps, ceramics, and blazons.

What is perhaps most remarkable is the Venetian painters' intimate knowledge of Near Eastern costume. During his visit to Constantinople in 1479–81, Gentile Bellini made portraits of Sultan Mehmet II and figure studies of local men and women from different social groups, including soldiers and scribes; in each instance, he painstakingly described their costumes. He and his pupils later drew on his studies in their paintings, which accounts for their strikingly detailed representations of Ottoman turbans and dress. Later, the Bellini protégés Vittore Carpaccio and Giovanni Mansueti became veritable experts in Mamluk dress and its decorum, most likely as a direct result of increased Mamluk-Venetian diplomatic relations at the end of the fifteenth and beginning of the sixteenth century. For Venetian Renaissance painters, stock drawings, or simili, of Muslim figures became prized possessions, passed down from one generation to another and circulated among workshops for reuse.

By 1525, the last canvases painted in the Oriental mode for the Venetian confraternities were in place, many of the city's most important Orientalist painters had died, and the Ottomans had conquered the Mamluk Empire. The Venetian tradition of setting large narrative scenes in the Islamic world had no followers in the late sixteenth century, when portraits of Muslims, most often Ottoman sultans, or the inclusion of a single Muslim figure in a religious scene were more characteristic.

During the second half of the sixteenth century, costume books emerged as a popular new genre and reflect a greater curiosity about foreign cultures derived from travels and new discoveries. Venice and the Veneto, where at least nine examples were published between 1540 and 1610, played a leading role in the costume book's early development. The most famous and important example is

Cesare Vecellio's Degli abiti antichi et moderni di diverse parti del mondo of 1590, which became a model of the genre. It includes more than 500 illustrations and pays special attention to Venetian and Ottoman dress.

By the sixteenth century, Venice's relations with her Muslim neighbors became increasingly complex. Venetian merchants continued trading in the eastern Mediterranean, but Turkey's aggressive navy made travel more precarious. As a result, Venetians began representing Muslim subjects in less sympathetic ways. Turbaned men were frequently stereotyped as aggressive warriors or ridiculed as acrobats in Venetian paintings, drawings, prints, and even in wooden ship decorations.

Even in the changed political environment, the Islamic Near East continued to occupy a place in the collective imagination of Venetians. Wealthy patrons commissioned paintings with Muslim subjects, such as Turkish women relaxing in the sultan's harem, to decorate their private palaces. These scenes serve as an important prologue to the new Orientalism, a pan-European phenomenon, of the nineteenth century.

Collecting Islamic Art in Venice

The presence of Islamic art in Venice can be documented from the middle Ages until today. The earliest objects to arrive in the city—such as the luxurious relief-cut glass and rock crystal vessels from Fatimid Egypt in the Treasury of San Marco—can perhaps best be interpreted as spolia, or booty, rather than as a sign of an appreciation of Islamic art per se. Over the centuries, however, Venetian merchants and diplomats definitely developed a taste for Islamic ceramics, textiles, arms and armor, metalwork, and manuscripts and displayed them in their homes as works of art alongside objects from other periods and places. Perhaps no greater testament to the esteem of Islamic artifacts in Venice can be found than the portraits of

Venetian patrician families with one of their most prized possessions, an oriental carpet.

By the eighteenth and nineteenth centuries, so much Islamic art had accumulated in Venice's palaces and churches that the city became an important destination for collectors of Islamic art, such as Wilhelm von Bode of Germany, wanting to make new acquisitions. Provenance research reveals that many Islamic art objects now in Western European collections passed through Venice first. Major examples still remain in the city today, however, and the number of Venetian museums and churches with works of Islamic art is truly impressive; they include the Biblioteca Nazionale Marciana, the Basilica and Treasury of San Marco, the Museo Civico Correr, the Fondazione Giorgio Cini, and the Museo Franchetti alla Ca' d'Oro.

Venice's Principal Muslim Trading Partners: the Mamluks, the Ottomans, and the Safavids

Venice and the Mamluks

Venice's economic and diplomatic relationship with Egypt, Syria, and other areas along the eastern Mediterranean shore was tied, in particular, to the Mamluks (1250–1517), the powerful Islamic rulers who both halted the advance of Mongols west of Iraq and expelled the last of the Crusaders from the Holy Land in the second half of the thirteenth century. The Mamluk capital of Cairo, a city of around 200,000 inhabitants, was the greatest metropolis of its age. In this and other principal cities of the sultanate, Mamluk rulers built impressive mosque complexes, funerary structures, and urban palaces.

The Mamluks inherited from the Fatimids (909–1171) and Ayyubids (1171–1260) the role of middlemen between South and Southeast Asia and Europe in the valuable spice trade and in the movement of other goods by land and sea through the Damascus and the Red Sea routes. Venice consistently sought favorable privileges for its merchants and through these efforts became the Mamluks' main European trading partner.

Several cities under Mamluk control had a permanent Venetian diplomatic representative with regular access to local authorities. Ties between the Venetian oligarchy, nobility, and merchant class and the Mamluk court and its retinue were particularly strong. The longest reigning doge of Venice, Francesco Foscari (r. 1423–57), was even born in Mamluk Egypt.

Mamluk rule finally came to an end when Syria and then Egypt fell to the Ottomans in 1516–17. It was in the years leading up to this event that commercial exchange between the Mamluks and Venice intensified. As a result, a dazzling array of goods—textiles, spices, metals, medicines, pigments, precious stones, glass, and paper—traveled in both directions. Mamluk trade and, in some cases, direct artistic influence shaped the fashion in Venice for Islamic-style bookbindings, the development of inlaid metalwork, and the taste for blue-and-white ceramics in the fifteenth and sixteenth centuries.

Inlaid Metal-work

Under the Mamluks, metalwork intricately inlaid with silver and gold flourished in Damascus and Cairo. In the late fourteenth century, however, as the Mamluk elite suffered an economic decline, the European export market became increasingly important for these wares. By the early fifteenth century, new shapes and decorative styles developed in response to European tastes, and Latin inscriptions could sometimes be found on Islamic metalwork in addition to Arabic ones.

Venice played a crucial role in the trade of Islamic metalwork in the Mediterranean. Shipping documents reveal that Venetians exported large quantities of copper and brass to the Near East; in return, they imported finished inlaid vessels. Mamluk basins, ewers, candlesticks, and incense burners found a place in the finest Venetian homes and churches, and some were even customized with the coat of arms of Venetian noble families. Local craftsmen admired the skill and design of Islamic metalwork too and frequently imitated it.

The connection between Venice and Mamluk metalwork is so strong that a myth arose in the nineteenth century that Arab or Persian craftsmen must have lived and worked in the city, producing "Veneto-Saracenic" pieces for the local market. One craftsman in particular, Mahmud al-Kurdi, has long been associated with this theory. Recent research, however, suggests that al-Kurdi most likely was active in western Iran. Indeed, it is highly improbable that Muslim metalworkers could have ever set up shop in a city as tightly regulated by the guilds as Venice.

Venice and the Ottomans

The Ottoman Empire existed from 1281 to 1924 and at the height of its power in the sixteenth and seventeenth centuries included Anatolia, the Middle East, parts of North Africa, and much of southeast Europe. No other Muslim power in history has rivaled its longevity and extent. Because so many major Near Eastern entrepôts eventually fell within the confines of the vast Empire, including Bursa (1326), Constantinople (1453), and Damascus (1516), Venetians perforce developed commercial and diplomatic relations with the Ottomans. "Being merchants," the Venetian ambassador to the Sublime Porte wrote in 1553, "we cannot live without them." Territorial disputes in the Balkanic border region led to the Ottoman-Venetian wars of 1463–79, 1499–1503, 1537–40, and 1570–73, but both parties generally sought peaceful coexistence rather than conflict in the name of trade. So important was the Ottoman Empire to the Venetians that the ambassador to the Sublime

Porte was regarded as the most senior post in the Venetian diplomatic service and was the highest paid. Venice itself received regular visits from Ottoman dignitaries, as numerous documents attest.

Venice relied on the Ottomans for wheat, spices, raw silk, cotton, leather, and calcified ashes for the Murano glass industry. In return, Venice exported finished goods, namely glass, soap, paper, and textiles. In addition, it also produced maps, clocks, portraits, and luxury arts. Trade with the Islamic world made an indelible imprint on the decorative arts of Venice. Pottery, parade armor, furniture, bookbindings, textiles, pattern books, and inlaid metalwork are just some of the many Venetian arts in which distinctly Ottoman techniques and/or motifs can be observed.

Venice and Persia

Because of distance, Greater Iran did not have as strong a link to Venice as the Mamluk and Ottoman Empires did. Nevertheless, both the presence of Venetian merchants on the eastern coast of the Black Sea and the importance of the trade routes passing through Persian cities favored diplomatic and commercial exchange from the time of Mongol dominance in the region in the late thirteenth century down to its rule by the Safavid dynasty (1501–1722).

The need to maintain political equilibrium in the Mediterranean is often what spurred diplomatic relations between Venice and Persia. For example, Christendom, including Venice, sought an alliance with the Mongol Ilkhanids (1256–1353) against the Mamluks and the Mongols of the Golden Horde. In the fifteenth century, there were envoys between Venice and Tabriz—the industrious capital of the White Sheep Turcomans in northwest Iran, where a large array of luxury goods were traded—to occupy the Ottomans, and therefore to weaken them, on both their European and eastern Anatolian borders. According to legend, the Turcoman envoy of Uzun Hasan (r. 1468–78) presented the celebrated "turquoise" (in reality pale blue-colored glass) cup in the Treasury of Saint Mark as a gift to Venice in 1472.

Thanks to trade, large numbers of objects, manuscripts, textiles, and Persian carpets passed through Venice or were collected and remained in the city. A glimpse of this wealth can be found today in works dispersed in collections such as the Museo Civico Correr and the Biblioteca Nazionale Marciana. On the diplomatic level, the most important testimony of the exchanges between the Safavid shahs and the Venetian doges are a number of sumptuous silk and silver-wrapped-thread carpets of the so-called Polonaise type. Today in the museum of Basilica San Marco, these carpets were draped in front of the high altar of the church during religious festivals, used as a floor covering to display objects from the Basilica's Treasury, or laid beneath the doge's bier at his funeral.

Islam - Between Tradition and Modernity

The end of the Ottoman's Empire unleashed a renaissance in literature and the arts. Traditional arts had suffered under ailing economies and the transfer of patronage from urban regional centers to the Ottoman court. By World War I, artists had turned to Western art as a representative form of modern expression. As a result, a new separation emerged between traditional art in all its forms and what came to be known as the fine art of easel painting. Traditional arts such as painting on glass and leather, woodwork, glassmaking, metalwork, textiles, and wall frescoes were considered naive and repetitive, relying less on intellect and more on archaic traditions. Painting on glass is one example of a dying tradition that ended with the passing of the last Syrian painter in this genre (Abou Subhi al-Tinawi, Muhammad Ali fi al-Sham).

By mid-century, many of the countries in western Asia that was under European dominance gained their independence. These new nations claimed a renewed political as well as cultural identity. Iraqi artists joined poets and architects in advocating a modernity that embraced the rich and diverse local heritage. Reminiscent of Islamic civilization's success in creating a new culture that embraced and synthesized the diverse cultural characteristics of the societies it conquered, modern artists continued to select, reshape, and explore new ways to create contemporary art. They drew from an accumulation of sources: prehistoric, Mesopotamian, Hellenistic, Roman, Byzantine, Islamic, Persian, Coptic, and Indian. New expressions emerged in regional art, Islamic art, and between art and poetry.

Religious Art

Christian doctrine and the monastic way of life were first established in Syria and Egypt. In the early Christian era, Syrian artists were among the first to paint icons, illuminated manuscripts, and church murals. In the twentieth century, Christian art continued to flourish in Armenia, Cyprus, Lebanon, Palestine, Syria, Sinai, Crete, the Balkans, and Asia Minor. Iconographers followed the canons of the Eastern Orthodox Church with variations in style that reflected the diverse cultures of the region. Twentieth-century Arab iconographers continued this traditional art, passed from one generation to the next (Milad al-Shayeb, Saint Panteleimon). Icons were sought after by pilgrims and tourists to the Holy Land and monasteries in the region. Several modern artists, inspired by this tradition, produced new interpretations that combined the religious and the secular (Elias Zayat, Last Supper).

Islamic Art

While manuscript and book arts such as illumination, miniatures, and bookbinding declined, Arabic writing known as khat (calligraphy) continued to flourish. Since Islam does not favor human-based imagery and limits its use to secular buildings and illuminated manuscripts, Arabic calligraphy continued to be used as the single most prominent element in religious architecture. Because Arabic is the revered language of the Qur'an, Arabic calligraphy, long considered a sacred art, was regarded as the visible embodiment of the divine word. Among the most popular forms of calligraphy were quotations from Qur'anic verses, the Traditions of the Prophet, and Arabic proverbs, as well as representations of God's attributes. The elasticity of Arabic writing permitted an infinite number of forms, allowing artists to explore traditional Islamic calligraphy by using contemporary styles and techniques. These modern calligraphers followed any one of the myriad of classical styles, and at the same time introduced new interpretations in composition and media (Hashim al-Khattat, Untitled). Aside from their aesthetic value, Arabic letters are imbued with meaning and symbolism; their abstracted forms gave Arab artists a means of asserting their heritage within prevailing Western artistic trends.

Twentieth-century artists have explored calligraphy and geometric forms within an Arab-Islamic cultural context, in the process creating a new artistic vocabulary for modern art. Basing their work on Islamic geometric art and mathematical values, some artists revitalized the traditions of harmony and symmetry (Kamal Boullata, Eppur si muove no. IX), while others mastered Islamic techniques of ceramics (Wasma'a Chorbachi, The Mystery of Supplication). The contemporary free-style of calligraphy first appeared in Iraq around 1950. In contrast to formal styles of Islamic calligraphy, artists rendered letters in a free and abstracted form (Madiha Umar, At the Concert). In 1971, a group of Iraqi artists exhibited works that deconstructed the Arabic letter, thereby giving it a new dimension, which sparked a discourse on the theoretical implications of the abstracted Arabic letter. Modern calligraphic artists also used a word or phrase to convey a direct message, or they created compositions from the shapes of Arabic words. Others incorporated indecipherable cursive writing within the body of the work to evoke the illusion of writing (Jumana El-Husseini, Untitled) or used the letter as a structural element (Wijdan Ali, Karbala Series: Hussein). Some have been inspired by the medieval Sufi practice of studying the numerical and symbolic value of Arabic letters (Shakir Hassan al-Said, Objective Contemplations).

Image and Word

With its rich symbolism and imagery, Arabic poetry has captivated generations of Arabs since the pre-Islamic era. Similar to classical calligraphy, Arabic poetry traditionally has been subject to rigid rules. However, in the second half of the twentieth century, the boundaries of poetry gave way to a freer verse. Today, poetry remains a potent and ever-popular form of expression.

Literature, particularly poetry, has had a long and productive relationship with the arts of the twentieth century. Arab artists inspired by poetry have produced diverse works—from fiber art to engraving—devoted to classical and popular Arabic poetry (Rafa Nasiri, Homage to al-Mutanabi). Many modern art critics have been poets and authors who formed close relationships with artists. Collaborations between artists and poets have produced books in which the fusion of image and word manifests an aesthetic synergism that is not meant to be an illustration but rather a transformation of two languages—the visual and the written. Other artists inspired by modern poetry have underscored its visual aesthetic while retaining its literary value (Etel Adnan, Allah).

6

The Indo-Islamic Architecture

Indian architecture took new shape with the advent of Islamic rule in India towards the end of the 12th century AD. New elements were introduced into the Indian architecture that include: use of shapes (instead of natural forms); inscriptional art using decorative lettering or calligraphy; inlay decoration and use of coloured marble, painted plaster and brilliantly glazed tiles. In contrast to the indigenous Indian architecture which was of the trabeate order i.e. all spaces were spanned by means of horizontal beams, the Islamic architecture was arcuate i.e. an arch or dome was adopted as a method of bridging a space.

The concept of arch or dome was not invented by the Muslims but was, in fact, borrowed and was further perfected by them from the architectural styles of the post-Roman period. The Muslims used the cementing agent in the form of mortar for the first time in the construction of buildings in India. They further put to use certain scientific and mechanical formulae, which were derived by experience of other civilizations, in their constructions in India. Such use of scientific principles helped not only in obtaining greater strength and stability of the construction materials but also provided greater flexibility to the architects and builders. This amalgamation of the Indian and the Islamic elements led to the emergence of a new style of architecture called the Indo-Islamic Architecture.

One fact that must be stressed here is that, the Islamic elements of architecture had already passed through different experimental phases in other countries like Egypt, Iran and Iraq before these were introduced in India. Unlike most Islamic monuments of these countries, which were largely constructed in brick, plaster and rubble, the Indo-Islamic monuments were typical mortar-masonry works formed of dressed stones. It must be emphasized that the development of the Indo-Islamic architecture was greatly facilitated by the knowledge and skill possessed by the Indian craftsmen, who had mastered the art of stonework for centuries and used their experience while constructing Islamic monuments in India. In simple terms the Islamic architecture in India can be divided into religious and secular. Mosques and Tombs represent the religious architecture, while palaces and forts are examples of secular Islamic architecture. Forts were essentially functional, complete with a little township within and various fortifications to engage and repel the enemy.

Mosques:

The mosque or masjid is a representation of Muslim art in its simplest form. The mosque is basically an open courtyard surrounded by a pillared verandah, crowned off with a dome. A mihrab indicates the direction of the qibla for prayer. Towards the right of the mihrab stands the mimbar or pulpit from where the Imam presides over the proceedings. An elevated platform, usually a minaret from where the Faithful are summoned to attend the prayers is an invariable part of a mosque. Large mosques where the faithful assemble for the Friday prayers are called the Jama Masjids.

Tombs:

Although not actually religious in nature the tomb or maqbara introduced an entirely new architectural concept.

While the masjid was mainly known for its simplicity, a tomb could range from being a simple affair (Aurangazeb's grave) to an awesome structure enveloped in grandeur (Taj Mahal). The tomb usually consists of solitary compartment or tomb chamber known as the huzrah in whose centre is the cenotaph or zarih. This entire structure is covered with an elaborate dome. In the underground chamber lies the mortuary or the maqbara, in which the corpse is buried in a grave or qabr. Smaller tombs may have a mihrab, although larger mausoleums have a separate mosque located separately from the main tomb. Normally the whole tomb complex or rauza is surrounded by an enclosure. The tomb of a Muslim saint is called a dargah. Almost all Islamic monuments were subjected to free use of verses from the Holy Koran and a great amount of time was spent in carving out minute details on walls, ceilings, pillars and domes.

The Delhi Style of Architecture

The Delhi or the Imperial Style of Indo-Islamic architecture flourished between 1191-1557 AD and covered Muslim dynasties viz., Slave (1191-1246), Khilji (1290-1320), Tughlaq (1320-1413), Sayyid (1414-1444) and Lodi (1451-1557). The first Islamic sultanate structures were built of disparate dismantled pieces of Hindu temples, after which came an era of carefully planned structures and precincts, later assimilating and incorporating Hindu elements and workmanship.

The earliest construction work of this period was began by Qutubuddin Aibak, who started erecting monumental buildings of stone on Qila Rai Pithora, the first of the seven historical cities of Delhi associated with Prithviraj Chauhan. The Qutb Mosque (1192 AD) is one such building, whose arcaded aisles were composed of pillars carved in the Hindu style. Named as the Quwwat-ul-Islam Masjid, it is considered as the earliest mosque in India. The mosque has beautiful Islamic calligraphy, the arabesque designs and pillars with pre-Islamic Hindu motifs. Aibak got a series of arches constructed to screen the Hindu pillars of the sanctuary. Qutub-ud-din Aibak also started the construction of Qutub Minar in 1192 (which was eventually completed by Iltutmish in 1230). The Qutub Minar, built to commemorate the entry of Islam, was essentially a victory tower, decorated with several calligraphic inscriptions. The diameter of the Qutub Minar is 14.32m at the base and about 2.75m at the top. It measures a height of 72.5m and contains a spiral staircase of 379 steps. Another interesting monument constructed during this time was the Adhai-din-ka-Jhopra, located beyond the Ajmer darga in Rajasthan. It was constructed in 1153 AD and converted into a mosque in 1198 AD.

Shamsuddin Iltutmish (1211-1236 AD) was another great building monarch of the Slave dynasty. He extended the Quwwat-ul-Islam Masjid (1229 AD) and built the tomb of his son Nasiruddin Mohammed in 1231 AD, which is locally known as the Sultan Ghari. He also started his own tomb (Iltutmish's Tomb) located in the Qutub Minar complex in 1235 AD. This tomb employed the "squinch" system of construction in which a square hall is converted into an octagon by projecting a small arch across the angle of the square hall. Iltutmish is also credited with constructing two lesser-known monuments near Delhi called the Hauz-i-Shamsi and the Shamsi-Idgah. The tomb of Balban constructed in 1280 AD represents the first true arch built in India, which is produced by following the scientific system originally formulated by the Roman engineers.

Allauddin Khilji established the second city of Delhi at Siri, built the Alai Darwaza near the Qutub Minar and dug a vast reservoir at Hauz Khas around 1311AD. The well-decorated Alai Darwaza, which served as an entrance gateway to the mosque at the Qutub complex, marks the evolution of another innovative feature in the Indo-Islamic architecture. The Jamaat Khana Masjid near Nizamuddin in Delhi and the Ukha Masjid in Bharatpur in Rajasthan were also built during this period.

The rulers of the Tughlaq Dynasty also undertook considerable construction activities, including building three of the seven ancient cities of Delhi. Ghiyasuddin Tughlaq (1320-1325 AD) built Tughlaqabad, the third city of Delhi, in 1321-23 AD. The Tomb of Ghiyasuddin Tughlaq, built of red sandstone, is an irregular pentagon in its exterior plan and its design is of the pointed or "Tartar" shape and is crowned by a finial resembling the kalasa and amla of a Hindu temple. Delhi's fourth city Jahanpanah was built by Mohammad-bin-Tughlaq in mid-14th century. Feroz Shah Tughlaq (1351-1388 AD) was undoubtedly the greatest builder among all the rulers of the Tughlaq dynasty. He himself wrote in Fatuhat-i-Feroz Shah "among the gifts which God bestowed on me, His humble servant, was a desire to erect public buildings". He built Ferozabad, Delhi's fifth city, in 1354 AD. The famous Firoz Shah Kotla ground is the only remnant of its past glory. Feroz Shah Tughlaq is also credited with founding the fortified cities of Jaunpur, Fathabad and Hissar. His construction works were of a unique simple style characterised by the use of inexpensive materials. The medieval rulers, who were used to the convenience of choosing new locations for starting new constructions, rarely adopted restoration of previous buildings. It was only Feroze Shah Tughlaq who took up large-scale restoration works and repaired hundreds of monuments, including the Qutub Minar which was damaged by lightening in 1369 AD. The Kali Masjid (c.1370 AD), the Khirki Masjid (c.1375 AD) and the Kalan Masjid (c.1375 AD) also belong to this period, the last two being raised on a tahkhana or substructure of arches.

In the 14th century under the Timurid rulers, Islamic architecture underwent a change. The narrow horseshoe arch was replaced by the true arch, an idea imported directly from Persia. However, Indian masons weren't completely convinced of its holding power. They began using wooden beams as supports, and eventually the four-centred arch minus the beam support came into vogue. During the Sayyid and the Lodi Dynasties, more than fifty tombs of different sizes were constructed. The Lodis introduced the concept of double domes built one upon the other, leaving some space in between. Two different types of tombs with octagonal and square plans respectively began to be constructed. The Tombs of Mubarak Sayyid (d. 1434 AD), Muhammad Sayyid (d.1444 AD) and Sikander Lodi (d.1517 AD) are all of the octagonal type. The square tombs are represented by such monuments as the Bara Khan Ka Gumbad, Chota Khan Ka Gumbad, Bara Gumbad (1494 AD), Shish Gumbad, Dadi Ka Gumbad and the Poli ka Gumbad. The Tomb of Isa Khan (1547 AD), the Tomb of Adham Khan (1561 AD), Moth ki Masjid (c.1505 AD), Jamala Masjid (1536 AD) and the Qila-i-Kuhna Masjid (c.1550 AD) belong to the final phase of the Delhi style of architecture.

The Provincial Style of Architecture

The Provincial Style of Architecture encompasses the architectural trends and developments noticed in different provincial capitals in India, but specifically in Punjab (1150-1325 AD), Bengal (1203-1573 AD), Gujarat (1300-1572 AD), Jaunpur (1376-1479 AD), Malwa (1405-1569 AD), Deccan (1347-1617 AD), Bijapur (1490-1656 AD), Khandesh (1425-1650 AD) and Kashmir (1410 onwards). The Pandua and Adina mosques are the earliest architectural examples in Bengal. The tomb of Akhi Surajuddin, the Kotwali Darwaza, the Dakhil Darwaza and the tomb of Sultan Jalaluddin Mohammad Shah (1414-1431 AD), known as the Eklakhi Tomb, served as prototypes for the subsequent Islamic architecture of Bengal. The other important buildings of Bengal include Tantipara Masjid (1475 AD), Chamkatti Masjid (1475 AD), Lotan Masjid (1480 AD), Chota Sona Masjid (1510 AD) and the Qadam Rasool Mosque (1530 AD).

Under the Sharqi dynasty Jaunpur became a great centre of art, culture and architectural activity. During the rule of Shamsuddin Ibrahim (1402-1436 AD) several palaces, mosques, tombs and other buildings came up, the most prominent being the Atala Masjid built in 1378. Later other important buildings were produced that include Khalis Mukhlis Masjid (1430 AD), Jhangiri Masjid (1430 AD) Lal Darwaza Masjid (1450 AD) and the Jami Masjid (1470 AD).

Gujarat witnessed significant architectural activity for over 250 years starting from Muzaffar Shah's declaration of independence from Delhi and the formation of the Sultanate of Gujarat in 1307 AD until the conquest of Gujarat by the Mughal Emperor Akbar in 1500 AD. The early phase of the architecture belonging to the 14th century is represented by the Tomb of Baba Farid and the Adina Masjid at Pathan, Jama Masjid of Bharuch (1300), Jami Masjid at Cambay (1325) and the Hilal Khan Qazi's mosque in Dholka (1333). Under the rule of Ahmed Shahi (early 15th century) and Mahmud I Begarha (1459-1511) different types of mosques, tombs and gateways were built at Ahmedabad, Dholka and Sarkhej. Ahmedabad is a city full of architectural masterpieces which include Sayyid Alam's mosque (1412), Teen Darwaza (1415), Tomb of Ahmed Shah (1440), Rani-ka-Hujra (1440), the Jami Masjid (built by the city's founder Sultan Ahmed Shah in 1423), Qutubuddin's mosque (1454), Rani Sipri Mosque (1505), Sidi Bashir's Mosque (1510), which is famous for its "shaking minarets", Rani Rupmati Masjid at Mirzapur (built between 1430 and 1440) and the Kankaria Lake, constructed in 1451 by Sultan Qutb-ud-Din.

The cities of Dhar and Mandu of the Malwa province provide examples of distinct architectural elements in the form of polychromatic ornamentation of buildings, which was obtained by the use of coloured stones and marble as well as by means of encaustic tiles. The earliest buildings of this period are the Kamal Maula Masjid (1400) and the Lat Masjid (1405) at Dhar and the Dilawar Khan Masjid (1405) and the Malik Mughis mosque (1452) at Mandu. The architectural activity took a new turn with the establishment of the capital at Mandu, especially under the rule of Hoshang Shah (1405-1435). Important buildings in Mandu are the Jahaz Mahal (a 120 meter long 'ship palace' built by Sultan Ghiyas-ud-din-Khilji between two artificial lakes Munj Talao and Kapur Talao), Taveli Mahal with two wells called Ujali and Andheri Baoli, Hindola Mahal, Dilawar Khan's Mosque, Hoshang Shah's Tomb, Ashrafi Mahal and the Jami Masjid built by Mahmud Shah Khilji I. As Mandu or the 'City of Joy' was associated with the romance of the poet-prince Baz Bahadur and Rani Roopmati, many buildings are devoted to them like the Baz Bahadur's Palace and Roopmati's Pavilion. The city also has several gateways like the Delhi Darwaza, the Alamgir and Bhangi Darwaza, Rampol Darwaza, Jehangir Gate and Tarapur Gate.

The architecture of the Deccan is marked by its distinct originality and independence of style, unlike the architectural styles of the other provinces which combined both the temple architecture and the Islamic building ideals. It derived its elements from the architectural styles of the Sultan of Delhi and that of the distant Persia.

These aspects are best illustrated by the evolution of tombs in the Deccan. The earliest specimen afforded by the tomb of Allauddin (14th century) was an imitation in toto of the Tughlaq style of Delhi. The tombs of the 15th century built by the Bahmani rulers of Bidar depict distinct Persian elements dexterously combined with those of the Delhi style. Finally, the tombs of the Qutb Shahi dynasties of the 16th and 17th centuries show a fully developed bulbous or "Tartar" dome, indicating its complete evolution by the amalgamation of various differing styles. The earliest period of architectural development started in 1347 when Allauddin Bahman Shah constructed the Gulbarga Fort and the Jami Masjid at Gulbarga. The second phase is represented by the architecture of Bidar initiated by Ahmed Shah

(1422-1436), which includes the Bidar Fort, Mahmud Gawan's Madrassa and the Ali Barid's Tomb.

The Qutub Shahi and Nizam Shahi dynasties contributed greatly towards the development of the Deccan style of architecture. The best architectural specimen is the Charminar built in 1591 by Mohammed Quli Qutb Shah. Often called "Arc de triumph of the East", it is a beautiful structure with four intricately carved minarets built with granite and lime-mortar. The Mecca Masjid, located near the Charminar, is another architectural beauty. It was started in 1614 by Abdullah Qutub Shah and completed in 1687 by Aurangzeb. The Golconda Fort built by Mohammed Quli Qutb Shah in 1525 was an impregnable fort of great strategic importance to most of the rulers. The Qutb Shahi Tombs are a cluster of six magnificent tombs situated a kilometer north of Golconda Fort's Banjara Darwaza. These are built in a unique architectural style which is a mixture of Persian, Pathan and Hindu forms. The tomb of the fifth king of the Qutb Shahi dynasty and founder of Hyderabad - Mohammed Quli Qutb Shah is one of the largest and most imposing of these monuments. The Chowmahalla Palalce built in 1750 by Nizam Salabat Jung was designed along the lines of the Shah's palace in Tehran and consists of a group of palaces each used for a specific purpose. It consists of the Khilwat, Aftab Mahal, the Tahniyat Mahal and the Durbar Hall. The Falaknuma Palace built in 1870 by Nawab Vikar-Ul-Ulmara; the Prime Minister of Hyderabad is a rare blend of Italian and Tudor architecture.

The Adil Shahi dynasty of Bijapur constructed several mosques, tombs and palaces. The development of the dome reached its acme during their reign. They also borrowed some elements like the use of symbol of crescent from the Ottoman Empire. The most distinct monument of this period is, undoubtedly, the Gol Gumbaz built by Mohammad Adil Shah, which is largest masonry dome in the world. The dome is 51metres high and has a diameter of 37metres. The dome is an engineering marvel since it stands unsupported by any pillars. It also has an excellent acoustic system. Bijapur is also famous for the Sat Manzil, Ibrahim Roza, Bara Kaman, Mehtar Mahal, Nagar Khana and the Gagan Mahal. Ibrahim Roza is the tomb of Adil Shai Sultan Ibrahim II (1580-1627 AD).

The Islamic architecture of Kashmir is typified by use of woodwork. The log construction using deodar trees for the construction of wooden bridges called kadals or the wooden shrines called ziarats are the best illustrations of wooden architecture of Kashmir. The mosque of Shah Hamdan in Srinagar and the Jami Masjid at Srinagar built by Sikandar Butshikan (1400 AD) are the typical examples of the wooden architecture of Kashmir. The Mughals tried to revive the art of stone building in Kashmir in the 16th and 17th centuries. The Fort of Hari Parbat, the Pattar Masjid (1623) and the Akhun Mulla Shah's mosque (1649) are illustrations of these efforts.

Sher Shah Suri of the Sur dynasty also made noteworthy contribution to the Indo-Islamic architecture. The town of Sasaram in Bihar is an excellent illustration of the Suri monuments, which are in the form of four tombs viz., Sher Shah's Tomb, the tomb of his father, Hasan Sur Khan built in 1535, the tomb of his son Salim Shah and the tomb of Alwal Khan, the chief architect of Sher Shah. The tomb of Sher Shah Suri is an architectural masterpiece that was to have a profound impact on the evolution of Indo-Islamic architecture.

Sher Shah's another great contribution was the completion of the sixth city of Delhi called the Shergarh or Dilli Sher Shai around the Purana Qila area in 1540s. The Purana Qila has three main gates – the Humayun darwaza, Talaqi darwaza and Bara darwaza. The Qila-i-kuhna masjid built by Sher Shah Suri in 1541AD is one of the most fascinating buildings in the Purana Qila.

The Mughal Style of Architecture

The Mughal rulers were visionaries and their own personalities reflected in the all-round development of various arts, crafts, music, building and architecture. The Mughal dynasty was established with the crushing victory of Babar at Panipat in 1526 AD. During his short five-year reign, Babar took considerable interest in erecting buildings, though few have survived. The mosque at Kabuli Bagh at Panipat in Punjab and the Jami Masjid at Sambhal near Delhi, both constructed in 1526, are the surviving monuments of Babar. His son Humayun laid the foundation of a city called Dinpanah ("refuge of the faithful") at the Purana Qila in Delhi but the city could not be completed. The Mughal Empire briefly fell to the Suris in 1540 but was re-established by Humayun in 1555. The Persian influence into the Mughal architecture was largely a result of Humayun's observance of this style at the court of Shah Tahmasp during the period of his exile. However, the Persian elements could manifest and mature only several years after his death, as is evident in the Humayun's Tomb at Delhi, which was designed in 1564 by his widow Haji Begum as a mark of devotion, eight years after his death. Humayun's Tomb represents an outstanding landmark in the development and refinement of the Mughal style. In fact the design of the Taj Mahal was modelled on this tomb.

Architecture flourished during the reign of Akbar (1555-1605). The chief feature of the architecture of Akbar's time was the use of red sandstone. In principle the construction was of the trabeate order, although the "Tudor" arch was also used. The domes were of the "Lodhi" type, while the pillar shafts were many-sided with the capitals in the form of bracket supports. One of the first major building projects was the construction of a huge fort at Agra. The massive sandstone ramparts of the Red Fort are other impressive examples. The most ambitious architectural exercise of Akbar, and one of the most glorious examples of Indo-Islamic architecture, was the creation of an entirely new capital city at Fatehpur Sikri. It has been described as "a frozen moment in history". The buildings at Fatehpur Sikri blended both Islamic and Hindu elements in their architectural style. Its structures have been modelled after the simple canvas tents used by semi-nomadic ancestors of the Mughals. The free-standing pavilions are constructed as stone analogues of the tents. The Buland Darwaza, the Panch Mahal and the Darga of Saleem Chisti are the most imposing of all the buildings of Fatehpur Sikri. The Diuwan-e-Khas is another fascinating structure in the complex which was designed for private audiences. It is of cube-like form with an elaborate central column connected to the four corners by bridges. The square plan, although of Central Asian origin, would have represented to the Hindu craftsmen the "mandala" model of the cosmos. There are several palaces in the complex including Jodaha Bai's Palace and the houses of Miriam, the Sultana and Birbal.

Akbar's successor Jahangir (1605-1627) concentrated more on painting and other forms of art than on building and architecture. However, some note-worthy monuments of his time include Akbar's Tomb at Sikandra near Agra, which was completed in 1613. This monument represents a major turning point in Mughal history, as the sandstone compositions of Akbar were adapted by his successors into opulent marble masterpieces. Jahangir is the central figure in the development of the Mughal gardens. The most famous of his gardens is the Shalimar Bagh on the banks of Lake Dal in Kashmir. The adjoining Nishat Bagh built by Asaf Khan also belongs to this period. The Jahangir's Tomb at Shadera near Lahore, built by his wife Nur Mahal, is another outstanding architectural production of this time.

The style of Mughal architecture found expression of exceptional splendour during Emperor Shah Jahan's reign (1628-1658). The single most important architectural change was the substitution of marble for the red sandstone. He demolished the austere sandstone structures of Akbar in the Red Fort and replaced them with marble buildings such as the Diwan-i-Am and the Diwan-i-Khas. In 1638 he began to lay the city of Shahjahanabad beside the river Jamuna. The Red Fort at Delhi represents the pinnacle of centuries of experience in the construction of palace-forts. Outside the fort, he built the Jama Masjid, the largest mosque in India. Shah Jahan built the Jami Masjid at Agra in 1648 in honour of his daughter Jahanara Begum. The Wazir Khan's mosque in Lahore built in 1634 is another fine example of the Mughal art during Shah Jahan's time. However, it is for the Taj Mahal, which he built as a memorial to his beloved wife, Mumtaz Mahal, that he is most often remembered. The high point of the Mughal architecture during the Shah Jahan's time was the mellow marble has subtle low relief carving, lace like jalis, exquisite inlays, pietra dura and calligraphy. The pietra dura work was first incorporated in the Itamad-ud-Daula's Tomb at Agra built by Ghyas Beg, father of Nur Jehan. The extensive decoration of the interiors of monuments with precious and semi-precious stones using the pietra dura technique, which developed in Florence in the 16th century, and the use of pictures, jewellery and metal-works indicate considerable European influence on the Mughal art of this period.

Jahan Ara, daughter of Shah Jahan, was also a generous patron of architecture and showed an eclectic taste in building spacious gardens, mosques, madrasas and serais. She built the famous Begum Ka Bagh and Begum Serai at Delhi. She also built her own tomb near the shrine of the dargah of Hazrat Nizauddin.

The architectural projects of Aurangazeb's reign (1658-1707) are represented by the Bibi-ki-Maqbara, the tomb of Aurangzeb's wife Begum Rabia Durani, which is a poor replica of the famous Taj Mahal and is a fine example of Mughal architecture in the Deccan region. The death of Aurangazeb in 1707 led to the decadence of Mughal architecture. Aurangazeb's daughters Zeb-un-nissa and Zinat-unnisa Begum also contributed in a small way in carrying forward the Mughal trend of architecture. Zinat-unnisa Begum built the Zinat-ul-Masjid at Daryaganj in Old Delhi built in 1711, while Zeb-un-nissa built her own garden and tomb at Nawankot near Lahore. Qudsiya Begum, the wife of a later Mughal ruler, Ahmad Shah, built the Sunheri Masjid in 1751 opposite the west gate of the Red Fort. The last Mughal Emperor Bahadur Shah Zafar's favourite wife Zinat Mahal built the Zinat Mahal in the Lal Kuan bazaar in Delhi. However, the only significant monument built in the post-Aurangazeb time in Delhi was the Safdar Jung's Tomb built in 1753 by Mirza Mansoor Khan.

The Post-Mughal Style of Architecture

Avadh (Oudh) Style

During the later half of the 18th century and the first half of the 19th century, a distinct form of architecture flourished under the Nawabs of Avadh (Oudh), whose first manifestation was noticed in the form of Safdar Jung's tomb, built in the honour of Safdar Jung (1739-1753), who was the nephew of the first Nawab of Oudh. The city of Lucknow witnessed large building enterprises under Nawab Asif-ud-Daula (1775-1795). The most representative architectural achievement of this period is the Bara Imambara built by the Nawab in 1784. Absence of pillars in the main hall and simplicity of style and symmetry are its unique features. On the western side of the Bara Imambara is the Rumi Darwaza in which ornamental designs radiate from the base to the top on both the sides in the most expressive manner. A 67-metre clock tower was built near the Rumi Darwaza in 1881. The Chota Imambara or Husainabad Imâmbâra built by Muhammad Ali Shah as his tomb, and the Shahnajaf Imambara, housing the tomb of Nawab Ghaziuddin Haidar are other note-worthy buildings following this style of architecture.

Towards the middle of the 19th century, the architectural style of Avadh began to be impregnated with elements from European sources. Major General Claude Martin (1735-1800) built a large and pretentious building at Lucknow, then known as "Constantia", which was one of the first large buildings of the European style built in North India. This building, which had several Palladian elements, set the tone for the development of a hybrid style of architecture in Lucknow depicting a degenerative combination of Mughal and Gothic styles. The best examples of this style of architecture are the Chattar Manzil built by Nawab Naziruddin Haider and the Kaiser Bagh built by Nawab Wajid Ali Shah between 1845 and 1850. The Chattar Manzil is an imposing building, whose main attractions are the underground rooms and a beautiful dome surrounded by a gilt umbrella. The Kaiser Bagh is a quadrangular park with a baradari (pavilion) and yellow-coloured buildings on three sides. The Roshanwali Koti and the Begum Koti at Hazratgunj are other buildings where the Italian style is more prominent.

Punjab Style

In Punjab a distinct style of architecture developed under the influence of the Mughal style. It was characterised by certain indigenous features like the multiplicity of chattris or kiosks, the use of fluted dome generally covered with copper or brass-gilt and enrichment of arches by numerous foliations. This architecture was best manifested in the construction of the Golden Temple at Amritsar in 1764 built by the fourth Sikh Guru Ramdas.

7

History of Taj Mahal

The Taj Mahal is a large 17th century mausoleum complex, located on the south bank of the River Yamuna in Agra, India. The Mughal Emperor Shâh Jahân commissioned the mausoleum for his favourite wife, Mumtaz Mahal from whom the name is derived. Whilst the white domed marble mausoleum is the most familiar part of the monument, the Taj Mahal is an extensive complex of buildings and gardens that extends over 22.44 hectares and includes subsidiary tombs, waterworks infrastructure, the small town of 'Taj Ganj' and a 'moonlight garden' to the north of the river. Construction began in 1632 Common Era, (1041 AH), and was completed in 1648 CE (1058 AH).

Etymology

The Taj Mahal was variously referred to by 17th century CE Mughal chroniclers writing in Persian as Rauza-i munauwara, meaning 'building of the illuminated tomb', Rauzi-i muqqadas, 'the holy tomb' (carrying strong religious significance being the same name as the tomb of the prophet Muhammad at Medina) and the Imarat-i rauza-i mutahhara, 'building of the pure tomb'.

The present name derives from a European corruption of 'Mumtaz Mahal' which appears to have become its popular name at the time when Europeans arrived in significant numbers.

Origins and Architecture of the Taj Mahal

The architecture of the Taj Mahal represents the finest and most sophisticated example of Mughal architecture. Its origins lie in the moving circumstances of its commission and the culture and history of an Islamic Mughal Empire adapting to rule a largely Hindu populace.

The distraught Mughal Emperor Shah Jahan commissioned the mausoleum upon the death of his favourite wife, Mumtaz Mahal. Whilst the white domed marble mausoleum is the most familiar part of the monument, the Taj Mahal is an extensive complex of buildings and gardens that extends over 22.44 Hectares[a] and includes subsidiary tombs, waterworks infrastructure, the small town of 'Taj Ganj' and a 'moonlight garden' to the north of the river. Construction began in 1632 CE, (1041 AH), on the south bank of the River Yamuna in Agra, India and was completed in 1648 CE (1058 AH). The design was conceived as both an earthly replica of the house of Mumtaz in paradise and an instrument of propaganda for the emperor.

Who designed the Taj Mahal is unclear; although it is known that a large team of designers and craftsmen were responsible including Shah Jahan himself, with Ustad Ahmad Lahauri considered the most likely candidate as the principle designer. The intention at its inception was to create the most beautiful building in the world. Few in its history have disagreed, with many finding the exquisite nature of its pietra dura decoration closer to lapidary than stonemasonry.

Post Construction History and Legacy

Immediately before the construction of the Taj, the first diplomatic links between European nations and the Mughals had been established. The subsequent history of the Taj would see it witness the decline of the Mughal Empire, the rise of the Maratha Empire, the increasing influence of the British East India Company and eventually see India become the 'Jewel in the Crown' of the British Empire until India's independence in 1947. The reputation of the Taj as an exquisite work of architecture extended across continents even before it was completed. The Taj's form, execution and setting provided something for people from many cultures and periods of history to praise.

After the construction of the Taj, riverside garden form became the preserve of imperial nobility in other areas such as Shahjahanabad (Delhi).[5] Aurangzeb wrote to Jahan in 1652 CE (1062 AH) to inform him that the dome was leaking during the rainy season and requesting repairs. Until his death of in 1707 the complex was kept in a good state of repair but his demise saw the beginnings of the decline of Mughal power. During the war of accession between the emperors successors and other Mughal nobles the Agra fort was plundered and the pearl sheet (chadar) which Jahan had commissioned as a cover for Mumtaz's mausoleum. The situation in Agra became particularly precarious in the 18th century as indigenous and foreign powers exchanged control of the city. In an attempt to re-assert Mughal control under the reign of emperor Muhammad Shah new city walls were constructed and the earliest known plans of the Taj Mahal were prepared. When the Jats sacked the fort in 1761, part of their spoils included the doors of the Taj Mahal.

European Reactions

For European neoclassicists, the rigorous symmetry and the coincidental similarity of its façade's tripartite composition to Roman triumphal arches made the Taj, although resolutely a product of indigenous and Islamic architecture, accessible to the European mindset. 19th century painters of the picturesque praised the (by then) overgrown naturalistic setting of the garden and the ruined Agra waterfront and the traditional conception of the Taj as a 'monument to love' was well publicised and captured the imagination of the romantics. The earliest European visitors to the Taj were both French - Jean-Baptiste Tavernier visiting in 1640–1641 CE (1050–1051 AH) and Francois Bernier in 1659 CE (1069 AH). Bernier gave the following description and Shah Jahan's motive for building it.

The British and the Taj

The first artist to arrive from Europe was James Forbes (artist) in 1781 swiftly followed by Johan Zoffany in 1786. The first overall views of the Taj were made by William Hodges (1783) and Thomas and William Daniell who came in search of 'the sublime, picturesque and exotic'. The British East India Company established a presence in Agra in 1785 and from 1786-1798 Major William Palmer, would stay in the garden towers of the Taj.

Influence

Thomas Daniell's Oriental Views (1808) and his other Indian watercolours and paintings would become the major instrument of influence upon British sensibilities both in India and back in the United Kingdom. He advised on the design of the gardens of Sezincote, which was visited by the Prince Regent in 1812 and so became a strong influence on John Nash's 1815 redesigns of the Royal Brighton Pavilion. The interior designs of this and later buildings such as parts of Osbourne House for Queen Victoria, and Elveden Hall in Suffolk for Duleep Singh both demonstrate an eastern exoticism that can trace its influence to the Taj Mahal. For other eastern parts of the British Empire, particularly those with Islamic sensibilities, Mughal architecture provided a useful language to express imperial buildings. Accordingly, Kuala Lumpur has a very fine Moghul railway station.

Contemporary chronicles and court histories make it clear that Shah Jahan intended the Taj Mahal to be acclaimed by the entire world. It can be argued that he was almost entirely successful in this pursuit. The building has inspired admiration that transcends cultures and geography; so much so, that the personal and emotional responses to the building have consistently eclipsed the scholastic appraisals of the monument. Some of these responses and leaps of the imagination are now so old or compelling that they are imbedded in a global psyche and are often repeated as fact in opposition to the scholastic consensus. Others have attempted to use or promote misinformation about the Taj for political or self-serving advantage.

A longstanding popular tradition holds that an identical mausoleum complex for Shah Jahan was to be built in black marble instead of white on the site of the moonlight garden. Known as the 'black taj' this idea can trace its roots to the fanciful writings of an early european traveller called Jean-Baptiste Tavernier who visited Agra in 1665 whilst Jahan was incarcerated in the Agra Fort. The story suggests that Shah Jahan was overthrown by his son Aurangzeb before the black version could be built. Excavations of the moonlight garden were carried out in the 1990s and found no evidence of such foundations in the ruins of the garden, only white marble features discoloured completely to black by pollution and the frequent flooding of the site. Speculation continues that the black taj may refer to the reflection of the Taj in the large pool of the garden or possibly the reflection, seen by Jahan in his last days from Agra fort, through imperfect mirrors.

The lack of complete and reliable information as to whom the credit for the design belongs, has led to innumerable speculations. The most notable and frequently repeated is that the Taj Mahal's architect was Ustad Isa from Ottoman Turkey. Reliable sources suggest that the story is fictious and is born of the readiness of the British in the 19th century to believe that such a beautiful building should be credited to a European architect. Local informants are also reported to have supplied the British with fictitious lists of workmen and materials from all over Asia.

A related and earlier notion, first documented by the Spanish friar Sebastian Manrique in 1641, suggests the monument was the work of the Venetian goldsmith called Geronimo Veroneo.

In a pattern typical of many of the world's most famous buildings, a number of stories describe, often in horrific detail, the deaths, dismemberments and mutilations which Shah Jahan inflicted on various architects and craftsmen associated with the tomb. More conservative stories moderate the idea to that of a contract signed by those involved in the building's construction committing to have no part in any similar design. No evidence for these claims exist.

There is an often-repeated story that Lord William Bentinck, governor of India in the 1830s, planned to demolish the Taj Mahal and auction off the marble. There is no contemporary evidence for this story, which may have emerged in the late nineteenth century when Bentinck was being criticised for his penny-pinching Utilitarianism, and when Lord Curzon was emphasising earlier neglect of the monument, and presenting himself as a saviour of Indian antiquities. According to Bentinck's biographer John Rosselli, the story arose from Bentinck's fund-raising sale of discarded marble from Agra Fort and of the metal from a famous but obsolete Agra cannon. However, others, led by the Archaeological Survey of India, still believe and argue that a sale by the British East India Company was planned under Lord Bentinck's watch, though no satisfactory buyers were found.

In recent years, elements within India have become interested in the ideas of P.N. Oak. He claims that the origins of the Taj, together with all the other historic structures in the country currently ascribed to Muslim sultans, pre-date the Muslim occupation of India and have a Hindu origin. In 2000 India's Supreme Court dismissed Oak's petition to declare that a Hindu king built the Taj Mahal and reprimanded him for bringing the action.

A more poetic story relates that once a year during the rainy season, a single drop of water falls onto the cenotaph, paralleling the Bengali poet Rabindranath Tagore's description of the tomb as "one solitary tear hanging on the cheek of time". Another myth suggest that if the silhouette of the finial, set into the paving of the riverside forecourt, is beaten then water will come forth. To this day officials at the Taj Mahal find broken bangles surrounding the silhouette.

The Taj Today and its Future

Conservation

Pollution from small scale industry and an oil refinery 40 km north of Agra threatened to discolour the marble and weaken the sandstone of the complex and provoked the establishment of the 'Taj Trapezium' in 1982 to restrict such activities within an area of approximately 50 km radius around Agra. In the same year the complex was awarded UNSECO world heritage status. Criticism has been made that although the Taj Mahal and Agra Fort both enjoy this status, the contextual surroundings of the Agra waterfront and its traditions of residential and pleasure gardens remain unprotected. The case for conservation is in opposition to the interests of those trying to improve Agra's economic activity, who naturally see the restrictions imposed by the UNESCO heritage status as limiting.

In 1984 an emissions-free green belt was established around the complex because the Taj Trapezium measures had proved ineffective. In 1996, after a Supreme Court ruling, further measures were taken to reduce pollution, including the ban of polluting vehicles within 500 m and iron foundries in the wider vicinity. It also removed the shops and bazaar traders from within the Taj complex and established a no-build zone within 200 m. The full appreciation of the Taj Ganj and its integration with the rest of the complex did not come until after the ruling and so now, if the law were applied to the letter, all new building in the Taj Ganj would be prohibited.

Research is currently being undertaken to determine the original planting scheme with the intention of replanting the garden with the original Mughal design. This will mean the loss of the historic 1906 garden design but the more ecological methods of gardening proposed will benefit the local community.

Taj Heritage Corridor Project

In July 2003 work was stopped on the construction of a US$1.8 billion project that would have linked the Taj Mahal and the Red Fort with 2km of riverside walkway flanked by shopping malls, restaurants and tourist facilities. India's Supreme Court ordered the stoppage and an investigation into why the project was started despite numerous irregularities in the procurement of the work and the planning of a design within the Taj trapezium. UNESCO voiced concerns that the work that had been carried out to the Jamuna river bank had diverted the flow of the river, changed the water table and created mass landfill, leading to a possible risk for the Taj's foundations and further detrimental effects to other heritage sites downstream. The body requested an explanation and conducted its own investigations to determine whether the monument should be put on the "World Heritage in Danger" list. The resultant political scandal engulfed the Uttar Pradesh government. The Central Bureau of Investigation was called in and the Chief Minister Mayawati Kumari is currently facing corruption charges although further accusations have been made that delays bringing the cases to court are the result of political pressure.

Wakf Case

In 2005 an attempt was made to designate the Taj Mahal as a wakf property (an inalienable religious endowment in Islam, typically devoting a building or plot of land for Muslim religious or charitable purposes). This would have taken legal ownership of the Taj from the government, administered by the Archaeological Survey of India to the Uttar Pradesh Sunni Central Wakf Board and entitled them to a 7% share of the profits to be used for maintenance. The Sunni Central Wakf Board argued that the complex was willed as a wakf property by Shah Jahan, that the Indian Supreme Court had previously observed that all mosques and graveyards are wakf property. The Shia Wakf Board responded by filing its own claim asserting that since Mumtaz Mahal was a Shia then it was a Shia wakf property. The case had implications in Indian law that would have either required the Ancient Monuments Act and the Central Wakf Act to be modified to exclude protected monuments of national importance from the purview of the Wakf Act or to allow all such properties to cede to the Wakf board. In the event the Supreme Court found in favour of the Archaeological Survey of India who had argued that there was considerable historical evidence to support the claim that the complex had been in the ownership of the Government since the British abolished the waqf that financed the tomb's upkeep in 1803 and assumed responsibility for it themselves.

Tourism

The Taj Mahal attracts 2 million visitors every year of whom 200,000 come from overseas, making it one of the most popular international attractions in India. Most tourists visit during the cooler months of October, November and February. Polluting traffic is not allowed near the complex and tourist must either walk from the car parks or catch an electric bus. The Khawasspuras are currently being restored for use as a new visitors' center.

Compiled lists of recommended travel destinations often feature the Taj Mahal, which also appears in several listings of seven wonders of the modern world. The most recent of which was the result of an Internet poll of 100 million people. The poll itself drew criticism, particularly from UNESCO who argued that the wonders of the world should not be drawn from a popular vote, and other criticism which highlighted the attendant statistical skews in polls for 'wonders' in countries with large populations.

The crowning jewel of Indo-Islamic architecture, the Taj Mahal is one of the world's most beautiful and beloved structures. The monument was built in Agra, India, for Mumtaz Mahal, the favorite wife of Mughal emperor Shah Jahan. Construction of the tomb began in 1632 and employed more than 20,000 laborers for 20 years. During the reign of Shah Jahan, the structure was known simply as the rauza, the tomb. Later, the mausoleum would be called the Taj Mahal, a derivative of the name Mumtaz Mahal.

According to the French jeweler Tavernier, who claimed to had seen the construction of the Taj Mahal from beginning to end, the white marble monument was erected at a time when the resources of the Mughal Empire were such that only the finest materials were utilized for the structure and its embellishment and when the quality of the craftsmanship available in northern India was probably superior to that of any previous period.

Known for its symmetry, the Taj Mahal sits on a raised platform surrounded by four minarets. Inside are delicate mosaic works and marble walls adorned with intricate patterns of inlaid precious stones. The emperor Shah Jahan is said to have celebrated the anniversary of his wife's death in the mausoleum, kneeling before the cenotaph of white marble studded with gems and semiprecious stones, as prayers were offered up for the peace and repose of the empress' soul.

Mumtaz Mahal, whose name means Chosen One of the Palace, had been more than the emperor's wife. Indeed,

Shah Jahan had a number of wives. But Mumtaz Mahal was the love of his life. She was his best friend and his most trusted political adviser. Mumtaz Mahal bore 14 children; seven of them survived. She died in 1631 after giving birth to a healthy baby girl.

After his wife's death, Shah Jahan reportedly locked himself in his rooms and refused food for eight days. According to legend, when the emperor emerged from his seclusion, his black beard - visible in many Mughal miniature paintings - had turned completely white.

For the monument to his wife, Shah Jahan chose a site occupied by sprawling gardens on a bend in the left bank of the Yamuna River. Author Christine Moorcroft writes in The Taj Mahal (1998) that Shah Jahan may have chosen this specific site because of its beauty and because there was a clear view of the site from the imperial palace at the Red Fort. Poet Rabindranath Tagore describes the monument as rising above the banks of the river "like a solitary tear suspended on the cheek of time."

Refuting the romanticism of the aforementioned, many contemporary historians contend that the Taj Mahal is a mausoleum far too imposing to commemorate the memory of one woman, even the favorite wife of an emperor, write Amina Okada and M.C. Joshi in Taj Mahal (1993). "Some historians believe", continue Okada and Joshi, "that behind the monument's beauty and majesty of form, behind the purity of its line, and behind the sober refinement of its decoration is an autocratic ruler vaunting his grandeur and munificence to the world. While the monument is clearly funereal, these historians also perceive a symbolic and allegorical significance for the mausoleum_a significance equally accounted for by the omnipotence of a sovereign infatuated with his own grandeur."

Even if the Taj Mahal represents just one more jewel in the imperial crown of Shah Jahan, note Okada and Joshi, the emperor still must be credited with having made of the death of a spouse a symbol of lasting beauty. He bequeathed to India and the world its most beautiful mausoleum.

Following the standard Mughal architectural arrangement, write Sheila S. Blair and Jonathan M. Bloom in The Art and Architecture of Islam (1994), the tomb is set in a large quadripartite chahar bagh garden that measures about 1,900 feet by 1,000 feet. The tomb stands at the north end of the garden along the riverbank balanced by a large gateway on the south. In plan and massing, note Blair and Bloom, the mausoleum refines the model provided by Humayun's tomb at Delhi. However, the great bulbous tomb of the Taj Mahal is set on a higher drum; its octagonal rooms in the corners are more logically connected; and the tomb is framed by four tall minarets.

The carefully balanced image, reflected in the water channel dividing the garden, is enhanced by the superb polish and detailed carving of the marbles, write Blair and Bloom. Built in red sandstone on the sides of the platform and enshrining the mausoleum are two structures: a mosque (masjid) to the west and a guest house (mihman khana) to the east.

Visitors to the Taj Mahal will discover the ingenious, harmonious perspective of the gardens and canals which towers the massive form of the mausoleum. At the intersection of the canals, the shimmering waters of a wide ornamental pool reflect the vaporous silhouette of the Taj Mahal and the outline of the tall, elegant cypress trees, underlining the subtle symmetry of the whole.

In the book Islamic Art (1991), Barbara Brend writes that the mausoleum, flanked by attendant structures, stands on a terrace at the north end of the garden; it is thus seen as the culmination of a perspective, its marble surfaces changing hue as the sun crosses the sky and being reflected in the watercourses.

The Taj Mahal has restrained pietra dura decoration that forms vining floral designs. Above these beautiful floral patterns are extensive calligraphic inscriptions in black lettering. Most of the text is short verses from the Qur'an emphasizing eschatological themes, particularly the Day of Judgment. "It has been suggested", write Blair and Bloom, "that the epigraphic program designed by calligrapher Amanat Khan was meant to drive home the message implicit in the building's form and location - that the tomb was an allegorical representation of the Throne of Allah above the Garden of Paradise on the Day of Judgment."

The beauty of the pietra dura of the Taj Mahal and of the forts at Agra and Delhi still inspire numerous artists from all over the world. Moreover, write Okada and Joshi, the four canals clearly symbolize the four rivers of Paradise mentioned in the Holy Qur'an and seen by the Prophet Muhammed during his miraculous ascent to Paradise (al-Mi'raj). The symbolic and allegorical nature of the garden and the canals at Taj Mahal is not surprising considering the funereal nature of the monument it enshrines. The Qur'anic inscription on the southern facade of the Main Gate gives unequivocal credence to the comparison of the Taj Mahal with the Garden of Paradise, where the appeased souls of the dead find their ultimate refuge. This inscription says:

(It will be said to the pious): O (you) the one in

(complete) rest and satisfaction!

Come back to your Lord, — well-pleased (yourself)

and well-pleasing unto him!

Enter you, then, among My honored slaves,

And enter you My Paradise!

- *The Holy Qur'an,* Surah Al-Fajr: 89:27-30

The Taj Mahal contains 16 chambers, eight each on two levels that surround the octagonal funerary chamber surmounted by a surbased inner dome. In the funerary chamber are found the cenotaphs of Mumtaz Mahal and Shah Jahan, enclosed in a baluster of delicately perforated marble and studded with semiprecious stones. As dictated by Islamic tradition, write Okada and Joshi, the bodies of the emperor and his spouse are buried with their faces toward Mekka (the Holy Muslim city in the Arabian Peninsula) with the husband on his wife's right side.

To a student of Islamic architecture, writes Gavin Hambly in Cities of Mughul India (1964), the first and most enduring impression left by this incomparable monument is its Persian origin. This is architecture in the Safavid style. The Taj Mahal - in its perfection of space and proportion, in the classical perfection of its shape, in its combination of monumentality and delicacy, and in the quality of its decoration - represents the culmination on Indian soil of the Persian genius at work. Hambly quotes art historian, Hermann Goetz who writes:

(The Taj Mahal) "is a work of the finest Safavid taste. Except for the use of the most immaculate Makrana marble which translates the gay and gaudy Persian taste into the dreamy, languid spirit of later Mughal art, there are in the Taj Mahal only a few other deviations from Safavid orthodoxy - the Rajput chahtris around the dome, some differences in the proportion of the dome and dome drum (common, however, in the Deccan), and also the minarets, probably inspired by Mahmud Khilji's tomb at Mandu. It is one of the freaks of history that this 'Wonder of the World,' which is least characteristic of Mughal art, has become the classic representative and emblem of Mughal civilization.

The construction of the Taj Mahal was entrusted to a board of architects under imperial supervision, as was customary during the reign of Shah Jahan. The architects involved included Abd ul-Karim Ma'mur Khan, Makramat Khan, and Ustad Ahmed Lahwari.

Born in Lahore, Ustad Ahmed was not only a renowned architect but also a mathematician and astronomer of high repute. Besides the Taj Mahal, the Red Fort in Delhi should be attributed to him as well.

Okada and Joshi write that the monument stands as testimony to the technical skills and scientific knowledge of its builders. This is evident from the excellent handling of material and the perfect use of constructional devices: the arches used in raising the grand dome and distributing its heavy weight evenly, the method of laying the foundation, and the subtle manipulation of minute details. The entire complex is planned in such a way that the apparent organic unity of the whole does not obscure the individuality of any part, nor does it detract from the prominence of the Taj Mahal proper.

One more name that remains closely associated with the Taj Mahal, in particular with the superb calligraphic inscriptions displayed in the geometric friezes on the white marble, is that of the ingenious calligrapher, Amanat Khan, whose real name was Abd ul-Haq. This incomparable calligrapher, write Okada and Joshi, came to India from Shiraz, Iran, in 1609. Shah Jahaṇ conferred the title of Amanat Khan upon this Iranian as a reward for the calligrapher's dazzling virtuosity. In all probability, Amanat Khan was entrusted with the entire calligraphic decoration of the Taj Mahal. During Jahangir's reign, Amanat Kahn had been responsible for the calligraphic work of the Akbar mausoleum at Sikandra, and for that of the Madrasah Shahi Mosque at Agra.

It is quite possible that Amanat Khan was responsible for the choice of the epigraphs of the Taj Mahal, that is, the Qur'anic verses and other religious quotations appearing on the mausoleum. He signed his work inside the calligraphic inscription on the left side of the southern iwan - Amant Khan al-Shirazi, followed by the date (1638-39 AD). The calligrapher's signature bears witness to his status and renown at the court, since many of his peers remained anonymous.

The sinuous and austere letters in black marble inscribed with heraldic precision on the walls of the mausoleum heighten the whiteness of the marble and undeniably contribute to the ornamental richness and beauty of the edifice. There are 22 different Qur'anic Surahs or verses inscribed on the tomb, more than on any other monuments built during the reign of Shah Jahan. This makes the Taj Mahal an extremely exceptional funeral monument. Moreover, the locations of the calligraphic inscriptions correspond to a precise iconographic plan, Okada and Joshi note.

Also adding to the beauty of the Taj Mahal is the extraordinary delicacy of the floral motifs that embellish the marble surface. These floral motifs are sculpted in marble in sober relief (munabbat kari) or inlaid with semiprecious stones (parchin kari) that produce incandescent reflections. Other diverse kinds of flowers open in graceful arabesques and cover in profusion the imperial cenotaphs and their enclosures showing the dazzling virtuosity of the Mughal lapidaries.

The stone flowers of the Taj Mahal, depicted with a stamp of realism and with a soft lyricism, captivate the visitor with their grace and colorful freshness, write Okado and Joshi. In Islamic culture, flowers and roses are often seen as symbols of the Kingdom of Allah. Thus, the Taj Mahal's allusion to Paradise can be seen in the motif of flowers carved on the funerary chambers of the mausoleum, as well as on the plinths of the inner iwan. Accompanied by fruit or bunches of grapes, the vases of flowers express the abundance that awaits the faithful in Paradise.

The court poet Abu Talib Kalim, wishing to pay homage to the virtuosity of the imperial lapidaries, wrote these verses to glorify their art:

They set stone flowers in the marble

That by their color, if not their perfume, surpass real flowers.

In 1663, Francois Bernier, a Frenchman from Angers who spent 10 years in India, wrote about Delhi and Agra, the capital cities of the Empire of the Great Mughals. The Frenchman was very enthusiastic in his description of the Taj Mahal, which he considered far superior to "the shapeless masses of the pyramids of Egypt." Here is part of his description of the interior of the Taj Mahal:

The inside or concave part of the dome and the entire wall, usually from top to bottom, are covered with white marble. There is not a single spot that is not artistically wrought with its own beauty. Everywhere one perceives yashm or jade, the kind of stones that enrich the walls of the chapel of the Grand Duke in Florence. Everywhere there is jasper and several other rare and costly stones, presented in a hundred different ways, mixed together and set in the marble that covers the wall. Even the black and white marble floor tiles are decorated in like manner, with unimaginable delicacy and taste.

Francois Bernier in *Voyage dans les Etats du Grand Mogol,* new ed. 1981

In the 19th century, many artists in Europe, especially Britain and France, made delicate copies of these monuments in watercolor.

The historians of art refer to the encrustation of semiprecious stones studding the marble surfaces of the Taj Mahal and the forts of Agra and Delhi as 'hard stone', write Okada and Joshi. However, the authors continue, the Mughal and Persian chroniclers called this technique parchin kari. The process involves cutting with extreme care and then shaping thin sections of hard and semi-hard stones into tendrils and floral arabesques. When set in white marble, these cuttings blossomed into delicate, shimmering flowers. The Mughal lapidaries used parchin kari not only for arabesques and floral decoration but also for calligraphy in black marble and for the geometric and abstract motifs that are an integral part of the decoration of the Taj Mahal.

Unfortunately, the precious encrustations of the Taj Mahal aroused the greed of less delicate souls who unscrupulously did their best to appropriate the jewels, write Okada and Joshi. Many flowers with their Cornelian or yellow amber petals are irreparably mutilated, and many richly encrusted corollas are hollow today. At the end of 19th century, a French visitor wrote:

The Taj Mahal has not suffered from the injury of time, thanks to the excellence of the materials and the perfection of the workmanship. The two hundred and thirty years that have elapsed since it was built have not spoiled the luster of the marble or the countless wonders of the chiseling. All the defacement of the ornamental details is due to the hand of man.

The invasions and diverse troubles from which the country has suffered for two centuries have left a deplorable mark on all the monuments of Agra. After the pillage and removal of the precious metals of the portals, balusters, and diverse ornaments, the greed of the grasping soldiery was aroused by the encrustations of semiprecious stones decorating the two tombs and their enclosure. It would be difficult today to find a single flower, a single ornament intact. Tips of daggers, sabers, and bayonets have pierced and broken off fragments of these charming, delicate mosaics. I am sorely afraid that when travel is increased a hundredfold in the interior of India, thanks to the railway, bringing streams of visitors to Agra daily, it will cause irreparable damage to the Taj Mahal.

F. Devay, 1867, *Journal d'un voyage dans l'Inde anglaise (Journal of a Trip Through English India)*

One interesting architectural concept, note Okada and Johsi, is that the Taj Mahal, with its picturesque setting, chaste appearance, plastic delicacy, superfine ornamentation, and gentle molding of contours, is a feminine specimen of building art. Scholar E. B. Havell sees in the Taj Mahal an intentional attribute to the 'Lady of the Taj,' Mumtaz Mahal.

Havell writes that the monument's entire concept and every line of its expression reflect the radiance and beauty of the Empress. For Havell, the Taj Mahal is India's tribute to the grace of womanhood, the Venus de Milo of the East. Thus, the Taj Mahal can be interpreted as a glorious and profound symbol of love.

8

Characteristics of Islamic Art

Two dominant features of Islamic art and architecture, the importance of calligraphic ornamentation and the form of the mosque, are intimately related to the Islamic faith and were developed in the early days of the religion.

Prophet Muhammad was a wealthy merchant of Mecca who underwent a profound series of revelations when he was about 40 years of age and began to preach a new faith. His teachings, or the revelations, are contained in the Koran, one of the great books of religious inspiration. The rich linguistic and poetic heritage of the Arabs (see Arabic Language; Arabic Literature) contributed to the feeling of deep respect given to the Koran. Its centrality in Islamic culture and the particular gracefulness of the Arabic writing system led to the use of the written word, especially Koranic passages, as inscriptions on mosques and to the development of calligraphic styles and ornament in all branches of Islamic art.

In ad 622, the year that established the Islamic calendar, Muhammad made his flight (hijra) to the city of Yathrib (later Medina). There, a community of believers developed who worshiped in Muhammad's house compound. The common prayers of the new community in this simple setting—an enclosed oblong courtyard with huts (the houses of Muhammad's wives) along one side wall and a rough portico (the zulla, originally for shade) at one end for the poorer followers— established the mosque form. Almost all mosques, therefore, repeat the plan of Muhammad's house, being composed essentially of an enclosed courtyard (sahn), a building at one end for prayer, and arcades (riwaqs) on the sides.

The first followers of Muhammad, coming from the Arabian Peninsula, had no native artistic traditions comparable to those of the Empires they subsequently conquered, which they then took as their starting point. As Islam spread, its art forms developed, modified by the different climatic conditions and available materials in the lands of Islamic conquest, and absorbing and adapting indigenous art styles. Motifs from one area soon became universal in the vast Islamic world.

Islamic art thus developed from many sources. Roman, Early Christian, and Byzantine styles were taken over in early Islamic architecture; the influence of Sassanian art—the architecture and decorative art of pre-Islamic Persia under the Sassanids—was of paramount significance; Central Asian styles were brought in with Turkic and Mongol incursions; and Chinese influences had a formative effect on Islamic painting, pottery, and textiles.

Historical Sequence

The sequence of the development of Islamic art—from the 7th to the 18th century—may be classified in three periods. The formative period of Islamic art was roughly coexistent with the rule of the early leaders of Islam, the Umayyad Aliphs (661–750), who extended Islam from Damascus, in Syria, to Spain. The middle period spans the time of the Abbasid Aliphs (750–1258), who ruled Islam from Baghdad, in Iraq, until the time of the Mongol conquest. This Aliphate, famed for its promotion of learning and culture, was the most illustrious in Islamic history. It was in this middle period that the influence of Iranian art forms became significant. The period from the Mongol conquest to the 18th century may, for convenience, be termed the late period of Islamic art. See also ALIPHATE.

Within this sequence, distinctive art styles can be defined in different parts of the Islamic world, associated with various dynasties of rulers. Styles mentioned in this article—besides Umayyad and Abbasid art—include those of the Seljuk Turks, who ruled Iran from the mid-11th century to 1157; the Il-Khanids, a Mongol people who controlled eastern Iran from 1256 to 1349; the Timurids, the greatest patrons of Iranian culture, who ruled western Iran from 1378 to 1502; and the Safavids, rulers of all Iran from 1502 to 1736. Art also flourished under the Ottoman Turks, rulers of Turkey from 1299 to 1922, who extended their Empire to Egypt and Syria in the 16th century. Earlier in Egypt (and Syria), distinctive styles were associated with the Fatimid reign (909–1171) and that of the Mamelukes, who established control in 1250.

Architecture

The few and relatively simple rituals of the Islamic faith gave rise to a unique religious architecture, comprising the mosque (masjid), a place of community gathering and prayer, and the madresah, or religious school. Important among the various characteristic forms of Islamic secular architecture are palaces, caravansaries, and cities, the elaborate planning of which shows concern for the all-important access to water and for provision of shelter from heat. A third type of building important in the Islamic world is the mausoleum, serving both as an actual tomb for a ruler or holy man and as a symbol of political power. All these structures—religious and secular— share many organic and decorative features.

Mosques

Muslims call the direction in which they pray the qibla, and for his first two years at Medina, the Prophet prayed facing toward Jerusalem. He then received a revelation that the true qibla lay in Mecca, and this has been the qibla for prayer ever since, determining the orientation and spatial organization of all mosques throughout the world. The qibla is marked by a decorative mihrab, or niche, within the mosque.

Mihrab

When the Muslims conquered Syria in 636, they took over for use as mosques many of the basilican churches that abounded there. These basilicas were long, triple-arched buildings with pitched roofs and with the altar at the eastern end (see BASILICA,). The new worshipers placed the mihrab on the southern wall and made new entrances in the northern wall. Thus, the congregation prayed across the aisles.

Courtyard

When such an adapted basilica was combined with an enclosed courtyard having arcades at the side, it contained all the basic features of the Prophet's house at Medina. The first Mosque of al-Aqsa at Jerusalem (before 670) was adapted in this way from the Royal Stoa of Herod, a ruined basilica. In later examples, more long aisles were added to the end of the courtyard—as in the great 8th- to 10th-century Mosque of Cordoba, Spain—and any resemblance to churches with their focus at the narrow end disappeared. Such additions were made in response to population growth, but the process of adding on is analogous to a feature characteristic of all Islamic art: the infinite repetition of patterns.

Minaret

During the lifetime of the Prophet, the call to prayer at Medina was made from a rooftop, in imitation of the Jewish practice of blowing the shofar (ram's horn) or the early Christian use of a clapper to summon worshipers. It seems likely that a Syrian tradition of marking the corners of a building by four short towers was the origin of the minaret—a tower at the corner of the mosque courtyard (or, as at Samarra, Iraq, freestanding)—from which, after Muhammad's lifetime, the call to prayer was customarily sounded. The Umayyad Mosque, or Great Mosque, at Damascus (705–15), built around an earlier basilican church, is the best-preserved example of an early courtyard mosque with a minaret. A dome, of later construction, in the sanctuary, or prayer hall, marks the main one of the four mihrabs on the qibla wall.

Dome

Domes, a great feature of all Islamic architecture, developed both from Sassanian and Early Christian architectural sources. The earliest surviving mosque is the Dome of the Rock (late 7th cent.) at Jerusalem, one of the great religious structures of the world; it marks the spot where, according to tradition, Muhammad ascended to heaven. This mosque has a dome set on a high drum and a centralized or annular (ringlike) plan with two ambulatories or corridors; the design is derived from Roman architecture, possibly in emulation of the 4th-century Church of the Holy Sepulcher, also in Jerusalem. The Dome of the Rock, therefore, does not conform to the basic mosque plan. Its dome is gilded, and all its other surfaces are covered inside and out by colorful tile mosaic.

Influences from Turkic peoples were increasingly felt as Islam spread and developed. Thus, the mausoleum built at the beginning of the 10th century for the ruler of Bukhara, in Central Asia (the place of origin of the Seljuk dynasty), was of great architectural significance. This square brick building had a dome resting on squinches (small arches that span the corners of the square) instead of on pendentives (spherical triangles, or rounded triangular sections of vaults) as used in the Byzantine world. Squinches ultimately were derived from Sassanian Iran; they are more easily built than pendentives, and the device thus led to the spread of domed mosques, mausoleums, and other types of buildings throughout the Islamic world.

Under the Ottomans, mosques were built reflecting the Byzantine heritage of Turkey. Thus, the magnificent Selimiye Mosque (1568–74) built by the great Turkish architect Sinan at Edirne, Turkey, has a colossal dome ringed with smaller ones and with half domes, the same arrangement as HAGIA SOPHIA, (q.v.) in Ýstanbul, Turkey—a Byzantine church later converted to a mosque. Although also similar to Hagia Sophia in breadth, the Edirne mosque has many windows, providing much more light. This form—which Sinan also employed in two famous Ýstanbul mosques—influenced the design of mosques throughout Turkey, Syria, Egypt, Arabia, and North Africa.

Eyvan

In the Abbasid mosques of Iraq, an eyvan, an open, vaulted, two-story passageway or hall, was introduced into each side of the arcades surrounding the mosque courtyard. The eyvan had its roots in the architecture of Sassanian Iran.

Pointed Arch

Although the horseshoe arch is more typical of Islamic architecture, especially earlier examples, the pointed arch was also known. Probably of Syrian origin, adapted by the Umayyads, it was also characteristic of Abbasid mosques, and from Iraq it was carried to Egypt in the 9th and 10th centuries. In later Egyptian mosques, built under the Mamelukes (from the 13th cent.), the pointed arches have a Gothic profile, showing the influence of European architectural motifs transported by the Crusaders.

Mimbar and Maqqsura

The first known use of a mimbar, or pulpit, was in the mosque of Medina; originally used as a seat, it soon became a true pulpit for preaching. Another structural detail typical of some but not all mosques is the maqqsura, a screen or enclosure placed around the mihrab to protect the leaders of the community during services; this structure was developed after three early Aliphs were murdered.

Madresahs

Under the Abbasids, in the middle period, a new kind of religious building, the madresah, or religious seminary, was introduced in eastern Iran. Its form, based on Sassanian architecture, was taken over into a new kind of mosque that soon spread to many countries. The madresah and madresah-mosque have eyvans on four sides (with a larger one in front of the qibla), connected by two-story arcades. In the madresah these arcades lead to dormitories; in the mosque they are simply niches. In some late madresahs the courtyard is covered by a dome. The 11th-century Friday Mosque (the generic term for a mosque accommodating large congregations of worshipers) at Esfahan, Iran, is an early, great example of a madresah-mosque. In this building, as in tombs of the period, the muqarna motif, the stalactitelike ornamentation of vaulted roofs, was developed; a typically Islamic style of decoration, it consists of a honeycomb of niches with small projections, set into a vaulted roof or dome.

Later examples of madresah-mosques, both in Esfahan and both of the 17th century, are the Masjid-i-Shah with its high, pointed, tiled dome behind the main eyvan, and its interior surfaces and stalactites covered with tile; and the Masjid-i-Shaikh Lutfullah, with an even more extravagantly tiled dome.

Secular Architecture

During Umayyad and early Abbasid times, princes of the Aliphs' families built a number of desert palaces in Syria and Iraq. Some of these had hunting parks—like those of the late Sassanian kings—or domed baths, which were derived from late Roman types of buildings. Thus, these palaces demonstrate the synthesis of the Western and Eastern artistic heritage that characterized early Islamic art, and also demonstrate its relative freedom before the traditional proscriptions against figural art were codified, not in the Koran but in the Hadith (Traditions) in the 9th century. The Umayyad palaces featured mosaics, wall paintings, and plaster relief sculpture showing courtiers, animals, and even the Aliph himself; much of this ornament was derived from Sassanian tradition.

In the middle period, the Islamic world produced the greatest flowering of urban civilization yet seen. With the coming of the Mongols, however, many such cities were destroyed or reduced to villages, and the water systems on which they depended were also demolished.

Under the Abbasids, an entire administrative city, Samarra, was started—but never completed—in the desert near Baghdad. Within Samarra was an enormous walled building, 175 ha (432 acres) in extent and containing many gardens, which was a city in itself. It comprised offices, a mosque, baths, and living quarters. Some of the residential buildings had painted figural decorations, but the finest decorative work was of carved plaster in overall geometric patterns based on Turkish (Central Asian) motifs. Planned cities such as Samarra and Fustat (near Cairo, and known through excavation) are notable for their efficiently designed aqueducts and sewers; all the houses had baths and latrines.

Another Abbasid city-building project was the construction of the Round City (762) at Baghdad, known primarily from written descriptions because its site lies under the modern city. The Round City contained a series of concentric rings, with the Aliph's residence, mosques, and household in the center. The conception of the plan has its roots in Sassanian Iran.

Palace complexes, similar to that of Samarra, were built in later times at Cairo, at Madinah al-Zahra (Spain), in North

Africa, and in Ýstanbul where the Ottoman Turks in 1454 began the Topkapi Surayi, now the Topkapi Palace Museum. The tradition was continued also in the 14th century Alhambra Palace of the Moorish kings at Granada, Spain. Of particular note here is the Court of the Lions with a fountain surrounded by stone lions spouting water. These Alhambra lions have their counterparts in animal-shaped bronze and pottery vessels; although figural, their function keeps them within the category of decorative art.

In Iran, the last great buildings were those erected by the Safavids, whose contributions to secular architecture included bridges, polo grounds, and palaces built with wooden kiosks from which the ever-present fountains could be appreciated or polo matches observed. An art gallery, intended by Shah Abbas for his collection of Chinese porcelains, was also part of the palace.

The caravansary (or, in Turk., han) was the particular contribution of the Seljuks. These rest houses for travelers, built along the caravan routes, had an aisled hall and a courtyard for animals. Other types of buildings that were prominent in the history of Islamic architecture were public baths, bazaars (marketplaces), gardens as well as garden pavilions, and ribats, or frontier garrisons, extant examples of which are now found only in Tunisia.

Tombs and Mausoleums

Despite Islamic strictures against the building of elaborate tombs, mausoleums, erected as symbols of the power of departed leaders, became the most important structures of Islam, after mosques and palaces. Examples include the necropolis of domed tombs built outside Cairo by the Mameluke rulers of Egypt in the 15th century. In Samarqand (now in Uzbekistan), the Timurids constructed a necropolis, the Sah-i-Zindeh (15th–16th cent.), an impressive group of buildings with elegantly patterned brickwork and high tiled domes on drums. In Iran, under the Mongol conquerors, a special kind of tomb was developed. The large 14th-century mausoleum at Sultaniyah has a dome of double construction, giving greater height without added weight, on an octagonal base (originally with a tower at each corner). The most outstanding example of this form, it is the predecessor of one of the most famous of all Islamic mausoleums, the Taj Mahal (mid-17th cent.), in Agra, India, built by two Iranian architects.

Architectural Decoration

Plaster, patterned brickwork, and tile were used as decorative media in and on Islamic buildings; to this repertoire the Seljuks added glazed brick and tiles—the latter often luster painted like their pottery (see Pottery below). The city of Kashan, Iran, specialized in this production. Whole molded mihrab facings, composed of columnar bands of Koranic inscriptions, were made in luster faience, one of the earthenware styles used for tile. Tiles in various shapes, such as stars, were fitted together into wall panels. Timurid architecture featured mihrab coverings of brilliant tile mosaic, in which the individual colors were fired separately to achieve their fullest intensity. In the 15th century, tile ceramicists from Iran, which was still an important center, established tile production in Turkey. With the development of workshops at Ýznik, the Turks had their own superb source of tiles. In Safavid Iran, most new public buildings received splendid tile sheathings, and many older buildings were redecorated in the same way. These tiles included ones in gold and green, colors not previously used; the different colors were applied and fired together in patterns, rather than separately as before. The effect was different, and the individual colors were less brilliant.

Other Islamic architectural decoration included wood carving, occasionally inlaid with ivory—used on maqqsuras, mimbars, windows and doors, and various structural elements. Stone reliefs and marble inlays are found in buildings in Spain, Turkey, and Egypt (from the Mameluke period). Although not part of the building itself, mosque lamps and colorful prayer carpets may also be considered architectural decorations that veil and transform the building by introducing light and color.

Decorative Art

Islamic dicta on the permissible in art, collected in the Hadith, were similar to those of the iconoclastic movement (see Iconoclasm) during the time of the Byzantine Empire.

The idea behind the condemnation of making images of prophets and saints, and of adoring these images and tombs, was that such practices materialized worship, which belongs to God alone. Likewise, the creation of representational images by artists was condemned because only God is able to give life to creation. These prohibitions were always observed in religious contexts—in mosques, on mosque carpets, in the decoration of Korans and Koran boxes—but irregularly in the secular decorative arts, depending on the degree of orthodoxy usual under a particular ruler. At one Syrian desert-palace, Mshatta (early 8th cent.), which has richly carved stone reliefs on its walls, there is a sharp distinction between the reliefs on the mosque part of the complex, which are completely ornamental, and those on the other areas, which are figural representations of both fantastic and real animals. The effect of these prohibitions, even when figures of human beings and animals were represented, was to keep such figures within a decorative framework; unlike European artists, therefore, Muslim artists did not develop an understanding of anatomy, musculature, and perspective. On the other hand, instead of depriving artists of their ability to express their talents, these limitations on what was generally acceptable channeled their energies into the development of decorative patterns; based on geometric forms, Arabic script, and foliate shapes (later stylized as arabesques), this repertoire embodies the unique decorative genius of Islamic art.

The other main proscription from the Hadith that profoundly affected the development of the Islamic decorative arts was the condemnation of luxurious and precious materials. Thus, where the decorative art of other cultures may make lavish use of gold, silver, or precious gems, Islamic art is focused on ceramics, decorated bronze vessels, and wood carvings. Another reason for the attention given to unpretentious materials and fundamentally utilitarian objects was the rise of a large urban middle class; while this class was developing its connoisseurship its practical needs had to be considered.

Pottery

Perhaps the finest expression of the Islamic artistic impulse is found in pottery, which displays a degree of innovation and creativity comparable to that producing fine art in other cultures. POTTERY, (q.v.) was apparently collected by the prosperous middle class much as the Dutch middle class avidly collected portraits and genre paintings in the 17th century. The first period of ceramic innovation can be defined from pottery found in the excavations at Samarra. Imported Chinese porcelain in the Baghdad area stimulated the interest of Abbasid connoisseurs and potters, but the local clay could not produce such technically perfect works. Colorful green-and-yellow T'ang wares were imitated successfully, but to achieve a porcelainlike effect the Abbasid potters invented the tin glaze, which gave the pot a creamy covering. Some of these tin-glazed pots were overpainted with blue decorations (simple borders and one-word inscriptions), and this new ware is believed to have inspired the earliest blue-and-white porcelain of China (itself imitated by later Islamic potters).

The new technique of luster painting was also developed at Samarra. This involved painting with a metallic solution on a pot that had already been fired. It was then refired at a low heat, producing a shiny metallic pattern—

brown, greenish, or red—that seemingly transforms the pot into one of (prohibited) gold. This technique traveled to all parts of the world.

In northeastern Iran, in the late 8th to the 11th century, Nishapur (Neyshabur) and Samarqand produced other notable wares, in this case slip decorated. Slip is a thin layer of clay spread over the pot to make a ground for painted decoration; these potters rediscovered a technique that had a long history. Some of these pots, influenced by the Sassanian heritage, were decorated with figures of horsemen and a crowded field of ornament and calligraphy. On others the decoration was restricted to monumental Kufic inscriptions with small decorative motifs. Other important Iranian wares of this period are of the gabri type—on which the background or decoration is engraved to create a low relief effect—and the related graffito type, both of which imitate techniques known in metalwork. Like the lustered pottery, this ware can be understood as an acceptable substitute for a more costly material.

Under the Fatimids of Egypt, a large amount of important luster-painted pottery and other wares was made at Fustat. In Seljuk Iran, the potters made thin vessels with pierced walls covered in glaze in imitation of delicate Chinese porcelain, and another porcelainlike group with applied decorations in high relief. Other types of painted pottery were made in Iran at this time, including the famous luster-painted pottery and tiles of Rayy and Kashan. Some of these pots, and a special min'ai, or seven-color, enameled pottery, feature illustrations of poems and heroic scenes similar to Persian miniature paintings (see below). Pots were sometimes given charming animal shapes; a ewer, for example, might be decorated with a cock's head. Occasional small stools and boxes were also made of pottery.

In Iraq, in the years before the Mongol conquest, Raqqa was the center for the production of fine underglaze-painted pottery. Important ceramics were produced at Ýznik and

Kütahya, in Ottoman Turkey, well into the 18th century. Much of this was influenced by Chinese blue-and-white ware, but pots were also produced with typically Turkish floral patterns in turquoise, green, purple, brown, and black. The Safavid potters of Iran, also influenced by Chinese wares, produced beautiful blue-and-white ceramics that were exported to the West. Here, too, the production of polychrome and lustered ware continued into the 18th century.

Glass

Muslim artists also worked in glass, first with techniques used in Byzantium and Sassanian Iran, and then in new ways. Fatimid-cut glass, luster-painted glass, and stamp-decorated glass are of exceptionally high quality. In this period were also made a small number of exquisite carved rock-crystal vessels, comparable in quality to the cut glass. The enameled glass of 12th-century Syria, chiefly goblets and lamps, has never been surpassed in beauty; the decoration, in the form of inscriptional and patterned bands, is like that of contemporary bronzes. The Syrians retained their mastery of this glass craft in the late period and are known particularly for tapered and enameled mosque lamps.

Wood Carving and Ivory Carvings

Wood carving as architectural decoration has been mentioned above in connection with mosques. Exceptional woodwork was also done in Fatimid palaces, from which openwork figural panels with courtly scenes survive; some of this work echoes the Coptic (Christian Egyptian) heritage. Small pieces of furniture were also decoratively carved. Carved ivory boxes and carved elephant tusks were favored at the Fatimid court, and the tradition was continued in Arab Sicily. This delicate style of carving represented courtiers, animals, and foliage.

Bronze Work

Because of the stricture against precious metals, bronze was a favored material. Some of the finest pieces of Islamic bronze work have survived as parts of European church treasures. At first, Sassanian forms were adopted for bronze objects, but the Fatimid period produced some of the finest animal-shaped containers ever made, as well as candlesticks and plates. Important bronzes, engraved and inlaid with copper and silver, were made in eastern Iran, but the finest Islamic bronzes were the product of the workshops of Mosul (Iraq) in the 50 years before the Mongol conquest. Ewers, basins, and candlesticks were inlaid with silver and gold and contained bands of decorations, figures, and inscriptions of the most intricate workmanship. The fine inlaid Mosul bronzes of the 14th century tended to be even more purely decorative; Syrian workshops, however, continued to produce figural designs.

Manuscripts

Kufic script, a heavy monumental Arabic script suited to stone carving, appears in the earliest surviving Koran manuscripts. In these, the diacritical marks over the letters are sometimes painted in red, and the gold decorations between suras (chapters) contrast handsomely with the heavy black script. In the Seljuk period, a more cursive flowing script, Naskhi, developed. The two styles were often used for contrast in architecture and decorative contexts.

Leatherwork

Leather bookbindings with geometric patterns were also an important form of the decorative arts. The earliest examples were tooled and in relief; later bindings were stamped and gilded and, in the 16th century, enamel painted.

Painting

As in other Islamic art forms, where the Western concept of art for art's sake did not exist, painting too served definite purposes. Rather than an art of easel painting, it was an art of book illustration. The earliest Islamic paintings to survive in any number are miniatures illustrating manuscripts of Greek scientific texts translated into Arabic

(Arabic learning was the vehicle by which the learning of the classical world was transmitted to the West), the fables of Bidpai (fl. ad 300), and the Maqamat of al-Hariri (1054–1122), the narrative of a traveler's adventures. All of these paintings were derived from the 13th-century Baghdad school of manuscript illustration. The scientific illustrations are line drawings based on classical models, and the colorful secular paintings have a charming naivete, with only two or three monumental figures represented and landscape elements shown decoratively.

Persian miniature painting of the Mongol, or Il-Khanid, style flourished in 14th-century Tabriz, in Iran. Chinese influence in landscape details, the expression of emotion, and a complexity of composition characterized the new school. Many Persian epic poems were illustrated in this style, the greatest example being the 14th-century Demotte Shah nameh, a manuscript of Firdausi's great national epic. Miniature painting continued to develop in the 15th century in Herat (eastern Iran) under Timurid patronage. Bihzad, one of the notable Timurid miniaturists, was a master; many of his dramatic scenes are not confined within formal borders, and his figures have a psychological realism rare in this tradition.

The Ottoman rulers also patronized the art of the book; starting with the 14th-century artists from Tabriz, a Turkish school of miniature painting developed that recorded courtly and military life in a distinctive decorative manner. Safavid artists produced beautifully illustrated classics in their own style and, in response to European influence, broadened their scope to include figure drawing and portraits.

Miniature painting in Muslim India had its own special development from the 16th to the 19th century; it was much influenced by indigenous Indian art and often depicted individual rulers and ceremonial events.

Textiles

Textiles were highly valued as objects of luxury, and the finest medieval ones were made in workshops called tiraz, which were controlled by the Aliph. The tiraz system that imitated imperial Byzantine, Coptic, and Sassanian institutions, ended with the Mongol conquest. A gift from such a tiraz (often an inscribed robe of honor) was a most valuable possession. The word Tiraz was also used for the textiles themselves. These were often inscribed with the name of the workshop, the date, and the ruler's name.

In Egypt, many tiraz were of linen, and, under the Fatimids, beautiful silk tapestry bands containing gold threads were woven into them. Silk textiles were also manufactured in much of the Islamic world, and some were produced in official tiraz. Among the finest are 9th to 10th-century silks from the Bukhara region, and 10th to 11th-century silks from Iran, Baghdad, Egypt, and Spain. Despite Byzantine shipping blockades, such silks made their way to Europe with embassies. These silks had a profound influence on later Islamic, Byzantine, Sicilian, and Italian weavers and embroiderers. Even present-day words for textiles are often derived from the Islamic world, such as damask from Damascus. The coronation mantle of the Holy Roman emperors was embroidered by Islamic artists in Sicily, and Sicilian silks continued to be an influence in the 14th century, after the establishment of European silk workshops.

After the Mongol conquest, Chinese silks influenced Islamic weaving; this influence is seen in the first Islamic gold-brocaded silks and in specific decorative details. The Ottoman Turks produced new kinds of large-scale silk patterns featuring representations of carnations, tulips, palmettes, and the Chinese cloud-band motif. The patterned silk velvets and brocades of the Safavids are among the most beautiful textiles ever woven.

Rugs and Carpets

The earliest surviving Islamic knotted carpets are from Konya, in Turkey, made in the 14th century. These Konya carpets of blue, green, and red have an overall pattern based on natural forms; the border has an inscriptional band. Other distinctive geometrically patterned carpets were made under the Mamelukes in pale blue, red, and yellow. Several kinds of 16th-century Turkish and Egyptian carpets—Ushak, "Holbein," Cairene—survive; these occasionally were depicted in contemporary European paintings. Carpet weaving reached new heights under the Safavids of Iran, whose design repertoire included hunting scenes and garden motifs. A dated (1539–40) and signed example with floral designs, measuring nearly 12 m (40 ft) long, was woven for the Ardabil mosque and is now in the Victoria and Albert Museum, London. Safavid carpets of silk, in pastel tones with gold and silver areas, were woven specifically for the European market; although very beautiful, they mark the end of the purely Islamic tradition of carpet weaving.

Mughal art and architecture a characteristic Indo-Islamic-Persian style that flourished on the Indian subcontinent during the Mughal Empire (1526-1857). This new style combined elements of Islamic art and architecture, which had been introduced to India during the Delhi Sultanate (1192-1398) and had produced great monuments such as the Qutb Minar, with features of Persian art and architecture. Mughal monuments are found chiefly in N India, but there are also many remains in Pakistan. This article discusses these distinctive forms of art and architecture as they developed under a succession of Mughal emperors.

Humayun

The school of Mughal painting began in 1549 when Humayun (1530-56) invited two Persian painters to his court, then at Kabul. They came to direct the illustration of the Amir Hamza, a fantastic narrative of which some 1,400 large paintings were executed on cloth.

Achievements under Akbar

In architecture the first great Mughal monument was the mausoleum to Humayun, erected during the reign of Akbar (1556-1605). The tomb, which was built in the 1560s, was designed by a Persian architect Mirak Mirza Ghiyas. Set in a garden at Delhi, it has an intricate ground plan with central octagonal chambers, joined by an archway with an elegant facade and surmounted by cupolas, kiosks, and pinnacles. At the same time Akbar was building his fortress-palace in his capital, Agra. Native red sandstone was inlaid with white marble, and all the surfaces were ornately carved on the outside and sumptuously painted inside.

Akbar went on to build the entire city of Fatehpur Sikri (City of Victory) in which extensive use was made of the low arches and bulbous domes that characterize the Mughal style. Built in 1571 the choice of the site of Sikri reflected Akbar's gratitude to a Muslim saint at Sikri for the birth of his son. Courtiers soon followed suit and built homes surrounding the palace and mosque. The new city became the capital of the Empire, but in 1585 it was abandoned.

Under Akbar, Persian artists directed an academy of local painters. The drawings, costumes, and ornamentation of illuminated manuscripts by the end of the 16th century illustrate the influence of Indian tastes and manners in the bright coloring and detailed landscape backgrounds. Modeling and perspective also began to be adapted from Western pictures. Basawan, Lal, and Daswanth were Akbar's most famous painters.

Jahangir

Jahangir (1605-27) favored paintings of events from his own life rather than illustrated fiction. He encouraged portraiture and scientific studies of birds, flowers, and animals, which were collected in albums. Mansur and Manohar were among his famous painters. Jahangir, who resided at Lahore, built less than his predecessors but effected the significant change from sandstone to marble.

Shah Jahan

It was Shah Jahan (1628-58) who perfected Mughal architecture and erected at Agra its most noble and famous building, the tomb of his favorite wife, which is known as the Taj Mahal. A huge white marble building of simple, symmetrical plan, it is inlaid with colorful semiprecious materials and is set in an equally beautiful and symmetrical garden. The Taj Mahal continues the tradition of Mughal garden tombs, of which Humayun's tomb was the first. Shah Jahan established (1638) Delhi as his capital and built there the famous Red Fort, which contained the imperial Mughal palace. Painting also flourished during Shah Jahan's reign. Portraiture was most highly developed at his sophisticated court, and ink drawings were of high quality.

Decline under Aurangzeb

Under the orthodox Aurangzeb (1659-1707) the decline of the arts began, although his ornate Pearl Mosque (1662) at Delhi is worthy of mention. During his reign the Mughal academy was dispersed. Many artists then joined Rajput courts, where their influence on Hindu painting is clearly evident.

9

Understanding the Islamic Art

In the seventh century, in the decades following its inception, Islam's spread was startling, and the new faith quickly reached many diverse lands and cultures. A number of older art traditions (including Classical, Byzantine and Sasanian) were blended and modified—most obviously in the architecture of mosques—to serve the new ideology. Islamic art would always be multifarious (complex patterns of cross-fertilization, appropriation and synthesis, distant sources of inspiration, varied influences, and sectarian and regional differences), but certain unifying tendencies are constant: a reverence for the Word; a proscription against depictions of humans and animals (though there are a number of noteworthy exceptions, such as courtly arts, and illustrations by Iranian Seljuks, Safavids, and other heirs to Persian culture); and an equal prestige and esteem accorded to all genres and mediums. Writing—sacred, elegant and beautiful—was honored. Eschewing figural art, artists developed nonrepresentational geometric, vegetal and floral motifs into an elaborate repertoire of intricate, richly decorative patterns. Arabic script was also integrated into ornamental schemes.

In the eighth century, the Abbasid dynasty, based in Baghdad, supplanted the Umayyad dynasty (though art flourished under Umayyads in Muslim Spain), and held sway for five centuries. In Mesopotamia and Iran, architecture and painted ceramics were the result of Islamic art's encounter with the powerful artistic legacy of Persia. In the tenth century, during what some scholars regard as Islamic art's classical age, Fatimids from North Africa developed a rich tradition of textiles and ivory, and spur a revival of art in Egypt.

The imposing architecture of the Ayyubids and Seljuks is also a product of the classical age. The thirteenth century witnessed the destructive rise of the Mongols, though late in the century, their ruler converted to Islam and became an enlightened patron of art that now included elements imported from China; the Timurids succeeded the Mongols, and continued to generously sponsor art. Southwest of the Mongols, in Egypt and Syria, Mamluks spent lavishly on architecture, enameled glass, wares with precious metal inlay, and later, on carpets. In the fourteenth century, in the last outpost of Islam in Spain, the Alhambra was built on a hill above the city of Granada. Between the fourteenth and sixteenth century, the Ottoman, Safavid, and Mughal Empires rose to prominence. Ottoman art is distinguished by massive imperial architectural projects and by patterns of gracefully intertwining organic motifs produced by a royal studio. Safavid artists excelled at book illustration that combined opulence and specificity, and at related carpet designs. The exquisite art of the Mughals of India reflects their sensitivity to the delicacy of nature, but most famous is a royal tomb, the Taj Mahal. Over the last few hundred years, Islamic art has remained vital and adaptable, despite a sharp decline in royal patronage.

The unique beauty of Islamic art derives in large part from its longstanding rejection of depictions of humans and animals in religious art. Instead of portraits or stories from the Qur'an, mosques and manuscripts are adorned with flourishes of Arabic calligraphy, delicate tile work, layers of gold and intricate floral decorations. But attitudes towards figurative art have varied somewhat throughout the course of Islamic history and across different Islamic cultures. Animals and humans appear sporadically throughout the centuries, and there are many surviving examples of beautiful figurative art from the Islamic world, most of which come from the late medieval period in Iran. These depict events in the life of Muhammad, the prophets, scenes of Paradise and Hell, battles of Iranian kings, everyday life, and other human subjects.

Today, as is well known, figurative art is widely rejected in Islam and depictions of Muhammad are considered especially offensive. The following article seeks to provide a factual background for this, chronicling the history of figurative depictions in Islamic art, pinning down exactly what is prohibited in the Qur'an and hadith, and exploring the reasoning given for the special sensitivity to depictions of Muhammad.

At least when it comes to their official teachings, Judaism, Christianity and Islam agree that:

1. There is one great God who cannot be seen and that
2. Idolatry (worship of images) is one of the worst sins. These shared fundamental values have been interpreted in a variety of ways over the course of history when it comes to religious art, historical illustrations, and depiction of human religious figures.

In Judaism and Christianity, the creation of images for worshipping is specifically forbidden by the Second Commandment. Jews do not use images in religious rituals and never depict God, but have occasionally painted pictures of the prophets and biblical stories (for example in the 2nd-century synagogue at Dura Europos, Syria).

Christians began to depict Jesus as early as the 2nd or 3rd century AD (see our Jesus Image Gallery) in the catacombs, on tombs, and eventually in churches. The practice became widespread and common. But for a period in the 8th century and again in the 9th century, some Byzantine emperors and bishops condemned images of Jesus and the saints, calling it an innovation introduced by the devil that breaks the Second Commandment:

"Satan misled men, so that they worshipped the creature instead of the Creator. The Law of Moses and the Prophets cooperated to remove this ruin... But the previously mentioned demiurge of evil gradually brought back idolatry under the appearance of Christianity." (Iconoclast Council at Hieria, 754).

At the same time, other bishops and emperors strongly opposed this movement. They argued that: Christians do not worship images but the God who made them; that the images are not "false idols" (like images from other religions) but represent real things; and that they were depicting not divinity itself but Christ incarnate, who was after all a "figurative image" of God. This party won out by imperial decree in 843 AD, and religious images have been commonly used in Christianity ever since — except in Protestantism.

Like the Byzantine iconoclasts, Protestant Reformers of the 16th century believed that the veneration of images in Roman Catholicism amounted to idolatry. When churches became Protestant in Germany, Switzerland, and elsewhere, they were completely stripped of all religious statues and paintings on the walls were whitewashed. Protestant churches generally remain free of images today, yet many churches and families have modern portraits of Jesus hung on a wall.

Rules about Images in the Qur'an, Hadith and Islamic Law: Unlike the Hebrew Bible, and perhaps surprisingly, there is no commandment against making images of living beings in the Qur'an. But it does make clear that nothing should be honored alongside God:

"God does not forgive the joining of partners [Arabic: shirk] with him: anything less than that he forgives to whoever he will, but anyone who joins partners with God is lying and committing a tremendous sin" (4:48).

All the Islamic injunctions against making religious images come from the hadith, traditions recorded by various followers about what the Prophet said and did. Although not divine revelation like the Qur'an, hadith is considered binding when multiple trustworthy sources agree. Following are some examples of hadith on images:

"Ibn 'Umar reported Allah's Messenger (may peace be upon him) having said: Those who paint pictures would be punished on the Day of Resurrection and it would be said to them: Breathe soul into what you have created." (Sahih Muslim vol.3, no.5268)

"This hadith has been reported on the authority of Abu Mu'awiya though another chain of transmitters (and the words are): Verily the most grievously tormented people amongst the denizens [inhabitants] of Hell on the Day of Resurrection would be the painters of pictures...." (Sahih Muslim vol.3, no.5271)

"Narrated [Muhammad's wife] 'Aisha: Allah's Apostle said, 'The painter of these pictures will be punished on the Day of Resurrection, and it will be said to them, Make alive what you have created.'" (Bukhari vol.9, book 93 no.646)

"Narrated 'Aisha: The Prophet entered upon me while there was a curtain having pictures (of animals) in the house. His face got red with anger, and then he got hold of the curtain and tore it into pieces. The Prophet said, 'Such people as paint these pictures will receive the severest punishment on the Day of Resurrection.'" (Bukhari vol.8, book 73, no.130)

"Umar said, 'We do not enter your churches because of the statues and pictures.' Ibn 'Abbas used to pray in the church provided there were no statues in it." (Bukhari vol.1, chapter 54)

"'Aisha played with dolls while her husband Muhammad was with her. (Sahih Muslim vol.4, book 29 ch.1005, no.5981)

"Muhammad went to Fatimah's house, but turned back when he saw a figured curtain." (Sunan Abu Dawud vol.3, book 21, no.3746)

History of Images and Figurative Art in Islam: In the earliest days of Islam, a specifically "Islamic art" had not yet begun to develop and art in general was not a prominent issue. According to the Encyclopedia Britannica:

"Earliest Islam as seen in the Qur'an or in the more verifiable accounts of the Prophet's life simply do not deal with the arts, either on the practical level of requiring or suggesting forms as expressions of the culture or on the ideological level of defining a Muslim attitude toward images.... There is no prohibition against representations of living things, and not a single Qur'anic passage refers clearly to the mosque, eventually to become the most characteristically Muslim religious building."

But as the Islamic community grew and conquered a great deal of new territory, it came into contact with the religious art and architecture of other cultures and began to develop its own. By the mid-8th century there was a clear Muslim doctrine against the creation of images, as seen in the hadith above.

It is interesting that Islam came into contact with Byzantine culture at the height of the iconoclastic controversy. It is possible that those intensely negative associations of religious art influenced or strengthened Islamic views on the matter. Regardless, "it is likely that, more or less intuitively, the Muslims felt a certain reluctance toward representations from the very beginning.

For all monuments of religious art are devoid of any representations; even a number of attempts at representational symbolism in the official art of coinage were soon abandoned."

In the 8th and 9th centuries, Islamic art experimented with a wide variety of materials, techniques and designs, many of which were influenced by China and other parts of the world. But the decorative arts remained generally consistent in excluding depictions of humans and animals. Some minor exceptions are birds drawn from the folkloric past of the Near East and "occasionally human figures drawn in a strikingly abstract fashion."

Fatimid bowl from the 12th century, depicting a Byzantine Christian priest swinging a censer. (Victoria & Albert Museum, London) The art of the Fatimids (a Shi'ite dynasty that ruled 909–1171 AD) continued to focus mainly on calligraphy and decorative vines, but also frequently depicted animals and humans. The celebrated lustre-painted Fatimid ceramics from Egypt are especially distinguished by "the representation of the human figure. Some of these ceramics have been decorated with simplified copies of illustrations of the princely themes, but others have depictions of scenes of Egyptian daily life." The Fatimids also developed an art of manuscript illustration.

The Seljuk Turks sought to restore Islamic orthodoxy. They made many contributions to Islamic art and architecture, including monumental minarets, mausoleums of holy men (to which pilgrimages were made), citadels and madrasas. Paintings and sculptures of animals and people were among the decorations employed for the monumental new architecture, but the Seljuks were especially interested in geometry and mathematical proportion in art.

The Mamluks ruled Egypt, Palestine, and Syria from 1260 to 1517 and were very wealthy. The Mamluks are especially known for their splendid architecture, which included the Dome of the Rock in Jerusalem. Mamluk art seems to have been virtually devoid of human and animal depiction.

Meanwhile, in the Mongol period in Iran, Persian art became especially notable for its figurative art in wall painting and illuminated manuscripts. These include many narrative scenes of the Prophet, Iranian kings and other humans. Examples include the 56 minature paintings of the 14th-century Shah-nameh ("Book of Kings"); illustrations of the Jami' at-tawarikh ("Universal History of Rashid ad-Din"); and the Khwaju Kermani manuscript from 1396. The Iranian style of painting was influenced by Seljuk art, but more so by Chinese painting. The most celebrated Islamic painter was Behzad (1455-1536), who led an academy of art in Iran.

The Ottoman Turks (15th-19th centuries) are best known for their tiles and pottery, but also developed their own form of miniature figurative painting.

Ottoman miniatures do have a character of their own, either in the almost folk art effect of religious images or in the precise depictions of such daily events as military expeditions or great festivals. Among the finest examples of the latter is the manuscript Surname-i Vehbi (Topkapi Saray Museum, Istanbul) painted by Levnî in the early 18th century.

From this brief history, it is clear that figurative art (depictions of humans and animals) has made regular appearances in the Islamic world. However, figurative art has largely been a private and secular matter, with most mosques kept free of such imagery. As explained on the website of the Los Angeles County Museum of Art:

Contrary to a popular misconception, however, figural imagery is an important aspect of Islamic art. Such images occur primarily in secular and especially courtly arts and appear in a wide variety of media and in most periods and places in which Islam flourished. It is important to note, nevertheless, that representational imagery is almost invariably restricted to a private context. Figurative art is excluded from the decoration of religious monuments. This absence may be attributed to an Islamic antipathy toward anything that might be mistaken for idols or idolatry, which are explicitly forbidden by the Qur'an.

Today, the depiction of prophets and especially Muhammad is widely rejected. The 1976 film The Message, directed by Moustapha Akkad and starring Anthony Quinn, tells the story of Muhammad, but follows Islamic law by not showing Muhammad or even portraying his voice (it is filmed from his perspective).

But aside from the taboo about Muhammad, and despite the clear rules in hadith, only the most conservative Muslims (such as the Taliban) believe it is wrong to create images in general, such as portraits or photographs. The introduction of television into Saudi Arabia was widely protested at first because of its images, but is now a common part of Saudi life.

Depictions of Muhammad

The outrage and violence occasioned by the infamous "Danish cartoon controversy" perhaps had more to do with disrespect for Islam than depictions of the Prophet. But many of today's Muslims consider any public depictions of the Prophet Muhammad offensive and objectionable, no matter how respectful, and frequently request their removal. The reasons for this sensitivity to depictions of Muhammad are not immediately clear, since Muhammad is as human as anyone else, Islamic sources do not prohibit depictions of him any more than other images, and past Islamic art has depicted Muhammad.

Islamic scholars have explained that the main reason for the ban on depicting Muhammad is the fear that the images of Muhammad might be worshipped. Political scientist As'ad AbuKhalil, visiting professor at the University of Alifornia at Berkeley, explained:

"In the Holy Koran of Islam, the one sin unforgivable is that of polytheism. The prohibition is intended to protect the faithful from that sin. The fear was that intense reverence for the prophet might if unrestrained cross over into worship. In the 8th and the 9th centuries a general consensus banning such depictions arose among the clerics, but not all Muslims knew of it, paid attention, or obeyed."

According to Imam Talal Eid, director of the Islamic Institute of Boston:

"He [the Prophet] instructed his companions not to draw a picture of him, and this has been taken as a general prohibition. He also told them not to pray in places that have images. There also is a general prohibition against full statues. And — though today, of course, we find photos in all passports — many Muslims have felt some hesitance about permitting portraits of any kind."

Juan Cole, a professor of Middle Eastern history at the University of Michigan, told NPR.

"The fear was that, both in Judaism and Islam, if you represented a holy figure like a prophet who had discussions with the divine, there would be a danger of people worshipping the image." Muslims certainly do revere the Prophet extremely highly. As Professor of Islamic Studies John Esposito put it,

"To criticize the prophet Muhammad is as direct an attack as mocking or attacking the Koran, which is seen as the word of God or the sacred Scripture. Muhammad is seen as the living Koran. His life Muslims are to emulate."

Summary and Conclusions:

The above evidence might be summarized in the following facts:

Judaism, Christianity and Islam all consider idolatry a heinous sin.

The Qur'an does not prohibit making images, only worshipping them.

Hadith clearly and consistently prohibits all images of any living being, with special mention of punishment for painters.

One exception to this rule is dolls for children, probably because children are not considered in danger of worshipping them as idols.

Neither the Qur'an nor hadith mention depictions of Muhammad.

The hadith prohibiting images are directed at Muslims only (e.g. Muslims are instructed not to enter buildings where there are images, not to demand their removal).

Muslim outrage against depictions of the Prophet does not usually extend to outrage against all images.

The hadith prohibiting images do not call for Muslims to take action against those who make images, but instead say that God will punish them severely at the Day of Judgment.

Muslims have applied the prohibitions against images in various ways throughout history and there is still some variation today.

Figurative art of Muhammad and other humans has been a significant part of late medieval Islamic art. But it was generally limited to secular contexts and elite classes who could afford fine art.

Shi'ites tend to be more open to religious images than Sunnis.

The main reason given for not depicting Muhammad is to avoid the temptation to worship the image.

Neither the Qur'an nor hadith say that viewing an image accidentally is a sin, but in the hadith the Prophet teaches Muslims to avoid them.

Understanding Islamic Art of the 16th & 17th Centuries

Prince Sadruddin Aga Khan has one of the finest private collections of Islamic art in the world. The most striking feature of this marvellous collection is the fact that it required a mere thirty years to be put together. Obviously, the Prince is an aesthete and connoisseur of art. However, he is known to have relied upon scholarly advice from the noted Harvard University Islamic art historian, Stuart Cary Welch. Professor Welch who is curator of Islamic Art at Boston's Fogg Museum and New York's Metropolitan Museum, and has long acknowledged Prince Sadruddin's patronage and friendship, is quick to point out that ultimately, the Prince made the final decisions.

During the 1950s, while the Prince attended Harvard University, the appreciation of Islamic art had not approached its present level of demand. Discerning dealers in New York offered him fine and often rare examples of Islamic art. Gradually, the Prince acquired from European dealers in Paris and Geneva, where he still maintains a second home. He also bought from London dealers and bid regularly at Sotheby's and Christie's auctions on both sides of the Atlantic.

The Prince's Islamic art collection is comprehensive both in Muslim chronology and geography. He is constantly striving to strengthen his collection and upgrade its quality. Consequently, to concentrate his attention upon Muslim aesthetics, he recently sold his celebrated collection of African art. It would be difficult to summarize the enormous scope of Prince Sadruddin's collection. On the other hand, it is possible to stress the fact that his collection is best represented by the Arab, the Ottoman Turkish, the Safavid and Qajar Persian, the Mughal as well as Indian nineteenth century "Company" painting and manuscripts. Islamic decorative arts, ceramics and the minor arts, many of which can be found in the Prince's collection, will not be dealt with in this article.

Among the Arabs, calligraphy is the highest art-form. Muslims are people of the book. The Quran (Koran), the Muslim scripture, is the most revered Islamic text. So much so that even those Muslims who are unable to read Arabic, which is the sole language of the Quran, know a verse or two at least. Some Muslims, equally untutored in Arabic, can recite the entire Quran and know it by heart. The educated Muslims also share a similar interest in the Quran. Royal members of the House of Saud, such as the late King Feisal, knew the Quran, chapter and verse, and could recall any portion of this holy book at will.

Two types of written calligraphy were preferred, Kufic and cursive. Kufic, which originated from the town of Kufa in Iraq, is geometric, with a distinct rigidness.

Due to this physical characteristic, Kufic is ideal for chapter headings, as well as wall inscriptions on Muslim mosques and minarets. The cursive script, the more popular of the two, still used in newspapers, is precisely what the term implies, flowing and easily readable. Basically, all other Islamic scripts are variations of the Kufic and cursive, and all of them tend to be highly inventive and frequently seem like a new style. In Muslim architecture and in the Qurans, Muslims invariable used a combination of both the Kufic and the cursive scripts. But the numerous styles derived from the Kufic and cursive are utterly fascinating.

Prince Sadruddin possesses many copies of the Quran. Among all of them, he has one Quranic page which is an outstanding example of Islamic calligraphy. It dates from the early tenth century, approximately three hundred years after Prophet Muhammad's death in 632 A.D. As this page is from North Africa it is all the more interesting, for it sheds light upon a region generally considered late in the flowering of Islamic art. The lettering is written, in gold in Kufic style, on a blue vellum which is extremely rare. It is believed to be one of several folios, now housed in various collections, from a Quran presented to the mosque in Mashhad by Aliph as-Mamum (A.D. 813-837). Incidentally, a number of Qurans have been discovered recently in Yemen, all of them dating to the early years of Islam. Even in retrospect, this stunning sample from Prince Sadruddin's collection is a small but significant indication that the Arabs were diligent when it came to writing the word of Allah. Furthermore, the Prince's Quranic page attests to the fact that Muslims aspired to creating beauty within the confines of calligraphy.

Turkish history spans several centuries. An adventurous people, highly disciplined and efficient administrators, the Turks terrorised and disrupted many people. Then, in the wake of victory, they controlled vast territories that included portions of Central Asia, Western Asia and eventually Egypt. Many of the great Empires can be traced to Turkish ethnic origins such as the Mameluks, Timurids and Mughals. All of these people developed and integrated singular styles in art which are best defined by their dynastic names.

In 1453, when Constantinople fell to the Ottoman Turks, another new era in Islamic art emerged. These Ottomans employed the most adept and artistic calligraphers available. They commissioned splendid illuminated Qurans and enhanced the standards of the decorative arabesque. Above all, they developed the book into a single flowing concept. As a result the bindings (of handsomely hand-tooled leather) are as exciting as the pages themselves.

Prince Sadruddin has several examples of Ottoman calligraphies, manuscripts and paintings. Turkish arts thrived under Ottoman patronage. The thrills the Ottomans must have experienced at seeing the art of the Islamic book evolve under their aegis, can still be had from studying them. In fact, the Ottoman sultans acquired works of art for illustrated manuscripts and paintings, from all over the Muslim world - especially from Persia, and cities such as Baghdad, Damascus and Cairo, renowned for their skilled artisans and artists.

While the calligraphers were striving to produce their finest art for the sultans, these Ottoman sovereigns, with their prodigious concern for excellence, also turned to architecture.

As a result, there are distinct hints of architectural refinements in some of the Ottoman paintings in Prince Sadruddin's collection, including the portrait of Sultan Selim II and a portrait of an Ottoman official. A cursory glance at Muslim paintings will indicate an emphasis on headgear. A huge, tulip-shaped turban, favoured by Ottomans, is one such distinctive headgear among those worn by Muslims. It is a means of recognising the Turkish origin of the wearer. Ottoman paintings reveal the foremost achievements of Muslim portraiture west of the Tigris and the Euphrates. Those intrigued by these works of art would do well to study the Ottomans as they were painted in the West by Venetian painters such as Bellini, and by later masters such as Johann Kopenski. There is more pleasure to be derived once there is an understanding of Islamic art, rather than merely considering it an exotic aspect of world art.

There is no doubt that Prince Sadruddin's collection is particularly strong in Persian art, while again, the emphasis is on the art of calligraphy as applied to the Quran. The preference for this geographical area should not be surprising when one learns that Prince Sadruddin's ancestors came from Persia. Despite the change in his family's fortunes and notwithstanding contemporary politics, the Prince is warm-hearted towards Persia. It is Persia that contributed to the renaissance of Islamic art, and indeed, Persia is crucial to any discussion of Muslim cultural heritage.

Before nineteenth century, Perisan Muslim arts are best seen in ceramics. An exception to this is the Seljuk calligraphies (1055-1258), of which Prince Sadruddin owns several eleventh century example. The Seljuks are remembered for their arts, but Persia was transformed after the Mongol conquest in the thirteenth century. Despite this change the Il-Khans, who were descendants of the Mongols, patronised the arts of the book. For all its brief reign, this Il-Khanid age inspired generations of Persian painters.

All the same, Persian pictorial art is generally conceived as beginning under the aegis of the Timurids in the fifteenth century. It is in great measure the genesis of Persian painting. Moreover, subsequent painting in Persia and India is ultimately studied from Timurid sources as well, and as far as Islamic painting in Persia is concerned, the cities of Tabriz and Herat enjoyed the same kind of prestige as Florence and Rome in Renaissance Italy. Bihzad, for example, who is generally considered among the greatest Muslim painters, lived in Herat.

Iran embraced the Shiite sect of Islam at the time of the Safavid dynasty. The Sunni sect, which is larger, claims the majority of Muslims. Whereas theological discussion is not pertinent here, it is wise to remember that Prince Sadruddin, like his forebears, is Shiite. He is the son of Aga Khan III (1877-1957). Prince Karim the present Aga Khan, is Prince Sadruddin's nephew. The followers of the Aga Khan are a celebrated group among all Muslims. They are entrepreneurs with philanthropic interests who believe in the Aga Khan and accept his spiritual leadership. The Aga Khan's followers are based in Bombay, which has long served as their headquarters. Although many live in metropolitan cities such as Bombay, Karachi, Nairobi, Mombasa and Johannesburg, others are scattered around the world. Most of them are prosperous, self-confident and hard-working Muslims. These attributes represent a positive element and should be given greater attention than the lacunae of Islamic theology. In so far as Prince Sadruddin is concerned, until recently he served as the United Nations High Commissioner for Refugees and was nearly elected Secretary General of the United Nations, following the tenure of Kurt Waldheim. Such pragmatic achievements enable us to conceive the picture of a Muslim aesthete who is also a man of action. It is also possible, furthermore, to see Prince Sadruddin in the context of past Muslim patrons of art. The Safavids of Persia are a fine example.

Within the first generation, the Safavids (1502-1736) had established themselves as powerful patrons of art, no different from their Medici contemporaries in Renaissance Italy, the Mughals in India and the Ming emperors in China. The Safavids went so far as to accord calligraphers an esteemed position similar to that of painters. Shah Tahmasp (1524-1576), one of the most eminent Safavid patrons of painting, spent two decades in order to attract the best painters to his court. Having done so, he went ahead to inspire a stylistic harmony among his court painters. Such a royal incentive to paint had far-reaching consequences, some of which can be seen in Prince Sadruddin's collection.

Generations of Persian painters and patrons considered the "Shahnamah", the Persian epic by the poet Firdausi (933 - ca.1020), as their biggest pictorial challenge. In Persia, the "Shahnamah" held the sort of literary position that Homer's "Odyssey" had among peoples of the northern Mediterranean.

Prince Sadruddin has two pages from a "Shahnamah" made for Shah Tahmasp. On one page, attributed to the painter Aqa-Mirak, dated 1532, there is a rendering of the poet Firdausi, "Firdausi Encounters the Court Poets of Ghazna." On the second page, attributed to Muzaffar Ali, painted 1530-1535, is the legendary hero Rustam pursuing Akvan (the demon). Both these pages have been assigned to Tabriz, one of the two great Persian cities noted for its paintings.

However, Shah Tahmasp eventually lost interest in the arts while still in power. Soon, the neglected painters departed for new ateliers in Ottoman Turkey and Mughal India. There, at nearly opposite ends of Safavid Persia, these gifted artists contributed to the increased flowering of Islamic painting. This visual excitement is also garnered from Prince Sadruddin's collection.

Meanwhile, Persian patronage acquired a democratic trend in the final years of Shah Tahmasp. Shah Abbas I (1587-1629) and his successors discovered this egalitarian growth in the demand for inexpensive paintings. Besides the Shah and the aristocracy, the new patrons included bourgeois elements as well as career professionals such as soldiers. The physical form of drawings and paintings became a single page rather than an entire manuscript full of illustrations.

No doubt some of these single page paintings were meant to be subsequently bound in albums. At that time this popular concept - of the single page painting and drawing - appealed to patrons in India and Turkey as well. Images in these low-priced paintings tended to be introverted. These works of art also departed from the established tradition of anonymity and, on occasion, were signed. Gradually, Western painting influenced Persian art through trade, diplomatic ties, evangelist and maritime contacts. This Europeanised aspect of Persian painting developed a formidable style in the nineteenth century and is celebrated simply as Qajar painting. Among the Qajar dynasty paintings in Prince Sadruddin's collection is a striking portrait of Fath Ali Shah, dated 1819. Prince Sadruddin's great-grand-father, the first Aga Khan, was the son-in-law of Fath Ali Shah.

Indian Islamic art is syncretised with Hindu aesthetics. Even a casual glance at the similarities between the Hindus and Muslims of India is sufficient for a start. In religious practices, during festivals and occasions of mourning, including funerals, the two diverse religious groups come together in India.

The "Muharram" is a period of mourning for Ali and his family, including his sons, Hasan and Husain, and their followers. Ali, a cousin and son-in-law of the Prophet Muhammad, was martyred along with his family and followers. The Shiites accept Ali as the successor of the Prophet Muhammad. The Prophet had not nominated his successor. Ali's position had been challenged and he lost. This event, dating to the seventh century A.D. is commemorated with Shiites dressed in black and reciting elegies in front of "alums", the Shiite standards, usually free-standing calligraphy created in silver or copper, and at times even of gold. In the case of Indian Shiites, they carry the "taziya", a green or white paper mosque or mausoleum in miniature. The "taziya" is borne to the water's edge, then released in the water.

Similarly, the alums are also immersed in water. While the inexpensive, though religiously inspired taziya is left to float and disintegrate in the water, the alums, expensive and with considerable iconic significance, are returned to their special shrines or stored in religious treasuries until the following year. The rituals of the alums and the taziya are worth studying alongside Hindu customs that prevail during the festival of Ganesha, the son of Siva. Whether Muslims, with these rituals, follow Hindus, or vice versa, is unimportant. The fact that remains striking is the similarity in this case of the two diverse faiths of Indian people - Hindus and Muslims. There is a small wonder that among conservative Muslims outside the subcontinent, the Indian Muslims are treated as country cousins at best.

The early beginnings of Islam in India were limited to the coastal waters of the subcontinent. The Arabs arrived by sea and settled in Sind, now part of Pakistan, and also along the regions north of Bombay and at the tip of southern India. These events took place in the early eighth century

A.D. As most of these Arabs traded, India remained undisturbed until the Afghans descended into the plains of Hindustan in the tenth and eleventh centuries. All the same, Islamic art made little impact beyond Delhi, where the Sultanate was established and where some of its architectural remains can still be seen.

Late into the thirteenth century the Muslims suddenly seemed to gain control of northern India and by the fourteenth century, their presence was felt as far south as the Deccan plateau. The architecture of the Tughlaq dynasty (1320-1398) and the somewhat later dynastic consolidation of Muslim kingdoms in the Deccan led to wonderful cities being founded such as Bijapur, Bidar and Golconda. Prince Sadruddin has an entire manuscript of a 1399 Quran ascribed to Gwalior. It is a rare and important work of art, quite aside from its religious significance. By the time the Mughals arrived in India in 1526, traces of Islamic presence could still be felt among the Hindu majority.

By tradition, Hindus delighted in their scripture, but historiography, travelling accounts and memoirs were second nature to Muslims. Muslims kept journals. Imagine a boy of thirteen, standing inspired, conquering Hindustan, then setting out to landscape gardens. This was Babur (1526-1530), who founded the Mughal Empire (also known as the House of Timur) and continued writing his memoirs and composing poetry. Babur's son, though effete in comparison to the great Mughals, nonetheless played a vital role as an art patron. Humayun (1530 - 1556), Babur's son, exiled to Safavid Persia, brought back to India painters trained in the ateliers of Shah Tahmasp. Thus Humayun, often overlooked, is to be accepted as a catalyst.

Once Akbar (1556 - 1605) took charge of the Mughal Empire from his father Humayun, he extended it and improved his relations with the chivalric Hindus, the Rajputs. It was then that Muslim art experienced a metamorphosis in

India. Emperor Akbar has long epitomised the renaissance man in India. In fact he is credited with the Mughal renaissance.

With his government under control, a magnificent court that contained "Naorattan", nine of India's most gifted men in the highest echelons of his Empire, Akbar retained the best available painters. These talented artists synthesised the Mughal painting style from Persian, indigenous Indian and European sources. The realistic painting showed the diversity of Indian life, and included some specimens from the plethora of India's fauna and flora. The Akbari paintings concentrated on action.

Akbar's son Jahangir (A.D. 1605-1627) was a half Hindu, the son of Akbar's first wife, the Rajput Princess Joda Bai. Unlike the history painting and illustrations of religious epics under Akbar, both Hindu and Muslim, Jahangir championed individual portraits and natural history subjects.

Shah Jahan (1627 -1657), the Jahangir's son, turned more towards religion. He lived at a time when the Mughals were at the height of their prosperity, and the paintings of his court depict the formal elegance of Mughal India. A cold, distant, even somewhat restrained effect marked the paintings of an age best remembered for the Taj Mahal (completed in 1654).

So, from this rich spectrum, Prince Sadruddin has several examples of Mughal paintings, covering all the leading epochs. The early Mughal paintings show the Timurid strains, the Mongol links (obvious in their sinicised eyes) and the rock formations idealised in Chinese paintings. The Safavid elements mingled, the Hindus contributed, and what surfaced as Mughal art is well represented in Prince Sadruddin's collection. The "Pictorial Genealogy of Jahangir" is a painting that to my mind typifies the abiding enthusiasm which Muslim patrons of art have had for Islamic history. This is what I consider the "roots-syndrome" which is indicative of a continuing heritage.

Along with anonymous Mughal painters, there are such famous names as Abd al-Samad, Makund, Basawan, Mitra, Balchand, Abu'l-Hasan, Bishnadas, Muhammad'Ali; they are all represented in the Prince's Collection. This is not a "Who's Who" of Mughal painters but a sophisticated round-up of historical scenes, courtiers, gorgeous tulips and aged pilgrims - a synthesis, one might say, of the best Mughal paintings that have become available in the last thirty years. There are fine examples from the schools of Deccani painting. The 1650 "Floral Fantasy" is typical of the excellence for which the Prince aspired, when putting all these diverse Islamic works of art together.

Then there are the paintings from the twilight years of the Mughals and the British Raj, such as Story-teller, Dancer and Musicians, dated 1810 - 1820 from the Fraser Album that Sotheby's auctioned a few years ago. The setting is full of men eager to enjoy themselves, entertain and be entertained, simply by making music and there is an unmistakable air of revelry. The oral tradition of narration, so deeply ingrained in the Muslim psyche, is evoked in this painting. This was a world governed by poetry and enhanced by dancing.

It is this quality and the amazing diversity of all types of flowers from the vast fields of Islamic art, that one detects in the collection of Prince Sadruddin Aga Khan. The beauty of it all is the fact that the Prince is continuing to collect Islamic art. A very small portion of it has been on view at New York City's Metropolitan Museum of Art. A wider selection entitled "Arts of the Islamic Book," an exhibition curated by Anthony Welch and Stuart Cary Welch (the two scholars are unrelated) originated at the Asia Society in Manhattan in the autumn of 1982. From there it travelled to the Kimbell Museum, Fort Worth, Texas, and the Nelson Gallery-Atkins Museum, Kansas City, during 1983.

The most important building in the Islamic world was the mosque, followed by the royal palace. Mosques, as the centre of worship, were among the first buildings erected in the Islamic world. Many early mosques were in fact converted Christian churches or Zoroastrian fire temples in the newly acquired Islamic lands. Invading armies did not require elaborate buildings in which to pray; as long as they knew the direction of Mecca in order to face it when praying, Muslims were then - and are still today - able to perform their prayer duties.

The first mosques Muslims constructed, therefore, were simple squares. As the Islamic Empire grew in size and power, mosques became larger and more elaborate. In the areas around the Mediterranean Sea, most mosques followed a so-called "open plan," with a courtyard in the centre, roofed arcades, and the first minarets - towers that extend vertically from the mosque. Examples of this style include the Great Mosque of Kairouan (7th century), the Great Mosque of Damascus (early 8th century), and the Mosque of Cordoba in Spain (late 8th century). In Iran and Central Asia, a slightly different sort of mosque developed under the influence of Sassanid architecture. Four hallways led out from the open court, and minarets often came down to the ground, instead of resting on the top of the building. The Seljuk Masjid-i Jami in Isfahan (1072-92) and the Safavid Masjid-i Shah (1612-38) exemplify this style of mosque.

A third type was the domed mosque, common in Turkish Asia Minor. Although not a mosque, the 7th century Dome of the Rock in Jerusalem also had a dome, but the feature was not common at that time. Large domes were difficult to build, and the task was not regularly undertaken until the Ottomans conquered Constantinople in 1453 and sought to build a mosque to rival the grand Hagia Sophia, a magnificent domed Byzantine cathedral in the city. This was finally accomplished with the Selimiye Mosque at Edirne (1567-74), which had a larger dome than Hagia Sophia. Its Turkish architect, Sinan, was one of the most famous Islamic architects. He built the Sehzade Mosque in 1543 after the death of Suleyman I's son,

Mehmed. He also built the Suleymaniye Mosque (1551-57), whose roof still dominates the Istanbul skyline, and the Selimiye, completed in 1574 when Sinan was 80 years old. It is considered to be his masterpiece.

Islamic palaces were built in a unique way, because most of them were not meant to last longer than the ruler who inhabited them. Built from unbaked brick, or sometimes plaster, many palaces crumbled in the desert sun when abandoned. The Alhambra Palace in Granada provides a good example of this type of construction; it remains standing today, however, largely because Christian kings took it over and preserved it after the Christian reconquest of Granada in the 15th century. The largest surviving Islamic palace is Topkapi Palace in Istanbul, which was begun in the 15th century and underwent frequent additions until the 19th century. Islamic mauso-leums could also be grand structures, despite Islam's official discouragement of elaborate tombs. The Gur-i Amir, Timur's tomb in Samarkand (1405) is an example. Perhaps the most famous and elaborate Islamic tomb, the Taj Mahal in Agra, India (1632-47), was built by the Mughal Emperor Shah Jahan, and pioneered the use of white marble as a construction material.

In all Islamic buildings - from mosques, palaces, and mausoleums to houses, hospital, and schools - inner space was emphasised. An inner courtyard was common, as it offered not only space, but also protection from the wind and sun in hot climates. Symmetry was not as important as it was in European architecture, and Islamic buildings often featured additions that stretched out from the courtyard, undermining the balance of each side. Male and female sections of houses were separated, and an effort was made to allow as much natural light into the buildings as possible, because in Islam, as in other religions, light was considered a symbol of divine unity. Minimal furniture was again meant to contribute to the feeling of inner space.

Connections between art and Mathematics

Because they were now so intimately connected to a wide spectrum of intellectual treasures, Islamic scholars quickly embraced Greek philosophy and mathematics, translating and disseminating this knowledge for posterity. The cultivation of mathematical analysis, in particular, harmonized with their new spirituality. "Driven by the religious passion for abstraction and the related doctrine of unity — al-twahid, the Muslim intellectuals recognized in geometry the unifying intermediary between the material and the spiritual world.....

The works of Euclid and Pythagoras were among the first to be translated into Arabic." The study of geometry also fed an ardent preoccupation with the stars and astronomy. Traditionally Arabs used constellations to navigate through desert and sea, and to direct their daily prayers toward Mecca. Islamic scientists became expert astronomers and used... geometrical skills to measure the heavens.... [note 25] All this in turn nourished the Arabic passion for creating infinite, decorative tiling of star-shapes."

Properties of Polygons and Tessellations

The word tessellation comes from the Latin tessellate, a the small square stone or tile used in ancient Roman mosaics." Tiling and mosaics are common synonyms for tessellations. A plane tessellation is a pattern made up of one or more shapes, completely covering a surface without any gaps or overlaps. Some shapes tessellate without overlapping or leaving spaces and some do not... When we analyze a tessellation pattern, we are interested in the closed figure, or tiles, that form the overall design. The simplest class of closed figures is polygons. Circles are polygons, and squares and triangles, etc. are all closed figures that can be inscribed within a circle. Each has a perimeter and an area. Polygons are formed by line segments, that meet at their endpoints and are named according to the number of sides and angles they contain. Because of their symmetrical character we will be working with regular polygons: pentagons, hexagons, etc. A regular polygon is one with all its angles and sides congruent. The more sides a regular polygon has, the greater its angles. "Observe that as the number of sides in the regular polygon increases, the closer it comes to appearing like a circle. In addition, the circle encases every conceivable symmetry?

How Will this affect the Patterns?

Triangles are the simplest regular polygons with the most acute angles: 60 degrees. The angles of any triangle add up to = 180. Triangles, rectangles and hexagons are the only regular polygons that tile the plane by themselves. When hexagons fill the space around a point, three equal angles meet at a common vertex point and the sum of their angles divides evenly into the 360 degrees of a circle. This is true of the angles of triangles and squares, but not pentagons. Polygons larger than hexagons cannot tile the plane because they leave gaps or overlap. This is true of pentagons as well. Accordingly, when polygons larger than hexagons fill the space around a common vertex point, the sum of their angles does not divide evenly into 360.

Since the polygon angles get larger as the number of sides increases, the next time we could fill the 360 with equal angles would be when we had two angles measuring 180 degrees. This is a straight line and no longer a polygon. Therefore, unless we are using triangles, rectangles or hexagons, we will have to use more than one regular polygon whose angles add up to a sum that can be evenly divided into by 360 in order to tile a plane without gaps or overlaps. From this it is apparent that the circle and its symmetrical division are the basic feature of Islamic tiling.

The Circular Structure of Islamic Tessellation

The circle and its center are the point at which all Islamic patterns begin. Any regular polygon can be drawn within it by connecting points equidistant to each other on the circle's edge. However the circle must be repeated in order to create patterns.

When identical copies of a circle are placed together with their outermost edge touching so that they retain their separate identity while also becoming part of a larger shape, their centers rather than their edges become the point at which lines are connected.

When the centers of three united circles are joined by lines, an equilateral triangle is created.

Another interesting feature of this is figure is when the points on the edges of the circles (where they touch the other circles) are connected by lines, the lines also form an equilateral triangle within the larger triangle. The triangle is the simplest figure to which all other polygons can be reduced; Yet the symmetry of this figure is very complex. If three circles with half the radius of the original circles are drawn around the points at which the original circles touch the others, an exact replication of the original figure is created. This repetition can repeat infinitely.

The most important configuration of circles arises when six circles with equal radians are arranged around a seventh circle also with equal areas, so that the edge of each circle on the outside is touching the edge of the inner circle as well as the ones beside it. Figure 3c: From this configuration, the three most important polygons to Islamic art, the triangle, the square and the hexagon, can be formed.

By either connecting the centers of the circles with liens or by drawing tangents through the points at which the circles connect.

The equilateral triangle, the hexagon and the square are the three shapes that can tessellate and grow without leaving any gaps.

They represent an infinitely small and large growth system.

The principles of unity, abstraction and harmony with nature and the heavens, as fundamental to Islamic art, are symbolized in this circular geometry of the plane. The square and the rectangle have harmonious proportions, and the circle is the ultimate expression of unity.

The circle is not only the perfect expression of justice-equality in all directions in a finite domain—but also the most beautiful parent of all polygons, both containing and underlying them. From the circle comes the triangle, square and hexagon.

These three shapes are thus meant to symbolize "the square of the earth, or materiality, the triangle of human consciousness, and the hexagon, or circle of heaven.

Geometric patterns are constructed by the recurrence of geometrical forms, the resultant ordering of which is determined by the creative act.

When the systems of proportioning have been selected, the creation of patterns by infinite combinations of the geometric forms providing these systems of proportioning becomes possible. The designer thus has the freedom of choosing his systems of construction as well as the freedom of constituting the variations made possible by these systems. The geometric method therefore establishes an approach to art in which the execution and the aesthetics of the composition is systematically determined.

However, it cannot be regarded as a purely mechanical process on account of its capacity to accommodate human self-expression.

The reader must now conceive that the ability to exploit the freedom of expression by the geometric method necessitated a deep familiarity with the available systems of construction only acquired after long periods of experience. The knowledge gained in this field, being very broad and detailed, was only transmitted through apprenticeship.

The artistic achievement, as in music, was an abstract or intellectual beauty arising from order or 'truth', with expressiveness and originality based on the depth of knowledge and skill, in that order, the joyful pursuit of the usually 'anonymous' artist who thus wove his identity into his work.

10

Styles and Patterns of Islamic Architecture

Mosque as the main type of Islamic architecture must be built in the residential area of Islamic believers. The mosque building must comply with the general regulations of Islam. For example, the church must face the east so that pilgrims may hold worship service in the direction of the Holy Land, Mekka, namely, facing the west; no images are placed in the church and merely the holy niche behind the hall is taken as the object of worship; the decoration and pattern design of the mosque building is not allowed to use animal vein but merely the figures of plants or characters.

Since the difference in architectural technologies and materials in all parts of China and that in architectural scale, auxiliary buildings, characteristics of craftwork and local styles induced by requirements of use, mosque buildings of all shapes are produced. They can be divided into two categories according to form principles: architecture of the Hui nationality and architecture of the Uygur nationality.

Hui Mosque

The Hui Mosque is developed and formed by assimilating the workmanship of the traditional architecture of the Han nationality. It can also be said to be the Islamic architecture with the most oriental emotional appeal. First of all, according to the principle of courtyard style layout of the Han buildings, the buildings are combined into an enclosed courtyard house with a clear relationship of axial symmetry, such as the mosque in the Drum Tower Street in Chengdu of Sichuan Province and the mosque in Dahhuo Alley of Tianjin City.

Secondly a large quantity of building furniture of Chinese characteristics is applied, such as stone archways, screen walls, brick gate building, house style concierge. Even the Minaret building as the characteristic architecture of Islam is also constructed in the style of pavilion. Some mosques repeatedly apply above-mentioned building furniture in the overall layout and place more emphasis on the tradional characteristics of China. For example, the Jining Dongda Temple has four gates laid in front of the grand hall to make up the principal part of buildings.

Thirdlyÿthe roof combination of the Hui mosque hall is also an accomplished artistic creation. Owing to the generally quite large space depth of the worship hall and the problem of lighting and rain prevention to be solved, the worship halls of the Hui nationality mostly have combination style sloping roofs. Some even have five roofs that are joined together.

The mosque in Niu Street of Beijing, the Grand Temples in Tongxin and Weizhou of Ningxia, the grand mosque in the Shizui Mountain of Ningxia and the Xida Temple in Jining of Shandong Province are all in this style.

Fourthly, in order to further emphasize the gaudiness of the roof, the mosque has high and steep pavilions added to the combination roof. Take the mosque in the Dahuo Alley of Tianjin City for example. There are five square pavilions and hexagonal pavilions with doule eave roofs designed side by side at the back hall of the mosque. The pavilions have a long and thin proportion and exceptionally prominent vigor of toweringness and forcefulness. They are different in approach but equally satisfactory in result with the spire style Minaretbuilding of Arabic and Islamic architecture.

Lastly, the inner eaves of the Hui mosque apply a large quantity of traditional fitment and decoration techniques of the Han buildings. But it also combines with Islamic culture and initiates the new national art with fresh and pure emotional appeal. Take the worship hall of the mosque in the Niu Street of Beijing City for example. Its partition adopts the Central Asia style pointed arches and arches with Arabic characters and patterns. However, the arches are covered with the patterns of twisted-branch western lotus with red earth, dropping powder and stamping foil and hence produce blended artistic style and features. Moreover, the Chinese traditional brick sculpture and wooden carvings are also applied in the mosque in large quantities. Some carvings have almost become rare works of art.

Islamic Architecture of the Uygur Nationality

The buildings in South Xinjiang are most typical of the Uygur Islamic architecture. Since it is dry with less rain and clear-cut winter and summer in this area and it has a quite close contact with Central Asia in the history, the local buildings are mostly bungalows in the style of wooden post and close ribs or buildings with earthern arches and cove tops, which is very different from those in the hinterland. The Uygur worship temple and hall have an asymmetrical layout without a strict relationship of axial contraposition. The decoration of the Uygur worship hall is characterized by the application of geometrical pattern designs in large quantities. It forms the compostion of a picture with two or four consecutive sides by adopting all kinds of modes such as juxtaposition, symmetry, interleaving and circulation with constant changes. Its artistic style of delicacy amid uprightness is unique in the decorational patterns of

Chinese architecture. Islamic art has a recognisable aesthetic signature that somehow manages to express itself across an entire range of productions. The 'language' of this art, once established, was readily assimilated by each of the different nations and ethnicities that were brought within the Islamic sphere. Assimilated and built upon, because every region, at every period, produced its own versions of this super-national style. This extraordinary consistency of styles and artistic preferences in the Islamic world clearly derive from a deeper, social consistency. All Muslims hold to the same basic system of belief, all are familiar with the customary religious observations, and all – despite national and ethnic differences and rivalries – felt themselves to be Muslim first and foremost. This strong sense of identity and continuity tended towards a high degree of social, and artistic, conservatism. As a result, many forms and artistic concepts remained unchanged over the centuries - on the other hand, Islamic art has constantly demonstrated its capacity for the creative reinterpretation of accepted forms.

Much of the art of Islam, whether in architecture, ceramics, textiles or books, is the art of decoration – which is to say, of transformation. The aim, however, is never merely to ornament, but rather to transfigure. Essentially, this is a reflection of the Islamic preoccupation with the transitory nature of being. Substantial structures and objects are made to appear less substantial, materials are de-materialised. The vast edifices of mosques are transformed into lightness and pattern; the decorated pages of a Qur'an can become windows onto the infinite. Perhaps most importantly, the Word, expressed in endless calligraphic variations, always conveys the impression that it is more enduring than the objects on which it is inscribed.

Symmetry and Geometry

Another familiar characteristic of this art, which must also express something fundamental to the Islamic spirit, is its predilection for orderly, symmetrical arrangements in general and for purely geometrical decorative forms in particular. The influence of both religious and philosophical ideas on this aspect of Islamic art were examined earlier (in Background Notes #2 & #3 respectively), but the abstract, ideational nature of symmetry and geometry clearly fit with the Islamic taste for idealistic otherworldliness.

From a purely doctrinal viewpoint, geometrical designs, being free of any symbolic meaning (which is the case in Islamic art), could convey a general aura of spirituality without offending religious sensibilities. In addition, the purity and orderliness of patterns and symmetries could evoke a sense of transcendent beauty which, at best, would free and stimulate the intellect (rather than trap it in the illusions of mere representation).

There is a certain disregard for scale in Islamic art that derives from this perception. Similar kinds of patterning, for instance, might be found on a huge tile panel or on a bijou ornament. This is because decorative effects, in an Islamic context, are never mere embellishments, but always refer to other, idealised states of being. In this view, scale is almost irrelevant. For similar reasons Islamic ornemanistes usually opted for a-centric arrangements in patterning, avoiding obvious focal points – a preference that resonates with the Islamic perception of the Absolute as an influence that is not 'centred' in a divine manifestation (as in Christianity), but whose presence is an even and pervasive force throughout the Creation. A further analogy can be drawn between the patiently created repeats of the 'infinite' pattern (in all its varieties), and the familiar and unvarying customs of Moslem religious observances. In an Islamic context repetition is not tedious; on the contrary, it connects to the world of the spirit.

Whether in a religious setting or not, the work of Muslim artist/craftsmen always manages to convey a certain integrity, even nobility. In fact the distinction between art and craft-work is largely irrelevant in the Islamic world, but even when their works demonstrated surpassing skill and inspiration, the practitioners tended to remain anonymous. This is not surprising; in a culture whose ideal was submission to the will of Allah, it was quite natural to submit creative individuality to a perceived higher notion of beauty.

Earlier Islamic Art

It was seen earlier (in Background Note #1) that the Umayyad's were the first dynasty to rule the newly-established Islamic Empire (from the mid 7th- mid 8th centuries; 41-132 AH). During this early period, which was marked by conquest and consolidation, such art and architecture that was commissioned drew on pre-Islamic traditions (primarily those of Christian Byzantine and Sassanian Persia). Even so, there are clear signs of the emergence of Islamic aesthetic priorities. The main elements of decoration at this time derive from late-classical traditions of stone-carving, floor- and wall-mosaic and wall-painting, but plaster decoration, introduced from the Hellenised East, is also used.

This window-grill from the Umayyad Mosque, Damascus shows a direct continuation of the Syro-Roman tradition, Mosaic Decoration from the Umayyad Mosque, Damascus: This also shows an unbroken continuation of late classical Byzantine tradition of sacred architectural decoration. But the subject-matter, of a paradise landscape, is decidedly Islamic.

Facade of the Umayyad castle of al-Mushatta (detail of carved stone-work): The rich variety of floral and animal forms derives from both classical and oriental sources.

The replacement of the Umayyad dynasty by the Abbasid (in 750 CE/ 132 AH) saw the removal of the capital eastwards to Baghdad, and later to Samarra. These two great cities were enormously important for the development of

Islamic art and culture but, sadly, little has survived of either from the early period. From the fragments of architectural decoration that have been recovered there appears to have been a steady move away from naturalistic treatments, towards more abstract and repetitive forms. The long-established eastern traditions of plaster- and brick-work were adopted as the principle architectural materials in the Islamic East, and were to remain so for the following centuries.

By the early 9th/3rd century, Turks from Central Asia become an ever more dominant political force, and from this time on their tastes exerted a strong influence on Islamic art generally. At the political level, these incursions meant that the Islamic Empire began to fragment into rival factions, with local dynasties establishing themselves in various regions. Islamic art in these turbulent 9th -10th centuries (3rd-4th AH), is represented by local styles, usually based on older precedents, but always bearing the imprint of Islamic tastes and limitations: Stucco panel from Samarra; Ceramic bowl with decoration from Nishapur, Iran; 0th/4thcentury, Wooden frieze; Egypt; 9th/3rd century, Door panel; Egypt; Stucco decoration in mosque at Nayin; 10th/4th century, Stucco decoration; Ibn Tulun Mosque; Egypt; 9th/3rd century, Decorative brick work; Mausoleum of the Samanids; early 10th/4th century and Stylistic maturity; 11th - 12th centuries.

As indicated above, the Abbasid Aliphate began to lose political power, and it's Empire to fragment, at the turn of the 10th/4th century. The most serious consequences of this political turmoil, for Islamic culture as a whole, were the accompanying religious controversies and multiplicity of doctrines. In time, in a reverse of the status quo of earlier centuries, Shi'ism became the dominant creed among the various secessionist dynasties, and for a period this interpretation looked set to dominate the Islamic world.

But early in the 11thcentury there began a Sunni revival, which had both religious and cultural aspects. This movement, which saw itself as a restoration of traditionalism, was accompanied by an artistic revival that established many of the enduring forms of Islamic art and architecture – in particular, its canon of decorative art.

The Sunni revival, which began in Baghdad, gradually spread through the Islamic world. As it did so, it became associated with a range of new artistic and architectural forms, which became an identifying mark, a sort of symbolic language. These new stylistic terms were adopted by the Ghaznavids in Khorasan, the Seljuks in Iran, the Zangids in Northern Syria, and the Ayyubids in Egypt. The 'classic' style of Islamic ornament which used distinctive epigraphic, geometric and abstract vegetal elements first came to maturity during this period. This decorative canon was eventually taken up in every part of the Islamic world.

The three elements of the Islamic decorative canon began to appear as early as the Umayyad period, but they crystallised into their classic forms during the 'Sunni Revival'.

Calligraphy gives a visible form to the revealed word of the Qur'an and is therefore considered the most noble of the arts. It manages to combine a geometric discipline with a dynamic rhythm. Interestingly, none of its many styles, created in different places at different periods, has ever completely fallen into disuse. In the Islamic world it takes the place of iconography, being widely used in the decorative schemes of buildings.

Geometric patterns have always had a particular appeal to Muslim designers and craftsmen. They convey a certain aura of spirituality, or at least otherworldliness, without relating to any specific doctrine. In an Islamic context they are also quite free of any symbolic meaning. Above all they provide craftsmen with the opportunity to demonstrate his skill and subtlety of workmanship, and often to dazzle and intrigue with its sheer complexity.

Vegetal 'Arabesque' compositions are as ubiquitous in Islamic decoration as geometric patterns. It is difficult, without other indications, to determine where or when a particular composition of this genre might have originated. Like geometrical designs, these too are found across the entire range of mediums from book illustration to plasterwork; in ceramics, woodwork, metalwork and ivory-carving, even in carpets and textiles.

The Craft-group

As indicated earlier, there was no distinction between 'art' and 'craft' in the medieval Islamic world, just as there was no sharp division between notions of beauty and utility. The idea of the brilliant, lone individual artist was also absent. These are modern concepts. In fact, architectural and artistic productions generally tended to be the work of groups of anonymous craftsmen, whose occupations were usually hereditary and based within guilds or similar craft-groups. However, given that the subject area of 'the decorative arts of Islam' has such an extensive geographical and historical reach, and involved a great variety of craft skills, generalisations of any kind about this broad subject may be misleading. Among such a diverse range of artistic traditions there were bound to be huge variations in working practices, social status, and indeed of expressive intent, in so many and varied creative processes.

As I've indicated, by comparison with life in the modern world, medieval Islamic society was highly conservative. We can imagine that working practices, just like the designs and motifs that were used, often persisted for generations with little change. There was no formal training; skills were acquired in the workshops, and were often handed down from father to son. The apprentice/ master relationship was usually regularised however, and there is evidence that craft-groups were formed into guilds (which had similarities with the trade-guilds of medieval Europe). It seems also to have been the case that some of these guilds (in some periods at least) were affiliated to religious groups. Details of this kind are naturally difficult to uncover, as they tended to be bound up with the mystique and protectiveness of what were essentially closed professions. It is of more than passing interest though, that these religious connections were usually associated with Sufi fraternities, whose mystical outlook had been imbued with Neoplatonic concepts.

The production of specialised goods and of the particular skills involved was often localised, but these skills often took artisans far away from their home. Occasionally these movements were less than voluntary. In the turmoil of war craft-skills were generally prized as a form of booty and artisans could be carted off to the victor's base, sometimes en masse. Since the ruling power was usually the greatest patron of arts and architecture, it often happened that new artistic movements were initiated in this way. The dynasty founded by Timurlane was perhaps the most famous example of this effect. It occasionally happened that skilled craftsmen were welcomed as refugees after fleeing invasions and wars. The relative security of Fatimid Egypt attracted many mid-eastern artisans during the turbulent 11th/12th centuries, much to the cultural benefit of Cairo.

The transfer of skills and knowledge as a result of migrations and conquest is of course a time-honoured process. Huge numbers of skilled artisans from various traditions were brought into the Islamic fold as a result of the early conquests, and in the course of time these skills became part of the background of Islamic culture. But there was one craft technology in particular that was acquired in this way that had a profound effect on the course of Islamic civilisation on many levels (including the visual arts). This was the manufacture of paper.

The Role of Paper in Islamic Art and Architecture

Paper was a Chinese invention that had spread to Central Asia and Khurasan prior to the Islamic conquests of those regions. As soon as Islamic rule had been established in this eastern end of the Empire the usefulness of this product for bureaucratic and military purposes must have become obvious. The precise history of the uptake of this invention is somewhat hazy, but what is quite certain is that the relative cheapness and ease of production of paper ensured its rapid spread throughout the Islamic world during the 9th and 10thcenturies ($3^{rd}/4^{th}$ AH) – and that it transformed societies wherever it appeared. Paper was soon pressed into service by the Baghdad Aliphate, where it greatly facilitated their centralised rule, and Baghdad itself became one of many important centres of paper-making.

As paper became available throughout the Islamic world it was gradually adopted by artists and craftsmen. This usage began, naturally enough, among visual artists of higher status, calligraphers and those involved in the 'arts of the book'. The use of paper was slower among craftsmen at a lower social position (woodworkers, stonemasons, weavers etc,), partly because of the conservatism of their working practices, but also for cost reasons. As it became cheaper and more widely available however, paper became a standard tool in most crafts, and in the process it effected a transformation of the visual arts of Islam.

In essence, the adoption of paper into craft-based work-practices introduced a certain separation of the design process from that of manufacture. This was bound to lead to a greater degree of organisation in design right across the board, from architecture through to the humbler crafts of pottery and weaving. Later this separation of design and making gave rise to a stylistic 'centralisation', such as that exercised by the many Royal studios and workshops that were maintained by the Royal courts. Many dynastic styles were established and maintained in this way.

Paper was a common commodity in the Islamic world as early as the 12th century (6thAH) and was already being used by various (usually high-status) artisans to produce preliminary drawings for their work. In the following centuries the use of paper designs was gradually adopted as normal practice. This development undoubtedly fostered stylistic consistency across different mediums and promoted a common currency of style. There are many examples of close similarities between decorative motifs in architecture, book illumination and craft objects.

These is some evidence that the sort of complex patterning and arabesques that are such a characteristic feature of Islamic art first appeared as decorative elements of books (as did calligraphy, of course). As the 'arts of the book' enjoyed the highest status among crafts it seems very likely that these designs would have gradually filtered down to other mediums. It is also clear that once pattern-books and albums of design motifs came into being their repertoire could be applied to a whole range of artefacts, in different settings and at different scales. Designs could be copied, improved upon and, most importantly, they could travel.

It would certainly appear that there was, for centuries, a broad awareness and appreciation of the aesthetic aspects of ornament and a lively interaction between different crafts. The stylistic homogeneity of Islamic art referred to at the beginning of this note may have its foundations in Islamic cultural homogeneity, but its primary medium of transmission was paper.

The most important building in the Islamic world was the mosque, followed by the royal palace. Mosques, as the centre of worship, were among the first buildings erected in the Islamic world. Many early mosques were in fact converted Christian churches or Zoroastrian fire temples in the newly acquired Islamic lands. Invading armies did not require elaborate buildings in which to pray; as long as they knew the direction of Mecca in order to face it when praying, Muslims were then - and are still today - able to perform their prayer duties. The first mosques Muslims constructed, therefore, were simple squares. As the Islamic Empire grew in size and power, mosques became larger and more elaborate. In the areas around the Mediterranean Sea, most mosques followed a so-called "open plan," with a courtyard in the centre, roofed arcades, and the first minarets - towers that extend vertically from the mosque. Examples of this style include the Great Mosque of Kairouan (7th century), the Great Mosque of Damascus (early 8th century), and the Mosque of Cordoba in Spain (late 8th century). In Iran and Central Asia, a slightly different sort of mosque developed under the influence of Sassanid architecture. Four hallways led out from the open court, and minarets often came down to the ground, instead of resting on the top of the building. The Seljuk Masjid-i Jami in Isfahan (1072-92) and the Safavid Masjid-i Shah (1612-38) exemplify this style of mosque.

A third type was the domed mosque, common in Turkish Asia Minor. Although not a mosque, the 7th century Dome of the Rock in Jerusalem also had a dome, but the feature was not common at that time. Large domes were difficult to build, and the task was not regularly undertaken until the Ottomans conquered Constantinople in 1453 and sought to build a mosque to rival the grand Hagia Sophia, a magnificent domed Byzantine cathedral in the city. This was finally accomplished with the Selimiye Mosque at Edirne (1567-74), which had a larger dome than Hagia Sophia. Its Turkish architect, Sinan, was one of the most famous Islamic architects. He built the Sehzade Mosque in 1543 after the death of Suleyman I's son,

Mehmed. He also built the Suleymaniye Mosque (1551-57), whose roof still dominates the Istanbul skyline, and the Selimiye, completed in 1574 when Sinan was 80 years old. It is considered to be his masterpiece.

Islamic palaces were built in a unique way, because most of them were not meant to last longer than the ruler who inhabited them. Built from unbaked brick, or sometimes plaster, many palaces crumbled in the desert sun when abandoned. The Alhambra Palace in Granada provides a good example of this type of construction; it remains standing today, however, largely because Christian kings took it over and preserved it after the Christian reconquest of Granada in the 15th century. The largest surviving Islamic palace is Topkapi Palace in Istanbul, which was begun in the 15th century and underwent frequent additions until the 19th century. Islamic mausoleums could also be grand structures, despite Islam's official discouragement of elaborate tombs. The Gur-i Amir, Timur's tomb in Samarkand (1405) is an example. Perhaps the most famous and elaborate Islamic tomb, the Taj Mahal in Agra, India (1632-47), was built by the Mughal Emperor Shah Jahan, and pioneered the use of white marble as a construction material.

In all Islamic buildings- from mosques, palaces, and mausoleums to houses, hospital, and schools - inner space was emphasised. An inner courtyard was common, as it offered not only space, but also protection from the wind and sun in hot climates. Symmetry was not as important as it was in European architecture, and Islamic buildings often featured additions that stretched out from the courtyard, undermining the balance of each side. Male and female sections of houses were separated, and an effort was made to allow as much natural light into the buildings as possible, because in Islam, as in other religions, light was considered a symbol of divine unity. Minimal furniture was again meant to contribute to the feeling of inner space.

Decoration in Islamic architecture followed the pattern of Islamic art in general - images of humans or animals were discouraged, because of the danger of the image being revered in any way. Mosques were particularly free from pictorial imagery in their decoration, and were usually adorned with floral patterns, geometric shapes, or calligraphy.

Materials and Mediums

As indicated in Background Notes 4, the decorative arts in Islam are marked by a remarkable degree of stylistic consistency which has been applied to a broad range of materials, each of which had a craft-base of its own, the history of which often traces back to pre-Islamic times. The stylistic coherence within the Islamic world and the many variations of its basic themes across time, influenced as they were by local artistic traditions, are all part of the fascination of this art. In Muslim architecture virtually any surface may be regarded as worthy of receiving elaborate decoration and this is particularly apparent in religious architecture, but this principle extends out to woodwork, ceramics, textiles, metalwork, books and many other art forms.

Stonework

There is an East–West divide in basic Islamic architectural techniques that derives from earlier, pre-Islamic traditions. In the Persian/Iranian sphere of influence the principle building material tends to be brick, whereas in Egypt, Syria and Asia Minor, stone is far more common, at least for monumental building.

The earliest Islamic monuments, dating from the Umayyad period, clearly continue the Roman/Byzantine tradition in their typical structures and in their use of dressed and carved stone. These techniques continued under later dynasties in Egypt and Syria (the Fatimids, Zangids, Ayyubids and Mamelukes). This architecture is characterised by its monumental scale, its relative simplicity of form and a somewhat sombre tone. The deep carving, ordered in panelled schemes, with calligraphic bands and geometrical and arabesque motifs, make an impressive contrast against great expanses of undecorated surfaces.

In Asia Minor the Seljuks, and later the Ottomans, continued the traditions both of ashlar building and of stone carving. Under the Seljuks a more plastic style of stone-carving was introduced, based on the stucco work of their predecessors in Iran. This gave rise to a rich tradition of that used all the familiar elements of Islamic decoration in a dazzling profusion of examples. The strength and vitality of this tradition of carved stonework continued up to the beginning of the 16th/10th century, gradually becoming less exuberant during the Ottoman period.

A separate tradition of architectural stonework developed on the Indian sub-continent, again derived from pre-Islamic sources. The early Turkish conquerors of India introduced entirely new, and in many ways quite opposite, architectural concepts to the sub-continent, but the synthesis that arose from the meeting of Hindu and Islamic traditions produced a great range of marvellous buildings, and countless examples of exquisite carved and inlaid stone decoration.

Brickwork

As mentioned above, brickwork was the favoured building technique in the eastern Islamic provinces of Iraq and Iran, the tradition originating in the ancient civilisations of this area. Typically, however, in the hands of Muslim builders, brickwork was soon being used in quite novel and more decorative ways than in the past. In fact there is a well-defined progression in the use of brick in eastern Islam, from purely structural purposes towards ever greater decorative complexity.

The first stage (in the 11th/ 5th century) saw an increasing variety of brick bonds that created relief patterns of light and shade to great effect. The enthusiasm for this technique was such that some buildings featured dozens of different bond-patterns, veritable showcases of brick design.

Later, carved ornamental inserts were used to break up the tedium of plain bonding; these were soon moulded before being fired, in a whole variety of motifs. In the next stage these brick inserts were glazed, a technique that lead naturally on to entire walls and domes being invested with coloured glazed bricks, by which time the structural and decorative functions of brickwork had more or less separated out. Over time these glazed bricks were gradually reduced in thickness until they were virtually tiles – and the possibility of a whole new era of architectural ornament was created.

Ceramic Tiles and Ceramic Mosaic

Coloured glaze was part of the repertoire of decoration in the architecture of the Ancient middle-east, in both Egypt and Mesopotamia – by the time Islam arrived on the scene however, these techniques had been long forgotten. The earliest Islamic monuments made extensive use of mosaic as both floor and wall decoration, but these were very much in the still-flourishing tradition of late-Antiquity. It was not really until the 12th/6thcentury that architectural ceramics began to be used extensively in an Islamic setting (by way of the progression described above). The gradual development of suitable ceramic glazes, in both pottery and tile-work, represented a whole series of technological advances, and as such was as much a scientific/technological achievement as an artistic one. The enthusiasm for the intense colours produced by these techniques meant that they were eventually transmitted right across the Islamic world, from the Atlantic to Central Asia.

Ceramic tiles are found in most Muslim countries, using an extensive range of techniques that include high moulded relief, polychrome, lustre-ware and sgraffito. In addition, sophisticated techniques were developed that used pieces of cut-tiles, bonded together with plaster, to form elaborate, multi-coloured mosaic panels. The latter method was particularly favoured in the lands that came under Timurid influence (Iran and Transoxiana), and in the Islamic far-West (Spain and Morocco).

The broad area that fell under Iranian influence had a long, independent tradition of ceramic architectural revetment, known as kashi, which reached its first great achievement in the 14th/8thcentury and was sustained through the Timurid and Safavid periods. Each element of the traditional Islamic decorative canon, geometric and vegetal arabesque forms, together with calligraphy, is used but with great local variations of style.

The use of cut-tile mosaic seems to have come into favour in the Islamic West (the Maghreb) with the appearance of the Berber dynasties in the 12th-13th centuries (6th-7th). Known as zellij, it is almost exclusively dedicated to geometrical arrangements in this part of the world. The Maghreb (Spain and Morocco) had long followed an independent cultural existence, developing its own characteristic architectural and decorative forms. The particular specialty here was always an intense geometric patterning, a tradition that has lasted right up to the modern period.

Stucco/Plaster Work

Plaster was a well-established building material prior to the Islamic conquests both in Iran, where it had been used to cover rough, rubble walls for centuries, and to a lesser extent in the Classical, Mediterranean world. This was a readily available material in the Middle-east, and was used in Islamic architecture from the very earliest periods (in Syria and Iraq), from where it fairly rapidly spread to the rest of the Muslim world.

Its earlier forms followed late-Classical and Sassanian models, but Islamic tastes were soon asserted, inclining towards a flattening of the decorated surface, the emphasis on symmetry, its division into distinct, evenly laid-out panels, and the use of abstract rather than naturalistic motifs.

Plaster, a singularly useful material that leant itself to moulding and carving in a variety of ways, became a staple of Islamic architecture. Perhaps because of its plasticity as a medium it was less frequently used for purely geometric designs, and was more often used in vegetal-arabesque arrangements. It could also, of course, be painted or gilded.

In essence, plaster (on its own or in conjunction with ceramics) was the perfect medium for transforming surfaces - which was always the primary concern in Islamic architecture. In Islamic art generally, the underlying intention is bound up with the notion of the dissolution of matter, of transcendence.

Woodwork

Since wood is a comparatively scarce material in many parts of the Islamic world it perhaps not surprising that it enjoyed a higher status as a material than elsewhere and, at its best, displays the very highest levels of workmanship. Traditionally, it was used for doors and window shutters which are frequently inlaid, but the finest work is generally found on pulpits (minbar), the key piece of furniture in the mosque from which Friday sermons are preached. Many highly sophisticated techniques were developed to create intricate decoration; in the finer examples ebony and other precious woods are used as inlays, together with ivory and mother-of-pearl. The carving in these objects often has a concentrated, almost lapidary detail. In the Islamic world the skills of carpentry were traditionally associated with geometry. The 14th/8th century historian Ibn Khuldun (who was presumably expressing a generally held belief) asserted that all the leading Greek geometricians were masters of this craft. Some surviving examples of 12th/6th century woodwork indicate that the genre of complex, interlacing geometrical designs in the girih mode were relatively common by this time, and may have been expressed in this architectural medium before any other (after their probable invention as Qur'anic illumination in the 10th/4th century).

Book Illumination

As indicated above, the earliest appearances of the girih mode (the classical Islamic decorative style that includes both geometric and vegetal forms) are found in late 10th/4thcentury Qur'an manuscripts that are believed to have originated in Baghdad. It is thought likely that this style spread out to other mediums from this source. Although the precise mechanisms by which this style was transmitted are obscure, obviously it would have been facilitated by the widespread availability of paper soon after this time.

The three components of the Islamic decorative canon (calligraphy, of course, geometrical and vegetal arabesque arrangements) which were established in this medium continued to be a feature of the Islamic arts of the book, with every period making its own contribution to the genre. As the most elevated of all objects the Qur'an naturally always received the most respectful and inspired treatment, but there are also many examples of geometrical patterning and arabesque in secular book illustration. Clearly, the art of decoration was taken seriously in Islamic culture; patterns had a currency. Their appearance in the portable arts i.e. of the book, in craft-albums and working drawings, meant that existing examples could be reworked and improved upon, and those who specialised in decorative patterns could inspire new directions in this way. There are countless examples of intricate pattern in each of the major traditions of miniature painting (Turkish, Persian and Mughal Indian, in fact sometimes they are positively teeming with them. The exploration and playing with decorative ideas that is evident in so many of these works is probably indicative of a general interest in the subject in studios of various kinds. Sadly, apart from these examples and the few surviving folios and working drawings, the originators of the majority of these brilliant patterns and arabesques are likely to remain obscure.

Court Patronage and Cottage Industry

The distinction between the artistic and luxury goods that were commissioned and made in centralised, Royal studios and workshops, and those that were essentially the products of small-scale cottage industry, has already been remarked upon. This division, however, between central and independent manufacture in traditional Islamic cultures, was often a rather more complex business than this simple apportioning might suggest.

It was usually the case that Rulers and their court custodians were the chief arbiters of taste and fashion in all things, but in most periods there were thriving manufacturing centres of such goods as textiles, pottery, metalwork and glassware, with their own design traditions. Many fine articles were designed in Royal studios and manufactured in Royal workshops exclusively for use by the Court, and occasionally these productions were made available to other wealthy clients. In other cases designs were created in an official studio and the work then commissioned from independent artisans, many of whom worked in districts close to Royal palaces. Religious institutions were of course another major source of commissions.

These differences of origination, together with differences in local tastes and traditions, account for the greater variation of design in the arts of 'everyday objects', by comparison with the consistencies of the formal decorative modes in architecture. Symmetry, as always in Islamic design, was still the keynote, but the traditional decorative canon (of geometrical patterns, arabesque arrangements and calligraphy), while an ever-present and general influence on design, exerted less of a hold beyond architecture.

The design studios retained by Islamic ruling houses tended to exercise stylistic control and consistency across a whole range of mediums, including architectural decoration. In many case this stylistic continuity is fairly evident - the designs on Nasrid silks, for instance, have clear similarities with contemporary stuccowork. Textiles, partly because of the important role they played in courtly life and ceremonial, were frequently a focus for court designers and textile workshops themselves were actively encouraged by the ruling establishment in many periods. There are abundant examples of this sort of stylistic conformity across the arts in the Ottoman, Safavid and Mughal dynasties, and it is safe to assume that this was the case in earlier periods.

There is evidence from various Islamic periods of complex designs being prepared in design-studios and passed on to skilled artisans across a range of luxury items, including (at different times), metalwork, carpets, glasswork and ivory-carving. In fact a great many artistic products from the Islamic world, in all mediums, are characterised by highly organised arrangements with complex schemes of patterning that clearly indicate a prior design stage. The essential role of paper in this process has already been touched on (in Background Notes 4). Although very few examples survive, it seems extremely likely that the use of working drawings (and the inevitable appearance of pattern books and design folios), led to the creation of a design 'currency' among skilled artisans which enabled the continuous refinement of patterns, and their exchanges between mediums.

Egypt

Egypt was brought into the Islamic sphere in the first wave of conquests, in 639. With the Tulunid assumption of power (868-905 C.E.; 254–292 A.H.) it became an independent centre then, under the Fatimid dynasty (909-1171C.E; 297-567 A.H.) it assumed its enduring role as the cultural focus of western Islam. The architecture of the Mameluk period (13th–16th C.E.; 7th-10th A.H.) saw a continuity of earlier Egyptian traditions. But it also incorporated aspects of Iraqi and Syrian styles. Most of the buildings of these periods are of stone; in fact the general feeling conveyed by medieval Cairene architecture is that of a sombre stolidity. This is reflected in the various forms of architectural decoration. Of particular interest are the massive carved masonry domes, the rich polychrome marble inlays and painted ceilings. The somewhat severe beauty of this architecture is frequently lightened by the exquisitely carved and inlaid wood-work of doors and minbars.

India

India was partially conquered by the Arabs as early as the 8th c. C.E./2nd c. A.H. The influence of Islam was maintained over successive centuries until, by the end of the 16th century, the greater part of the Indian subcontinent was under the rule of the Islamic Mughal emperors. In its earlier periods Indo-Islamic art and architecture borrowed heavily from Hindu forms, but over time a distinctive Indian-Islamic cultural style was forged.

There is little that survives of early architecture, but the Qutab mosque and the extraordinary Qutab Minar in Delhi give some idea of these past glories. The majority of images here, however, are from the Mughal period (which lasted from the 16th-19thc. C.E.(10th-13th A.H.). Despite the fact that Indo-Islamic architecture represents, to a greater extent than in any other region, a fusion between the preexistent tradition (Hindu) and Islamic style, all the classic forms of Islamic architectural decoration are all well represented here.

The exquisite inlaid marble patterns of the Tomb of Itimud Ad Daula make it an architectural gem par excellence. The polychrome panels of the tombs of Humayun and Akbar are also of great interest, as are the many red sandstone decorative panels that grace the beautifully preserved city of Fatepur Sikri.

Iran

The Persian Empire succumbed to the newly islamicized Arabs in their early expansion (mid 7th c. C.E./ 1st c. H.E.) immediately after the conquest of the Byzantine Middle East. But this ancient culture, though subjugated, was never entirely assimilated, and in time the Persians came to influence and contribute more than any other race to the building of Islamic culture.

The Mongol, Timurid and Seljuk dynasties all left important monuments in Iran, but the greater number of the examples shown here date from the Muzzafarid (1314-1393 C.E.) and Safavid (1501-1786 C.E) periods (731-795; & 907-1200 A.H.). Glazed decoration was a feature of Persian architecture from the earliest times and is found in most periods, but it assumed an ever more important role under Muslim patronage, transforming the buildings to which it was applied. Muzzafarid and Safavid art revel in sumptuous decoration, their architectural decoration use brilliant colours and highly evolved decorative schemes to virtually 'dissolve' the buildings to which there are applied. Apart from their ceramic tiles and mosaics there are rich traditions here of decorative brickwork and carved stucco. The Mosques of Isfahan and Yazd show particularly fine examples of architectural decoration.

Morocco

In the far west of the Islamic world, Morocco has always retained a certain national separateness. Its distinctive artistic and architectural styles evolved more or less independently of the countries of the Middle East, but are strongly connected to those of Islamic Spain. Five major dynasties have ruled Morocco during the past twelve hundred years, each leaving their own architectural legacy in their own capital city. The principle surviving monuments, from which the photo-images here are drawn, are in or near the towns of Fez, Meknes and Marrakesh.

In its typical forms, Moroccan architectural decoration uses complex geometric ceramic mosaics in combination with intricately carved stucco. Finely carved and painted woodwork (particularly doors) are another common feature. All three modes of the Islamic decorative canon (geometric, arabesque and calligraphy) are expressed in a characteristic, somewhat intense style. This is a decorative art that makes a powerful impression, but it is on a human scale. Some of the finest examples of this somewhat cerebral ornamentation can be found in the various medieval Medersas.

Spain

Spain had an Islamic presence for some eight centuries, and for the three of these it was important enough to have its own Aliph, based in the Umayyad capital at Cordova, quite independent of Baghdad. After the fall of the Umayyad dynasty (in mid-11th c. C.E.; mid-5th A.H.) a series of minor dynasties ruled, until the Nasrid dynasty re-established political and cultural unity. At their court in Granada the Nasrids created a magnificent culture that recaptured some of the earlier glories. But this last stronghold of Islam in Spain was itself finally overcome by the Christian monarchs Ferdinand and Isabella in 1492 C.E.; 897 A.H. Hispano-Islamic art and architecture, in both major periods, was marked by an extreme aesthetic refinement. Miraculously, enough has survived in the Nasrid palace of the Alhambra in Granada to give us some idea of this marvelous art. Here practically every surface is decorated. Each wall has a dado of intricate ceramic mosaic, displaying a dazzling range of geometric patterns; above this, every wall surface is covered with moulded and carved plaster, creating a seemingly endless variety of arabesque forms, all of the panels are interwoven with bands of calligraphy. Although there is a definite consistency in the decorative scheme the overall effect is far from repetitive; it is perhaps the most exquisite architecture in the world. The Alcazar in Seville, though of a later date, and the palace of a Christian King, still resonates with the taste and workmanship of Muslim artist/craftsmen.

Syria

Syria, with its deep Classical and Christian cultural heritage, was Islam's first encounter with an advanced, urban civilisation. In fact, the conquest of Byzantine Damascus (in 635 C.E.; 14 A.H.) was a defining moment in Islamic history, and the first Muslim dynasty, the Umayyads, soon made Damascus their capital. The Great Mosque in Damascus, the earliest mosque to have survived more or less intact, is interesting for precisely these reasons; the mosaic decorations are in the Byzantine tradition, but reflect a new Islamic artistic sensibility, and the same leavening influence on late-classical forms is evident in other architectural features, such as the tracery windows.

In 1401 Damascus was occupied by Tamerlane, suffering terrible destruction as a result, an event from which the city never really recovered. A century later Syria was conquered by the Turks was absorbed into their Empire and became an Ottoman province.

There are, nevertheless, many interesting monuments in Syria, particularly those dating from the medieval period - the Sabrinye madrassa and the mosque of Taynabiye in Damascus; the Umayyad mosque, the al-Otrush mosque, the madrassa al-Faradis and the mashad al-Hussein in Aleppo, are all impressive and important from an art-historical perspective.

Transoxiana

The river Oxus in Central Asia, long before the region had become part of the Islamic world, had always been the traditional boundary between civilisation and barbarism. For the first three centuries of Islamic rule the barbarian nomads of the steppes beyond were held in check, as they had been for the Persians, and the cities of Bukhara and Samarkand prospered. But by the end of the 10th century (4thc A.H.) the infiltration of Turkish nomads, the 'Turkish Irruption', had began in earnest. This great movement of peoples, highly important for the future of Islam was, by turns, a highly destructive and an extremely creative force.

Very little architecture remains from the older Islamic civilisation of this region, but the Mausoleum of the Samanids (early-10thc.; 4thc. A.H.), whose surfaces, both internal and external, are entirely patterned with decorative brick-work, is an architectural masterwork. In fact this highly original building set an architectural style that was to be enormously influential throughout the eastern Islamic world.

Because of its geographical location the cities of this region were always in the front line of nomad incursions, and the two greatest of these, the Mongol and Timurid, had a devastating effect on the region. But there was a pattern of recovery; even these ferocious hordes were eventually civilised. In fact Timur made Samarkand his capital, and his descendants established a brilliant and influential culture. The majority of the surviving monuments in Transoxiana are in the style established by the Timurids, or their successors, the Shaybanids. This architecture is characterised by its monumental proportions and richness of their decoration, with entire surfaces being covered with ceramic tiles or glazed brick. Among the most impressive monuments are those of the Shakh-i-Zindeh and Registan complexes in Samarkand.

Turkey

Anatolia was conquered and brought into the Islamic fold by the Seljuk Turks in 1077 C.E. (470 A.H.). In common with other dynasties with nomadic origins they brought a new vigour and originality to the arts and architecture They were the first in Islamic architecture to use ceramic decoration on a monumental scale and the style that they pioneered in the 12th and 13th centuries (6th- 7th c A.H.) became a source of inspiration, particularly in the eastern Islamic world, for centuries to come. As well as using ceramics on a grand scale the Seljuks made an extensive use of fine stone-carving to decorate their monuments. In both mediums they took the art of patterning to new levels of subtlety and intricacy.

Seljuk power declined at the end of the 13th (7th) century, and their successors the Ottomans introduced entirely new architectural and decorative forms rejecting much of the traditional notions, but some aspects of this tradition were retained, notably in their use of complex geometrical wood-inlay patterns in doors and other woodwork.

The stunning use of ceramic decoration in the Seljuk period is exemplified by the interior of the Karatay Mederse in their capital, Konya; the splendid tradition of carved relief can be seen in the extraordinary Ince Minare Medrese (also in Konya), and in the many caravanserais strung out across Antolia

Peripheral Material

There is no one Islamic style. Many forms of artistic expression have evolved in the extended Islamic world over the centuries, but there are certain aesthetic priorities that have affected artistic style wherever the influence of Islam itself was felt. The emphasis on the decorative arts, and the fondness for pattern was, of course, always part of this. This part of the collections is concerned with three artistic traditions that, whilst outside the mainstream of the Islamic current, were clearly caught up in its general flow.

Jaiselmere

The fortified desert town of Jaiselmere in Rajastan was founded in the 12th century. Occupying a strategic position on the camel train routes between north-west India and Central Asia it prospered as a major entrepot and trading centre. The wealth and confidence that it acquired over the centuries are reflected in the extraordinary local tradition of stone-carving that decorates most of the older houses, shops and Havelis. Although the Bhatti Rajputs managed to resist direct conquest by the Muslim rulers of Delhi the predominantly geometric style of architectural decoration here clearly shows a strong Islamic influence.

Qatar

The sheikdom of Qatar on the Persian Gulf was too much of a backwater for most of its history to be able to boast of any splendid monuments of the kind found in the great urban centres, but in common with other Gulf States it does have a fine local tradition of carved plaster-work. The examples here are from the Old Amiri Palace complex and other public buildings

Sicily

Sicily was conquered by the Arabs in the 9th c. (3rd A.H.), and was ruled by Muslims for two centuries before it was reclaimed for Christendom by Norman adventurers. In the years of Islamic dominance there were strong links with Fatimid Egypt, which contributed to Sicily's sophisticated urban culture, an influence that later penetrated deeply into Italy. The cultural mix inherited by the Normans, which included Byzantine Greek as well as Muslim Arab influences, allowed the different artistic traditions to blend together, to great effect. The results of the Islamic influence on the Byzantine-geometric tradition can still be seen on the walls and floors of several monuments in Sicily, notably in the Cappella Palatina in Palermo and the Cathedral and Cloisters at Monreale. It is also evident in the ornate 13th century stonework on the façade of Palermo Cathedral.

11

The Evolution of Style

Consistency and Variety

Islamic art has a recognisable aesthetic signature that somehow manages to express itself across an entire range of productions. The 'language' of this art, once established, was readily assimilated by each of the different nations and ethnicities that were brought within the Islamic sphere. Assimilated and built upon, because every region, at every period, produced its own versions of this super-national style.

This extraordinary consistency of styles and artistic preferences in the Islamic world clearly derive from a deeper, social consistency. All Muslims hold to the same basic system of belief, all are familiar with the customary religious observations, and all – despite national and ethnic differences and rivalries – felt themselves to be Muslim first and foremost. This strong sense of identity and continuity tended towards a high degree of social, and artistic, conservatism. As a result, many forms and artistic concepts remained unchanged over the centuries - on the other hand, Islamic art has constantly demonstrated its capacity for the creative reinterpretation of accepted forms.

Much of the art of Islam, whether in architecture, ceramics, textiles or books, is the art of decoration – which is to say, of transformation. The aim, however, is never merely to ornament, but rather to transfigure. Essentially, this is a reflection of the Islamic preoccupation with the transitory nature of being. Substantial structures and objects are made to appear less substantial, materials are de-materialised. The vast edifices of mosques are transformed into lightness and pattern; the decorated pages of a Qur'an can become windows onto the infinite. Perhaps most importantly, the Word, expressed in endless calligraphic variations, always conveys the impression that it is more enduring than the objects on which it is inscribed.

Symmetry and Geometry

Another familiar characteristic of this art, which must also express something fundamental to the Islamic spirit, is its predilection for orderly, symmetrical arrangements in general and for purely geometrical decorative forms in particular. The influence of both religious and philosophical ideas on this aspect of Islamic art were examined earlier (in Background Notes #2 & #3 respectively), but the abstract, ideational nature of symmetry and geometry clearly fit with the Islamic taste for idealistic otherworldliness.

From a purely doctrinal viewpoint, geometrical designs, being free of any symbolic meaning (which is the case in Islamic art), could convey a general aura of spirituality without offending religious sensibilities. In addition, the purity and orderliness of patterns and symmetries could evoke a sense of transcendent beauty which, at best, would free and stimulate the intellect (rather than trap it in the illusions of mere representation).

There is a certain disregard for scale in Islamic art that derives from this perception. Similar kinds of patterning, for instance, might be found on a huge tile panel or on a bijou ornament. This is because decorative effects, in an Islamic context, are never mere embellishments, but always refer to other, idealised states of being. In this view, scale is almost irrelevant. For similar reasons Islamic ornemanistes usually opted for a-centric arrangements in patterning, avoiding obvious focal points – a preference that resonates with the Islamic perception of the Absolute as an influence that is not 'centred' in a divine manifestation (as in Christianity), but whose presence is an even and pervasive force throughout the Creation. A further analogy can be drawn between the patiently created repeats of the 'infinite' pattern (in all its varieties), and the familiar and unvarying customs of Moslem religious observances. In an Islamic context repetition is not tedious; on the contrary, it connects to the world of the spirit.

Whether in a religious setting or not, the work of Muslim artist/craftsmen always manages to convey a certain integrity, even nobility. In fact the distinction between art and craft-work is largely irrelevant in the Islamic world, but even when their works demonstrated surpassing skill and inspiration, the practitioners tended to remain anonymous. This is not surprising; in a culture whose ideal was submission to the will of Allah, it was quite natural to submit creative individuality to a perceived higher notion of beauty.

Earlier Islamic Art

It was seen earlier (in Background Note #1) that the Umayyad's were the first dynasty to rule the newly-established Islamic Empire (from the mid 7th- mid 8th centuries; 41-132 AH). During this early period, which was marked by conquest and consolidation, such art and architecture that was commissioned drew on pre-Islamic traditions (primarily those of Christian Byzantine and Sassanian Persia). Even so, there are clear signs of the emergence of Islamic aesthetic priorities. The main elements of decoration at this time derive from late-classical traditions of stone-carving, floor- and wall-mosaic and wall-painting, but plaster decoration, introduced from the Hellenised East, is also used.

This window-grill from the Umayyad Mosque, Damascus shows a direct continuation of the Syro-Roman tradition. Mosaic decoration from the Umayyad Mosque, Damascus: This also shows an unbroken continuation of late classical Byzantine tradition of sacred architectural decoration. But the subject-matter, of a paradise landscape, is decidedly Islamic.

The replacement of the Umayyad dynasty by the Abbasid (in 750 CE/ 132 AH) saw the removal of the capital eastwards to Baghdad, and later to Samarra. These two great cities were enormously important for the development of Islamic art and culture but, sadly, little has survived of either from the early period.

From the fragments of architectural decoration that have been recovered there appears to have been a steady move away from naturalistic treatments, towards more abstract and repetitive forms. The long-established eastern traditions of plaster- and brick-work were adopted as the principle architectural materials in the Islamic East, and were to remain so for the following centuries.

By the early 9th/3rd century, Turks from Central Asia become an ever more dominant political force, and from this time on their tastes exerted a strong influence on Islamic art generally. At the political level, these incursions meant that the Islamic Empire began to fragment into rival factions, with local dynasties establishing themselves in various regions. Islamic art in these turbulent 9th-10th centuries (3rd-4th AH), is represented by local styles, usually based on older precedents, but always bearing the imprint of Islamic tastes and limitations.

Stucco panel from Samarra;

Ceramic bowl with decoration from Nishapur, Iran;! 0th/4th century

Wooden frieze; Egypt; 9th/3rd century

Door panel; Egypt;

Stucco decoration in mosque at Nayin; 10th/4th century

Stucco decoration; Ibn Tulun Mosque ; Egypt; 9th/3rd century

Decorative brick work; Mausoleum of the Samanids; early 10/4thcentury

Stylistic maturity; 11th - 12th centuries

As indicated above, the Abbasid Aliphate began to lose political power, and it's Empire to fragment, at the turn of the 10th/4th century. The most serious consequences of this political turmoil, for Islamic culture as a whole, were the accompanying religious controversies and multiplicity of doctrines. In time, in a reverse of the status quo of earlier centuries, Shi'ism became the dominant creed among the various secessionist dynasties, and for a period this interpretation looked set to dominate the Islamic world. But early in the 11thcentury there began a Sunni revival, which had both religious and cultural aspects. This movement, which saw itself as a restoration of traditionalism, was accompanied by an artistic revival that established many of the enduring forms of Islamic art and architecture – in particular, its canon of decorative art.

The Sunni revival, which began in Baghdad, gradually spread through the Islamic world. As it did so, it became associated with a range of new artistic and architectural forms, which became an identifying mark, a sort of symbolic language. These new stylistic terms were adopted by the Ghaznavids in Khorasan, the Seljuks in Iran, the Zangids in Northern Syria, and the Ayyubids in Egypt. The 'classic' style of Islamic ornament which used distinctive epigraphic, geometric and abstract vegetal elements first came to maturity during this period. This decorative canon was eventually taken up in every part of the Islamic world.

The three elements of the Islamic decorative canon began to appear as early as the Umayyad period, but they crystallised into their classic forms during the 'Sunni Revival'. Calligraphy gives a visible form to the revealed word of the Qur'an and is therefore considered the most noble of the arts. It manages to combine a geometric discipline with a dynamic rhythm. Interestingly, none of its many styles, created in different places at different periods, has ever completely fallen into disuse. In the Islamic world it takes the place of iconography, being widely used in the decorative schemes of buildings.

Geometric patterns have always had a particular appeal to Muslim designers and craftsmen. They convey a certain aura of spirituality, or at least otherworldliness, without relating to any specific doctrine. In an Islamic context they are also quite free of any symbolic meaning. Above all they provide craftsmen with the opportunity to demonstrate his skill and subtlety of workmanship, and often to dazzle and intrigue with its sheer complexity.

Vegetal 'Arabesque' compositions are as ubiquitous in Islamic decoration as geometric patterns. It is difficult, without other indications, to determine where or when a particular composition of this genre might have originated. Like geometrical designs, these too are found across the entire range of mediums from book illustration to plaster-work; in ceramics, woodwork, metalwork and ivory-carving, even in carpets and textiles.

The Craft-group

As indicated earlier, there was no distinction between 'art' and 'craft' in the medieval Islamic world, just as there was no sharp division between notions of beauty and utility. The idea of the brilliant, lone individual artist was also absent. These are modern concepts. In fact, architectural and artistic productions generally tended to be the work of groups of anonymous craftsmen, whose occupations were usually hereditary and based within guilds or similar craft-groups. However, given that the subject area of 'the decorative arts of Islam' has such an extensive geographical and historical reach, and involved a great variety of craft skills, generalisations of any kind about this broad subject may be misleading. Among such a diverse range of artistic traditions there were bound to be huge variations in working practices, social status, and indeed of expressive intent, in so many and varied creative processes.

As I've indicated, by comparison with life in the modern world, medieval Islamic society was highly conservative. We can imagine that working practices, just like the designs and motifs that were used, often persisted for generations with little change. There was no formal training; skills were acquired in the workshops, and were often handed down from father to son. The apprentice/master relationship was usually regularised however, and there is evidence that craft-groups were formed into guilds (which had similarities with the trade-guilds of medieval Europe). It seems also to have been the case that some of these guilds (in some periods at least) were affiliated to religious groups. Details of this kind are naturally difficult to uncover, as they tended to be bound up with the mystique and protectiveness of what were essentially closed professions. It is of more than passing interest though, that these religious connections were usually associated with Sufi fraternities, whose mystical outlook had been imbued with Neoplatonic concepts.

The production of specialised goods and the particular skills involved were often localized. But these skills often took artisans far away from their home. Occasionally these movements were less than voluntary. In the turmoil of war craft-skills were generally prized as a form of booty and artisans could be carted off to the victor's base, sometimes en masse. Since the ruling power was usually the greatest patron of arts and architecture, it often happened that new artistic movements were initiated in this way. The dynasty founded by Timurlane was perhaps the most famous example of this effect. It occasionally happened that skilled craftsmen were welcomed as refugees after fleeing invasions and wars. The relative security of Fatimid Egypt attracted many mid-eastern artisans during the turbulent 11th/12th centuries, much to the cultural benefit of Cairo.

The transfer of skills and knowledge as a result of migrations and conquest is of course a time-honoured process. Huge numbers of skilled artisans from various traditions were brought into the Islamic fold as a result of the early conquests, and in the course of time these skills became part of the background of Islamic culture. But there was one craft technology in particular that was acquired in this way that had a profound effect on the course of Islamic civilisation on many levels (including the visual arts). This was the manufacture of paper.

The role of Paper in Islamic Art and Architecture

Paper was a Chinese invention that had spread to Central Asia and Khurasan prior to the Islamic conquests of those regions. As soon as Islamic rule had been established in this eastern end of the Empire the usefulness of this product for bureaucratic and military purposes must have become obvious. The precise history of the uptake of this invention is somewhat hazy. But what is quite certain is that the relative cheapness and ease of production of paper ensured its rapid spread throughout the Islamic world during the 9th and 10th centuries (3rd/4th AH) and that it transformed societies wherever it appeared. Paper was soon pressed into service by the Baghdad Aliphate, where it greatly facilitated their centralised rule and, Baghdad itself became one of many important centres of paper-making.

As paper became available throughout the Islamic world it was gradually adopted by artists and craftsmen. This usage began, naturally enough, among visual artists of higher status, calligraphers and those involved in the 'arts of the book'. The use of paper was slower among craftsmen at a lower social position (woodworkers, stonemasons, weavers etc,), partly because of the conservatism of their working practices, but also for cost reasons. As it became cheaper and more widely available however, paper became a standard tool in most crafts, and in the process it effected a transformation of the visual arts of Islam.

In essence, the adoption of paper into craft-based work-practices introduced a certain separation of the design process from that of manufacture. This was bound to lead to a greater degree of organisation in design right across the board, from architecture through to the humbler crafts of pottery and weaving.

Later this separation of design and making gave rise to a stylistic 'centralisation', such as that exercised by the many Royal studios and workshops that were maintained by the Royal courts. Many dynastic styles were established and maintained in this way.

Paper was a common commodity in the Islamic world as early as the 12th century (6thAH) and was already being used by various (usually high-status) artisans to produce preliminary drawings for their work. In the following centuries the use of paper designs was gradually adopted as normal practice. This development undoubtedly fostered stylistic consistency across different mediums and promoted a common currency of style. There are many examples of close similarities between decorative motifs in architecture, book illumination and craft objects.

These is some evidence that the sort of complex patterning and arabesques that are such a characteristic feature of Islamic art first appeared as decorative elements of books (as did calligraphy, of course). As the 'arts of the book' enjoyed the highest status among crafts it seems very likely that these designs would have gradually filtered down to other mediums. It is also clear that once pattern-books and albums of design motifs came into being their repertoire could be applied to a whole range of artefacts, in different settings and at different scales. Designs could be copied, improved upon and, most importantly, they could travel.

It would certainly appear that there was, for centuries, a broad awareness and appreciation of the aesthetic aspects of ornament and a lively interaction between different crafts. The stylistic homogeneity of Islamic art referred to at the beginning of this note may have its foundations in Islamic cultural homogeneity, but its primary medium of transmission was paper.

Materials and Mediums

As indicated in Background Notes 4, the decorative arts in Islam are marked by a remarkable degree of stylistic consistency which has been applied to a broad range of materials, each of which had a craft-base of its own, the history of which often traces back to pre-Islamic times. The stylistic coherence within the Islamic world and the many variations of its basic themes across time, influenced as they were by local artistic traditions, are all part of the fascination of this art. In Muslim architecture virtually any surface may be regarded as worthy of receiving elaborate decoration and this is particularly apparent in religious architecture, but this principle extends out to woodwork, ceramics, textiles, metalwork, books and many other art forms.

Stonework

There is an East–West divide in basic Islamic architectural techniques that derives from earlier, pre-Islamic traditions. In the Persian/Iranian sphere of influence the principle building material tends to be brick, whereas in Egypt, Syria and Asia Minor, stone is far more common, at least for monumental building.

The earliest Islamic monuments, dating from the Umayyad period, clearly continue the Roman/Byzantine tradition in their typical structures and in their use of dressed and carved stone. These techniques continued under later dynasties in Egypt and Syria (the Fatimids, Zangids,

Ayyubids and Mamelukes). This architecture is characterised by its monumental scale, its relative simplicity of form and a somewhat sombre tone. The deep carving, ordered in panelled schemes, with calligraphic bands and geometrical and arabesque motifs, make an impressive contrast against great expanses of undecorated surfaces.

In Asia Minor the Seljuks, and later the Ottomans, continued the traditions both of ashlar building and of stone carving. Under the Seljuks a more plastic style of stone-carving was introduced, based on the stucco work of their predecessors in Iran. This gave rise to a rich tradition of that used all the familiar elements of Islamic decoration in a dazzling profusion of examples. The strength and vitality of this tradition of carved stonework continued up to the beginning of the 16th/10th century, gradually becoming less exuberant during the Ottoman period.

A separate tradition of architectural stonework developed on the Indian sub-continent, again derived from pre-Islamic sources. The early Turkish conquerors of India introduced entirely new, and in many ways quite opposite, architectural concepts to the sub-continent, but the synthesis that arose from the meeting of Hindu and Islamic traditions produced a great range of marvellous buildings, and countless examples of exquisite carved and inlaid stone decoration.

Brickwork

As mentioned above, brickwork was the favoured building technique in the eastern Islamic provinces of Iraq and Iran, the tradition originating in the ancient civilisations of this area. Typically, however, in the hands of Muslim builders, brickwork was soon being used in quite novel and more decorative ways than in the past. In fact there is a well-defined progression in the use of brick in eastern Islam, from purely structural purposes towards ever greater decorative complexity.

The first stage (in the 11th/5thcentury) saw an increasing variety of brick bonds that created relief patterns of light and shade to great effect. The enthusiasm for this technique was such that some buildings featured dozens of different bond-patterns, veritable showcases of brick design.

Later, carved ornamental inserts were used to break up the tedium of plain bonding; these were soon moulded before being fired, in a whole variety of motifs. In the next stage these brick inserts were glazed, a technique that lead naturally on to entire walls and domes being invested with coloured glazed bricks, by which time the structural and decorative functions of brickwork had more or less separated out. Over time these glazed bricks were gradually reduced in thickness until they were virtually tiles – and the possibility of a whole new era of architectural ornament was created.

Ceramic Tiles and Ceramic Mosaic

Coloured glaze was part of the repertoire of decoration in the architecture of the Ancient middle-east, in both Egypt and Mesopotamia – by the time Islam arrived on the scene however, these techniques had been long forgotten. The earliest Islamic monuments made extensive use of mosaic as both floor and wall decoration, but these were very much in the still-flourishing tradition of late-Antiquity. It was not really until the 12th/6thcentury that architectural ceramics began to be used extensively in an Islamic setting (by way of the progression described above). The gradual development of suitable ceramic glazes, in both pottery and tile-work, represented a whole series of technological advances, and as such was as much a scientific/technological achievement as an artistic one. The enthusiasm for the intense colours produced by these techniques meant that they were eventually transmitted right across the Islamic world, from the Atlantic to Central Asia.

Ceramic tiles are found in most Muslim countries, using an extensive range of techniques that include high moulded relief, polychrome, lustre-ware and sgraffito. In addition, sophisticated techniques were developed that used pieces of cut-tiles, bonded together with plaster, to form elaborate, multi-coloured mosaic panels. The latter method was particularly favoured in the lands that came under Timurid influence (Iran and Transoxiana), and in the Islamic far-West (Spain and Morocco).

The broad area that fell under Iranian influence had a long, independent tradition of ceramic architectural revetment, known as kashi, which reached its first great achievement in the 14th/8thcentury and was sustained through the Timurid and Safavid periods. Each element of the traditional Islamic decorative canon, geometric and vegetal arabesque forms, together with calligraphy, is used but with great local variations of style.

The use of cut-tile mosaic seems to have come into favour in the Islamic West (the Maghreb) with the appearance of the Berber dynasties in the 12th-13th centuries (6th-7th). Known as zellij, it is almost exclusively dedicated to geometrical arrangements in this part of the world. The Maghreb (Spain and Morocco) had long followed an independent cultural existence, developing its own characteristic architectural and decorative forms. The particular specialty here was always an intense geometric patterning, a tradition that has lasted right up to the modern period.

Stucco/Plasterwork

Plaster was a well-established building material prior to the Islamic conquests both in Iran, where it had been used to cover rough, rubble walls for centuries, and to a lesser extent in the Classical, Mediterranean world. This was a readily available material in the Middle-east, and was used in Islamic architecture from the very earliest periods (in Syria and Iraq), from where it fairly rapidly spread to the rest of the Muslim world.

Its earlier forms followed late-Classical and Sassanian models, but Islamic tastes were soon asserted, inclining towards a flattening of the decorated surface, the emphasis on symmetry, its division into distinct, evenly laid-out panels, and the use of abstract rather than naturalistic motifs.

Plaster, a singularly useful material that leant itself to moulding and carving in a variety of ways, became a staple of Islamic architecture. Perhaps because of its plasticity as a medium it was less frequently used for purely geometric designs, and was more often used in vegetal-arabesque arrangements. It could also, of course, be painted or gilded.

In essence, plaster (on its own or in conjunction with ceramics) was the perfect medium for transforming surfaces - which was always the primary concern in Islamic architecture. In Islamic art generally, the underlying intention is bound up with the notion of the dissolution of matter, of transcendence.

Woodwork

Since wood is a comparatively scarce material in many parts of the Islamic world it perhaps not surprising that it enjoyed a higher status as a material than elsewhere and, at its best, displays the very highest levels of workmanship. Traditionally, it was used for doors and window shutters which are frequently inlaid, but the finest work is generally found on pulpits (minbar), the key piece of furniture in the mosque from which Friday sermons are preached. Many highly sophisticated techniques were developed to create intricate decoration; in the finer examples ebony and other precious woods are used as inlays, together with ivory and mother-of-pearl. The carving in these objects often has a concentrated, almost lapidary detail. In the Islamic world the skills of carpentry were traditionally associated with geometry. The 14th/8th century historian Ibn Khuldun (who was presumably expressing a generally held belief) asserted that all the leading Greek geometricians were masters of this craft. Some surviving examples of 12th/6th century woodwork indicate that the genre of complex, interlacing geometrical designs in the girih mode were relatively common by this time, and may have been expressed in this architectural medium before any other (after their probable invention as Qur'anic illumination in the 10th/4th century; see below).

Book Illumination

As indicated above, the earliest appearances of the girih mode (the classical Islamic decorative style that includes both geometric and vegetal forms) are found in late 10th/4thcentury Qur'an manuscripts that are believed to have originated in Baghdad. It is thought likely that this style spread out to other mediums from this source. Although the precise mechanisms by which this style was transmitted are obscure, obviously it would have been facilitated by the widespread availability of paper soon after this time.

The three components of the Islamic decorative canon (calligraphy, of course, geometrical and vegetal arabesque arrangements) which were established in this medium continued to be a feature of the Islamic arts of the book, with every period making its own contribution to the genre. As the most elevated of all objects the Qur'an naturally always received the most respectful and inspired treatment, but there are also many examples of geometrical patterning and arabesque in secular book illustration. Clearly, the art of decoration was taken seriously in Islamic culture; patterns had a currency. Their appearance in the portable arts i.e. of the book, in craft-albums and working drawings, meant that existing examples could be reworked and improved upon, and those who specialised in decorative patterns could inspire new directions in this way. There are countless examples of intricate pattern in each of the major traditions of miniature painting (Turkish, Persian and Mughal Indian, in fact sometimes they are positively teeming with them. The exploration and playing with decorative ideas that is evident in so many of these works is probably indicative of a general interest in the subject in studios of various kinds. Sadly, apart from these examples and the few surviving folios and working drawings, the originators of the majority of these brilliant patterns and arabesques are likely to remain obscure.

Court Patronage and Cottage Industry

The distinction between the artistic and luxury goods that were commissioned and made in centralized, Royal studios and workshops, and those that were essentially the products of small-scale cottage industry, has already been remarked upon. This division, however, between central and independent manufacture in traditional Islamic cultures, was often a rather more complex business than this simple apportioning might suggest. It was usually the case that Rulers and their court custodians were the chief arbiters of taste and fashion in all things, but in most periods there were thriving manufacturing centres of such goods as textiles, pottery, metalwork and glassware, with their own design traditions. Many fine articles were designed in Royal studios and manufactured in Royal workshops exclusively for use by the Court, and occasionally these productions were made available to other wealthy clients. In other cases designs were created in an official studio and the work then commissioned from independent artisans, many of whom worked in districts close to Royal palaces. Religious institutions were of course another major source of commissions.

These differences of origination, together with

differences in local tastes and traditions, account for the greater variation of design in the arts of 'everyday objects', by comparison with the consistencies of the formal decorative modes in architecture. Symmetry, as always in Islamic design, was still the keynote, but the traditional decorative canon (of geometrical patterns, arabesque arrangements and calligraphy), while an ever-present and general influence on design, exerted less of a hold beyond architecture.

The design studios retained by Islamic ruling houses tended to exercise stylistic control and consistency across a whole range of mediums, including architectural decoration. In many case this stylistic continuity is fairly evident - the designs on Nasrid silks, for instance, have clear similarities with contemporary stuccowork. Textiles, partly because of the important role they played in courtly life and ceremonial, were frequently a focus for court designers and textile workshops themselves were actively encouraged by the ruling establishment in many periods. There are abundant examples of this sort of stylistic conformity across the arts in the Ottoman, Safavid and Mughal dynasties, and it is safe to assume that this was the case in earlier periods.

There is evidence from various Islamic periods of complex designs being prepared in design-studios and passed on to skilled artisans across a range of luxury items, including (at different times), metalwork, carpets, glasswork and ivory-carving. In fact a great many artistic products from the Islamic world, in all mediums, are characterised by highly organised arrangements with complex schemes of patterning that clearly indicate a prior design stage. The essential role of paper in this process has already been touched. Although very few examples survive, it seems extremely likely that the use of working drawings (and the inevitable appearance of pattern books and design folios), led to the creation of a design 'currency' among skilled artisans which enabled the continuous refinement of patterns, and their exchanges between mediums.

12

Spirituality in Islamic Art and Design

Islamic art and design is firmly based on the idea of unity; almost everything Islamic has its reference back to the idea of unity, of one God. Genuine Islamic architecture provides a vehicle, in that it is providing some sort of plastic form or experience through which the person experiencing the architecture can contemplate the idea of a divine unity.

The aim of all Islamic art and architecture is then to show this divine unity or to make the experiencee (if there is such a word) aware of the divine unity and the interrelatedness that exists within creation to the divine unity. One of the aims then is to lead the experiencee to this realization. Islamic art or design is aimed or geared towards doing that and is an expression of that principle in particular.

To begin to understand Islamic architecture is to understand the principles of Islam. It's such a diverse topic, we'll go through it and describe it in a nutshell, and see how we go. Even in this day and age of secularism and a bit of suspicion towards any sort of organized religion, we need to look at the principles upon which Islam is based so that we can look into how Islamic architecture then expresses that.

Islamic civilisation is based on the view that the revelation was propagated through the prophet Muhammad (PBUH) and I believe that in a few of the previous lectures that the life of the prophet Muhammed was the topic of the day.

That message or that revelation is the same pure and simple, the life principle that was propagated by the entire lineage of prophets starting from Adam, including Noah, Moses, Abraham and Jesus. The very word Islam, meaning peace, is well known; it can also be translated as submission. But the meaning I prefer is being at ease or being at one with the divine will. It's very important because it implies a harmony. And the creed of each of these prophets was simply that there's none worthy of worship except God and that particular prophet of the day was a messenger of God. In an Islamic view, Muhammad (PBUH) the seal of the prophets is that current prophet, he's the final prophet and therefore he's the current messenger of the day.

Therefore you have the creed of Muslims being "la ilaha illallahu, Muhammadur rasulullah": there is none worthy of worship except God, and the prophet Muhammad is the messenger of God. This statement or creed is in its simplicity the basic attitude that summarizes the spiritual aspect of Islam.

It's so simple: there's no priesthood in Islam; each Muslim has the responsibility or takif of being the best representative of God on earth that he can be or she can be. He or she has the capacity of fulfilling all the religious functions associated with the personal, the family and the social spheres.

In its universal sense Islam can be said to have three levels of meaning (sorry if this is a bit wordy and we're going into some in-depth topics; you're probably thinking what's this got to do with spirituality in art and design, but we're getting there).

The first basic level is that all beings in the universe are Muslim. This is somewhat of a revelation to most non-Muslims, that Muslims view all beings in the universe as

Muslim; that there is a basic surrendering to the Divine will from everybody and every creation.

For example, whether you are outwardly Muslim or not, there is a basic level of submission to natural laws. You need to sleep, you need to go to the toilet, you need to engage with others socially, and you have a range of other physical natural requirements. A cow would eat grass, and has no option except to eat grass, and doesn't think otherwise; doesn't think "oh, I feel like a burger tonight". It hasn't got that sort of will. A rock cannot help but fall if it's dropped. God has created these universal laws, and all obey them voluntarily or involuntarily, and in that way, all creatures are Muslims, because they're submitting to the will of God.

In actual fact, Muslims believe that all people are born pure Muslims, in a state of submission, and it's only their environment, and the impact of that, that makes them otherwise (afterwards). In other words, the innateness of basic human character is Muslim, and that is why when a person becomes a Muslim, other Muslims refer to them as being a revert not a convert, because you're coming back to Islam.

The second level is those who accept with their will the sacred laws of revelation, in that they assume they surrender their will to those laws. So the outwardly Muslim people are the second level (and these are not levels in term of hierarchy, but just different).

So when someone asks me "why do you fast?", I don't say to them "look, I'm fasting because it's good for my body, it's a cleanser, it's good because I can exercise some self control, its good because I can feel for the less fortunate, it's good because it creates a brotherhood with other people". These are all good side effects, but simply, I fast because God tells me to and has ordained it for me. So it's that level of people who obey, basically, God's commandments.

The third level is that of pure knowledge and understanding. It is that of the '`arif', or in English terms, the closest word that I've come across is the 'gnostic'. It is the level that has been recognized by Islam as the highest and most comprehensive. At the beginning we had a bit of calligraphy which said "'allama bil qalam" which implies "and God taught man by the use of the pen", so that the pursuit of knowledge and understanding has always been the highest pursuit that you could undertake as a Muslim.

The 'gnostic' is a Muslim whose whole life is being surrendered to God - he has no separate individual existence of his own - he's like the rest of creation in a way. He's like the cow, the bird, which has full submission to the creator and doesn't think to disobey or to be contrary. And like them he reflects the divine to his own degree.

And so this person or this gnostic is like the rest of creation; the difference is he does so actively; he submits actively whereas other creation does so passively. They do it by virtue of their character, their innateness. His participation is a conscious one and therefore his interaction with his environment is a conscious interaction.

Within nature there are many signs of the divine, and it's interesting that the verses of the text within the Qur'an are also called signs. In Arabic the word for verse in Qur'an is 'ayah', which actually means sign. So both nature and Qur'an speak of the presence of God, and they do so purely.

To the person or to the adherent of sacred law, the signs merely serve to be prescriptive - "do this!", "do that!", "do this!", "do that!" - but to the gnostic the Qur'anic signs and the signs within nature are symbolic. And if the symbolism of that text is to disappear completely and be reduced just to its literal meaning (and a lot of Muslims fall into this category at the moment), man will still know what to do in terms of his duty, but the symbolic aspects of his life will become unintelligible. The phenomena of nature would become just a mere fact, as we have in our daily lives today. "Nice day today". "Yes it is, its 25 degrees". "Oh, it's good weather for a BBQ". It is that very basic, factual analysis of the nature around us, instead of seeing the signs in nature that reflect the existence of divinity.

And this dry analysis or quantitative analysis of nature is precisely what the higher intellective capacity of Islamic culture does not accept. The spirit of Islam emphasizes by contrast the unity of nature, the unity which is the aim of Islamic design expressed in the different signs within nature and the Qur'an. So it can be said that the idea of unity is not just a basic principle of Islamic art and design, it actually dominates Islamic art and design.

Seyyed Nasr has mentioned that the very canon of art in Islam is abstraction. So what you will see then is that art and Islamic architecture and design tend to go towards abstraction rather than literal interpretation.

Unity cannot be represented directly. It can be symbolized, though even then only subtly and by hints. Islamically there's not one concrete symbol for unity; we don't have any sort of symbol that expresses unity. The basic creed of belief that I mentioned before, that there is none worthy of worship but God, is actually a statement that has negatives in it. "There's none worthy of worship but God". The abstract symbol of unity is negation; in other words we can sort of understand what God is by saying "he's not that", "he's not that", 'he's not that' and by elimination we can sort of get to know what he is. (I'm sorry, I'm using the word 'he'; it's very traditional in Arabic language to use the word 'he', but in Arabic the word for God, 'Allah' - as you probably would know - is actually genderless; God is not he or she, so don't take it that way).

For instance, in Surah Ikhlas, one of the verses in the Qur'an, God devotes a chapter to describe him. And you'd think he'd devote the biggest chapter, but it's only three verses. It says in that chapter "Say God is one"; and then the negatives come into it. It says, "He does not beget, nor is He begotten", so he's not born nor does he give birth; "And there is nothing like unto Him". And that's the end of the verse, that's the end of the chapter. So through that negation; "He does not beget, nor is He begotten and there is nothing like unto Him" we can start to understand the nature of God. He's not like a man; he's not like his creations. He doesn't get tired, he doesn't get sleepy. He doesn't suffer like we suffer; he doesn't have any of the corporeal constraints that we have, because he created all those things. So in that way we know what God is by knowing what he isn't.

So the traditional Muslim designer looks upon all artistic work as sacred, and he studies it according to those levels that I mentioned before.

The first is the law as contained in essence in the Qur'an, and exemplified by the prophet, and thereafter by scholarly tradition and jurisprudence as as taught by qualified masters. (Who are the qualified masters? There's very few of them around at the moment).

It covers every aspect of the social and the religious life of the believer. The catchphrase Muslims often say is "Oh, Islam is not a religion; it's a way of life". It's very simplistic, but it is like that; it's not simply something that we do as rituals, but actually permeates and goes through every aspect of your life. Even to the extent that going to the toilet is an act of worship, having sex is an act of worship, and so on. All the routine and other day to day acts that you might engage in, going to work and so on, can become acts of worship.

So first is the law. It's that basic "here are the laws, here are the requirements; you do these".

Second is the path. And this deals with the inner aspects of things, and this is where the spiritual life comes out.

For instance, a Muslim might pray a ritual prayer, before sunrise; and he or she might fulfil all the outward requirements of that prayer. He may first take ablutions and prepare for the prayer, and then engage in the prayer, face the correct direction, have the correct clothing on, face Mecca, make sure that the place where he's praying is clean, and all that sort of thing; and then recite all of the things that he needs to recite in that prayer; and yet really he has only completed that prayer on the level of law. On the level of path it would be issues such as the sincerity of the prayer that come into it; the modesty, the awe that that person experienced while they were praying; the utter devotion within the prayer. Those are the things that would come under consideration. That I class as the path.

And last is the absolute truth which lies at the heart of both of those approaches. Sayd Nasr again illustrates this point with a simile. If you can picture the law as being the circumference of the circle, the path is its radius, and the centre is where the truth is. So you can see that the law is dictated by the path (the radius) and it's all focused on the centre point, the one point which is the unity, the truth. From this concept you can develop a science of the universe, a science of the soul, and at its core a metaphysical intuition that appeals to all people.

The truth is there whether its recognized or not. It's still there. And it is the arousing of this intuition in all people, outwardly Muslim or not outwardly Muslim that is the main duty of the Muslim artist or architect.

What I'm saying is that truth exists always; it's just waiting to be recognized. And so when speaking about Islamic art it may be that work displays recognition of this truth; but it hasn't necessarily been completed by a Muslim. It could have been completed by a non-Muslim whose intuition, that basic innate quality, has led to that discovery. The artist may have recognized a sign; maybe not in the Qur'an, but maybe in nature; and abstracted it and expressed it. Therefore, in this context, it would be regarded as Islamic art. The problem has been in the last couple of centuries that where Muslims live, by and large, they have not been very free to pursue these sorts of discourses, this sort of discussion, these sorts of initiatives. And so really the challenge at the moment is because Islamic art and architecture has almost stagnated. It has stayed in the time of 200 years ago and hasn't really progressed.

And what we saw in the last century (post World War II) was the influx of Western ideals and principles in Islamic art and architecture, coming into the areas where Muslims are - to ridiculous levels. For instance, in the Gulf countries where you have, in the middle of the desert climate, a multi-story glass facade village that is kept cool by 24 hours of air-conditioning; and only because it can, only because they've got the dollars to pay for that.

Whereas in essence, the architecture, the expression of the architecture is not appropriate for that-area or that-culture. I was working with Rasem Badran in 1990 to 1992, and now in the last twenty years there was the recognition of the need to build a bridge from where Islamic art had left, stopped developing; a need to build a bridge from that point to this point. A lot has changed in that time; namely the use of materials has changed dramatically.

But the first port of call in trying to do that is to raise the awareness of the appropriateness of the architecture, and the appropriateness of that architecture in marrying into the Islamic culture and lifestyle, and how it was actually much more appropriate, because it was something that had not just popped up but had eventuated over a number of centuries and actually had holistic solutions to people's requirements. I'll go through some of those in a little while.

I'm talking very abstractly, and to bring some specificity to this talk, I'd like to share the spiritual aspects of Islamic design with regards to what I've been doing - I apologize I don't have Alhambra to show you, I don't Isfahan to show you; I've never been to those places (I'd love to) - I've only got the work that I've done to show you, and hopefully it will be enough to illustrate the points that I'm trying to get across.

Starting with ablution - on the level of law, we talked about it being one of the basic levels. The most important aspect of design in architecture is to facilitate the Muslim's functional needs, and one of those is ablution.

You'll find most things in Islam have a functional aspect to them and they have from that function developed a symbolic aspect, a deep and meaningful aspect. So ablution has a functional aspect, which is to keep clean. But at the same time ablution has a symbolic aspect in that it's cleansing, not just externally, but it's actually cleansing spiritually.

So the requirement to have ablution facilities is a basic level of law-type requirement in any design which services Muslims. The focus on wash areas is so that a person may perform proper ablution rituals including the proper use of the toilet (by the way, this picture is RMIT, but I think it's basically the same as the one that's at Melbourne University, it's almost the same prototype). In Islam, as I mentioned to you before, there are actually requirements and rituals as to how to even use a toilet. So we address that at RMIT and at Melbourne.

And we're addressing it in a different way in our bid for the Royal Women's Hospital redevelopment. Because you can just imagine if somebody unknowing about Islamic toilet requirements walked into a cubicle that had that! "What do I do with that?" I guess it wouldn't be too hard to work out. But nonetheless, what we are doing now in our Royal Women's Hospital bid consultancy is saying to them "let's make it a lot more subtle and convert all disabled toilets so that they're usable by people with a disability and by Muslims". Because what you need in a Muslim-friendly toilet is water to wash yourself; you need a lot of room; and the orientation has to be correct, and there are some other factors as well.

So the ramifications extend into the design of both community projects and also into residential projects.

We also, on the level of law, have to have a place to pray. Now a place to pray for me could be a two metre by one metre space, and that would be sufficient, as long as it was clean and as long as I could face the correct direction. Obviously on a community level it needs to be a bigger space for congregational prayers and so on.

It was a significant challenge because we were trying to marry the aspects of path (which I'll talk about a bit later) with aspects of law. Sure, we could facilitate the aspects of prayer; but it was very tricky because the building wasn't orientated in anywhere near the direction of Mecca. So we actually had to create false walls within the space, and not so much disorientate, as reorientate a person coming through the building. So they are coming into it fully confident that this is the direction in which I should pray, without someone having to tell them so. That's for prayer.

One of the other aspects is privacy. This is just a snapshot of a house we did in Eltham. You can see that by having, for instance, recessed windows, there's a shadow cast on the window constantly, and that allows for that privacy to occur. There are other reasons why we did the recessing; for shading so it wouldn't get the western sun and so on. But that's one of the aspects. On the level of law, we need to provide for privacy.

You'll find that a lot of the traditional Islamic houses are so focused on this aspect of privacy, it affects window placement, window shape. You have something called a 'mashrabiya', traditionally placed in front of a window, which is like a lattice screen; so a person inside can see towards outside but the person outside cannot see inside.

Also, the issue of privacy affected the traditional design of houses in that they were mostly inward focused. So unlike the traditional brick veneer home in suburban Melbourne on a quarter acre block which is outward focusing (all of the windows are facing outwards, you have a five to ten metre setback from the front yard, two to three metres on the sides, and so on), the traditional Islamic house would most likely have the courtyard inside and focus inwards. That way there is no restrictions on the windows, be they open, be they small. And the courtyard served other purposes both functional and symbolic. That was relating to the issue of privacy.

At Melbourne University for instance, the direction in which people needed to pray was towards the one that is shown in the picture. And we had the windows there; we didn't want to lose that light; but we didn't want people to lose their concentration and be distracted by what was happening outside. So we put the clouded glass in the windows and obscured the view, allowing the nice soft white light to come through, but containing that view. The other issue of law would be segregation. (If you haven't visited this facility, please do - it's open for everyone to have a look). In terms of segregation in this mosque or in this prayer facility we had to have the option of being able to segregate between males and females at various times, and so we had these large panels that were on a pivot (the bottom view shows them closed) and you were able to open or close them, and that served the purpose quite well.

In terms of orientation, as an issue of law as well - it was very important in any prayer facility that the person not be confused as to the direction of prayer. So we had, at RMIT as I mentioned, to reorientate the person so that they came around and they were focused to the correct direction. We had these lights, like tarmac lights, but on the ceiling, so you're actually guided by them and just follow these lights around to the correct direction.

On the level of knowledge and inner spiritual development that is the path, there are a number of things that we've been trying to tackle. And the main one is stimulation of the senses. Because through stimulating the senses, through the tools available to the architect such as light, matter (different materials), use of water, wind, color - these sort of tools - we are able to stimulate the senses.

RMIT was a huge challenge to us, because it was in a multistorey building. We had a space between two floors, whereas Melbourne University we had a 4 metre floor to ceiling space. So you can imagine, as with churches, as with any religious type building, you are really trying to focus on height, because height tends to be related to spirituality. We had three metres; and that was it (2.7m I think, something like that). We actually created a false dome in there, to give that sense of elevation. I think you would agree that this space gives the impression that it's a spiritual space, and that's what we were trying to do through stimulation of the senses, through light, through the use of color, and so on - forms such as the dome, the arch, and so on. We were trying to put across that it was a spiritual space.

After that in terms of the path (and I've put a few commercial samples here where really I should be putting some mosques), this image is trying to illustrate the concept of continuous space.

Similarily inside a mosque where you would have a dome we would treat that dome in such a way where if you're underneath that dome, firstly you feel like you're the focus, because you're actually a node geometrically of that dome, you're generating that form. But also if you look up at the surface, the way that it's treated, you wouldn't know where it ended and where it started, and again it's symbolic of the universe that it's there as a functional element. The concept of continuous space is something that you would put across in any Islamic architecture.

And similarly, at RMIT, the concept is that this space is continuing around a corner. The first thing you want to do when you come to this space is go and see what's around the corner.

One of the other aspects in terms of the path or the spirituality is simplicity and sublimity. Islamic architecture tends to be very sublime, very simple. Even when it's embellished, it tends to be very simple. That's a commentary on the fact that what we're not trying to do in Islamic architecture is to set up something aside from God to be worshipped or to be monumentalized.

In the early periods of Islamic architecture the focus was away from monumentality because of this notion that you are trying to set something up apart from God. And the focus was more on abstraction and simplicity. Perhaps Muslims lost their way when their focus came towards monumentality, embellishment, and decoration.

The concept that you have simplicity and sublimity is something that's common to most Islamic architecture, even in South-East Asia and other places aside from the Middle East. So that's basically how we've tackled it in Melbourne - we are a very small company, a very small firm. We're not an international firm by any means, and therefore the examples that you see are very limited. But that's what we've tried to do on our level - that's to tackle the issue of law, of basic requirements, and the issue of spirituality which is then to take that sensory aspect a bit further and try to evoke feelings of spirituality with that sort of sensual stimulation.

13

The Meaning of Islamic Architecture

The architecture of the Islamic world—its spectacle of domes and minarets, arches and interior mind-boggling geometric decoration—has fascinated and perplexed many Western observers who have had few ways of really understanding the buildings or the beliefs and ways of life of the Muslims for whom these buildings were designed and erected. Architecture is more than a history of form and style: it is a product of cultural and environmental factors and an expression of the way of life of the people who live in the buildings. With that point of view in mind, the London orientalist scholar, George Michell, and a distinguished cast of contributors, in 1978 created for the first time a book titled "Architecture of the Islamic World: Its History and Social Meaning." In 1995, this book, long available only in hardcover, was published in a rich paperback edition, making it available for $20 to a much larger audience. It is a classic created a quarter of a century ago yet ripe for our times. What does it say?

There is an architecture produced for and by Muslims that serves Islam as a religion and reflects special qualities inherent in Islam as a cultural phenomenon. What then are those qualities that set Islamic architecture apart from non-Islamic architecture? Note that Grube avoids simply cataloguing famous Islamic buildings, exploring instead how Islamic architecture serves and reflects basic Islamic cultural traits and needs. The most prominent quality of Islamic architecture as compared with non-Islamic architecture, according to Grube, is its concentration on the interior of buildings.

"One of the most striking features of all Islamic architectural monuments is their focus on the enclosed space, on the inside as opposed to the outside, the façade or the general exterior articulation of a building." The Muslim house typifies this quality best with its inner courtyard and high windowless walls interrupted only by a single low door, often joined with other houses connected by corridors and inner private passageways to produce a complex maze that resembles "the natural growth of coral reefs or cell-structures of irregular form." This unmistakable traditional Muslim appearance survives in many examples of ancient town centers including the casbahs, medinas, and "old cities" throughout the Islamic world [but also see Editor's Note below]. To see photos of these amazing complexes is one thing; to watch people move about in them is another. Fortunately, films exist that depict people using these building-hives, e.g., " The Battle of Algiers" and " Algiers" (Charles Boyer, Hedy Lamarr, 1938). Qualities of Islamic architecture that build on this theme of the enclosed space follow below.

Hidden Architecture

The emphasis on inner enclosed space in Islamic architecture, according to Grube, is accompanied by a "disregard for the outside appearance of a structure" by completely hiding it by "secondary adjacent buildings (for instance a bazaar). This 'hiding' of major monuments goes hand in hand with a total lack of exterior indication of the shape, size, function or meaning of a building. Even if a structure has a visible façade or a portal, these features tell us little, if anything, about the building that lies behind it. In other words, rarely does a façade give any indication of the inner organization or purpose of the building in question, and it is rare that an Islamic building can be understood, or even its principal features identified, by its exterior." Grube then gives the example of domes, which loom over the mass of a building and can be seen from afar. Yet, as one approaches the dome, it seems to "sink into the maze of small cupolas and roofs of surrounding structures." Grube concludes that "[i]n all times and in all regions of the Muslim world are 'hidden architecture'—that is, architecture that truly exists, not when seen as monument or symbol visible to all and from all sides, but only when entered, penetrated and experienced from within."

Absence of form Adapted to a Single Function

Closely related to the concept of a hidden architecture is the concept of a "striking and almost total absence of a specific architectural form for a specific function," for example, a dining room for eating and a bedroom for sleeping. As a result, Islamic buildings can be adapted for a variety of purposes and do not change their form according to functional demands. Rather the building form remains fixed and functions are adapted to fit within the contained internal spaces.

Absence of Building Directionality

Islamic buildings, according to Grube, usually lack an inherent local directional or axial quality. This means that the physical direction of the building is different from the functional direction. For example, if an ordinary person enters a Christian cathedral, it is by the front doors, which, when open, lead eventually to the altar, the metaphysical point of the building. The visitor who enters a mosque is generally drawn alongside the prayer hall, which is at right angles to the "metaphysical direction" as indicated by the mihrab. This can be disconcerting to a Western visitor who is used to a "logical sense of direction expressed in European architecture.

The mihra is a niche in one wall, which indicates the qibla. The qibla (stay with me here) is the direction of prayer. The direction of prayer is always towards Mecca. Thus any time a Muslim anywhere in the world enters a mosque, his eyes likely will train to the mihrab.

By locating the mihrab (dent in the wall), he receives an instantaneous and very personal orientation to (and reminder of) the physical point on Earth (Mecca) that is the source of his faith. If you were to float above the Earth, look down and draw a line between each mihrab of each mosque, the lines should converge on Mecca. Thus, Islamic buildings lack a local directionality, because the only direction that is really important is the (global) direction of Mecca.

Building form Irregularity

The lack of local building directionality is also "clearly expressed in the lack of balance between the various parts of a building complex. European architecture is generally designed as a complete balanced plan: Islamic architecture" is "never hampered by an inherent principle governing the whole and conditioning all parts in an equal manner." (p. 13) For example, even when the four-iwan courtyard plan (a balanced building conceived of in Iran) is used, it "soon disappears as a single balanced unit to become part of a greater complex.

The very possibility of enlarging a given structure in almost any direction by adding units of almost every conceivable shape and size to the original scheme, totally disregarding the form of the original structure, is a characteristic that Islamic architecture shares with that of no other major culture," contends Grube. (p. 13)

Interior Space's Visual Negation of the Reality of Weight and the Necessity of Support

Enclosed space, defined by walls, arcades, vaults, and lavish decoration, is the most important element of Islamic architecture, contends Grube. The main purpose of "[d]ecoration in Islamic architecture appears to be the creation of non-tectonic values, the dissolution of all those elements that in other architectural traditions emphasize the structure, the balance and counter-balance of loads and stresses—the actual mechanics of a building. Islamic architecture...is truly a negation of architecture as conceived in Europe, that is, of structure; it aims at a visual negation of the reality of weight and the necessity of support.

The various means by which the effect of weightlessness is created, the effect of unlimited space, of non-substantiality of walls, pillars, and vaults are all well known. They range from the usage of mosaic and painted decoration to "lustrous tiles..." Its effect is extraordinary and its function quite unmistakable.

It goes hand in hand with the non-directional plan, the tendency to an infinite repetition of individual units (bays, arches, columns, passages, courtyards, doorways, cupolas) and the continuous merging of spaces without any specific direction or any specific center or focus." (pp. 13-14) Grube notes that when a terminal spatial limit, such as a wall, is reached, artists decorate that wall with patterns that repeat themselves, leading on visually beyond the given limit of that wall surface. The same is true with the decoration of a vault or a dome.

Not all Islamic scholars would agree with Grube's assessment that a) there is such a thing as Islamic architecture and that b) its primary qualities are as summarized above. Grube is aware of this and he notes that he has made a start which is an important milestone by itself. "It will take many years of research, hardly in its infancy at the present time, satisfactorily to 'explain' the phenomenon of Islamic architecture, that is to say, to correlate the physical appearance of Islamic architecture in various parts of the Muslim world with the 'spirit' of Islam as it prevailed in any given region and period," he cautions.

14

Islam and Globalization

Islamic Universality

The Quran states that Islam is the universal religion and is a mercy to all creatures. Islam is a religion of peace. As a universal faith that has been subject to diverse interpretations Islam offers a living demonstration of qualities to which all human beings can relate: compassion, mercy, tolerance, and love. Bearing the label "Muslim" is no guarantee of living by its teaching since Muslims are not a single, homogeneous entity. Grave risks arise from thin-king that they are. Islam is more than a system of theology, it's a complete civilization. The classical history of Islam proved the Islamic universality: Islam rejects discrimi-nation, racism, and teaches men and women to disperse within the land and seek the bounty of God.

More clearly the tradition of the Prophet Muhammad instructs his followers to seek knowledge, even to China. Indeed, this hadith calls for globalization at doctrinal and practical levels. Islam became the global power when the peoples of Arabia, Africa, Europe and Asia admired and followed the Islamic civilization and culture. The presence of Islam has contributed to the welfare and the prosperity of the peoples. The civilized peoples closely related to the basics of Islamic doctrine, ethics, values, morals, law, and their customs. Islam and its history have taught globalization at the most general level, that refers to a process of change which affects all regions of the world in a variety of sectors including the economy, science and technology and to some extent – politics, the media, culture and the environment.

The characterization of globalization may be thought of initially as the widening, deepening and speeding up of worldwide interconnectedness in all aspects of social life, from the cultural to the criminal, the financial to the spiritual. The 12th Century was "The Golden Age of Islamic Globalization". The majority of Muslims are not located in the motherland of Islam, but Indonesia, India and Pakistan. The faces of Islam in these geopolitical locations are more moderate than what has developed in the Middle East. However, the global interaction among the people of Muslim countries does not only introduce moderate Islam, but also militant ideas and practices as the resistance to the common enemy, namely the West.

With this in mind, this chapter attempts to explain the nature of Islam, its interaction with the West and its responses to the Western global economy and military as part of the triggering factors of how global resistance towards the West is expressed in the most inhumane form, such as terrorism. This is not to say that terrorism is acceptable in Islam and to Muslims. Terrorism is not Islamic at all and will never become part of the Islamic teaching.

Unity in Diversity

Although Muslims maintain that there is one divinely revealed and mandated Islam, there are many Muslim interpretations of Islam. There are two major branches of opinion about political and religious leadership after the death of Muhammad: Sunnis (85 percent of the World's Muslims) and Shi'is (15%). There are diverse school of theology, law and mystical tradition that includes many Sufi orders or brotherhoods. Islam represents a basic unity of beliefs within rich cultural diversity. Islam practices itself in different ways within a vast array of cultures that extend from North Africa to Southeast Asia, as well as Europe and America.

As a world religion, Islam is practiced in diverse cultures in Africa, the Middle East, Asia, Europe, and America. Differences in religious and cultural practices are therefore wide-raging. Like all faiths, Islam has developed divisions, sects, and school of thought over various issues. Islamic law provides one of the clearest and most important examples of diversities of opinion. While many law schools existed, only a few endured and were recognized as authoritative. While all Muslims share certain beliefs and practices, such as a belief in God, the Quran, Muhammad, and the Five Pillars of Islam, divisions have arisen over questions of political and religious leadership, theology, interpretations of Islamic law, and responses to modernity and the West.

Perhaps nowhere are differences in Islam more visible than in responses to modernity. Since the nineteenth century, Muslims have struggled with the relationship of their religious tradition developed in pre-modern time to the new demands of the modern world (viz. religious, political, economic, and social demands). The issues are not only about Islam's accommodation to change but also about the relationship of Islam to the West, since much of modern change is associated with Western ideas, institutions, and values. Muslim responses to the issues of reform and modernization have spanned the spectrum from secularists and Islamic modernists to religious conservatives or traditionalists, "fundamentalists", and Islamic reformists. The other groups are more "Islamically" oriented but have different opinions as to the role Islam should play in public life.

Islam and the West

The highest tide of Islamic culture, 800-1100A.D., was coincident with the lowest ebb of European culture. While the Muslims enjoyed general standards of living equal to, if not surpassing those of the proceeding Graeco-Roman civilization, the Europeans were living in the semi-barbarous squalor and restricted regime of feudalism – a pattern unalleviated by comforts and luxuries. One of the strangest dramas of history is that at the very moment when Europe, prodded by contacts with the Islamic culture in Sicily and Spain and by the Crusades, began to recover from its prolonged descent towards darkness, Islam entered a decline that was to carry it down into the very fog of obscurantism from which it had helped to rescue Europe. "The spirit" of Islamic civilization developed more rapidly in the West synergized by the philosophy of capitalism in economy and secularism in the politics. Both capitalism and secularism supported by sciences, technology and the military had created the Superpower State, especially after the Cold War.

The Islamic civilization has a significant contribution to drive the Enlightenment in the West and the modern world. The immenseness of the Arab-Islam contribution can best realized by recapitulating the most significant of her activities, considering at the same time their impact to a Europe struggling upward through the barbarism of the Dark Ages. The Arabic-Islamic science and technology, reaching Europe via Sicily and Spain, awoke her from the Dark Ages in which she was slumbering. The detailed elaboration of the actual routes by which this transference took place have only recently been outlined by historians. A hundred years ago a statement of the full influence of the Arabic culture on Europe would have been incredible. But modern research has firmly established its incontestability.

The principles of Western political systems typically are democracy and the rule of law. Together democracy and the rule of law save people from arbitrary whims of dictators and tyrants, and make all people politically equal. Democracy was pioneered by ancient Athens. The rule of law is to a great degree a product of Islam. Democracy in the words of Abraham Lincoln is similar to the syura' in the Islamic concept derived from the Quran by Fuqaha. The West learned the scientific method from Islam and has used that method to develop, amongst many other things, technologies for communication that have shrunk the world. The global civilization may be regarded as the joint legacy of Islam and the West.

The three most influential thinkers of the Western civilization represented the three Abrahamic faiths: Ibn Rusyd (Averroes) the Muslim, Maimonides the Jew, and Thomas Aquinas the Christian. Rationalism initiated the new modern world and ignited the secularism that only takes the Christian's ethic; meanwhile, ethics are a changeable point of view on what is good or bad. Conceptually, Islam and the West were born within the tradition of monotheistic religion, - Jews and Christianity - referred to the Abrahamic faith. In the spheres of politics and economics Islam and the West are often in conflict, where as in knowledge and ideas they are often in harmony. When there is a rivalry between Islam and the West (Christianity) or between capitalism and Islam, one of the solutions is military power and war. Therefore, there is a significant relationship between the economy and politics on one side and belief and religion on the other.

The only super power State nowadays is the United States (U.S.) that has become the "World Cop" who always monitors and unashamedly forces the other State or States to be under its control. This condition is globalization or hegemony. The Western world as a whole previously clashed with other civilizations long before the Cold War of Ideology. Firstly, there was genocide against the native ancient civilization of the Americans. Secondly, there was later enslavement of millions of Africans for use in the so-called New World. Thirdly, there was the phase of European imperialism and colonialization of most of the world. Is the fourth phase the United States as an imperial superpower?

America has now become a new form of empire, controlling millions of people through a variety of inducements and intimidations. In addition, the global development that began after the Cold War left a vacuum from the influence of the two Super Powers or West and East Block represented by the USSR and the U.S. This area is well-known as the Middle East. The victory of the West pioneered by the USA, soon followed by founding the Israel State in the middle of the Middle East countries. The State, in the eyes of the world, inflicts injustice on the Palestinians. Muslims around the world consider the invasion of the Palestinian land as the core problem that creates the rebellion of the oppressed people (Palestinians) by the powerful and unjust state institution and government (Israel). Such rebellion is called "terrorism".

War on Terrorism

The lack of information and deeper misunderstanding of Islam may lead some to think that the war on terrorism is a war on Islam. That's why most Americans and Europeans think of Muslims as strange, foreign, and frightening, inevitably linked to headlines of terrorist events. This is not true since the war on terrorism is not a war on Islam. Islam and Islamic law have consistently condemned terrorism (the killing of non-combatants). Like the members of all religious faiths, Muslims have had to deal with religious extremism and terrorism from their earliest days.

The responses of the mainstream majority to groups like the Kharijites and the Assassins and more contemporary groups like Islamic Jihad in Egypt or al-Qaeda have been to condemn, combat, and marginalize them. From the origins, the Islamic community faced rebellion and civil wars, violence and terrorism, epitomized by groups like the Kharijites and Assassins. The Kharijites were a pious but puritanical and militant extremist group that broke with the Calip Ali and later assassinated him.

The Assassins lived apart in secret communities from which they were guided by a series of Grand Masters, who ruled from the mountain fortress of Alamut in northern

Persia. The Assassins' jihad against the Seljuk Dynasty terrorized the princes, generals, and ulama (scholars), whom they murdered in the name of the Hidden Imam. They struck such terror in the hearts of their Muslim and Crusader enemies that their exploits in Persia and Syria earned them a name and memory in history long after they were overrun and the Mongols executed their last Grand Master in 1256.

The response of Sunni Islam and Islamic law was to marginalize extremist and develop a political theory that emphasized stability over chaos and anarchy. This, of course, did not dissuade all from the extremist path. In more recent decades, alongside mainstream Islamic political opposition, terrorist groups have risen up to challenge the regime and terrorize their populations and attack foreign interests. Often they portray themselves as the "true believers" struggling against repressive regimes and in the midst of a "pagan" society of unbelief.

They attempt to impose their ideological brand of Islam and "hijack" Islamic doctrines such as jihad, claiming to be defending true Islam, to legitimate their illegitimate use of violence and acts of terrorism. In Egypt, groups like Egypt's Islamic Jihad and other extremist groups assassinated President Anwar Sadat and government officials, slaughtered tourists in Luxor, burned churches, and killed Christians. In Algeria, the Armed Islamic Group has engaged in a campaign of terror against the Algerian government. Osama bin Laden and al-Qaeda undertook a global war of terror against Muslim governments and America, distorting Islam and countering Islamic law in issuing their own fatwas (legal opinions) in an attempt to legitimate their war and call for an attack on civilians (non-combatants).

The Suicide Bombing in Jakarta, Bali and Poso by Indonesians terrorists under their commander of Malaysian citizenship "the late Dr. Azahari" and his close companion and successor Nordin Top. They have distorted the true Islam and seemed to endorse the mistaken view so common in the West that Islam is essentially a fanatical and violent faith. Terrorism has multiple faces and may be hiding under the name of a religion, philosophy, politics, or any other name. Terrorism is a way of life. It may be a part of the history of human civilization and culture. Defining terrorism is most important in order not to be changeable between "terrorism" and "the warrior of freedom".

The scholars have their own definition of terrorism based on their point of view and field, or they define it as the ruler's outlook. Anyway, how divers those definitions, but the might is the rulers' definition who enforce their definition to be accepted by the people either using military, political, economic, technology or cultural power. Terrorism may be derived from religious doctrine or motivated by any other beliefs. Terrorism may be come to the true when the terrorists regard themselves as the victim of a repressive and hypocritical regime that never takes care of them, for instance: the IRA, EPTA, and some groups of terrorists in Latin Ame-rica, and the intifada movement of the Palestinians.

The beginning of the terrorist's movement seems to be Hassan Bin Sabbah (1057 AD), the leader of the impressive movement in the Middle East, Hashashiyyin or Assassins as mentioned above. Meanwhile, Maximilien Robespierre of France was the father of modern terrorism, as claimed by the scholars. Vladimir Lenin (b.1870-1924) is the modern terrorist. His ideas and theories of terrorism are followed by his successor as Vladimir Lenin said. Joseph Stalin (d. 1953) is the master executive of terror. Furthermore, the greatest terrorist of the East was Mao Tse-Tung. Mao led a world class of terror. Mao believed that the government needed to be a dictatorship to remain in control; using terrorism as a means to oppress the people to obey all the governments will.

Mao modernized terrorism and made it more effective, more powerful and more horrific than before. America has been described as "conceived and born in violence". Noam Chomsky has stated that the USA is a rich and powerful country that practices international terrorism on smaller States. Noam Chomsky stated that Osama bin Laden has caused the USA to bomb poor countries, such as Afghanistan. Osama bin Laden is the creation of the U.S. For Kuwait, the U.S. is the savoir and the defender against Saddam' aggression.

For Egypt, the U.S. is the donor of millions of dollars in order to take Egypt out of alignment with countries against Israel. For Saddam Hussein, the U.S. is the big enemy who removed him from his crown.

For many countries of the world, the U.S. is a never ending Superpower State. There is no state in history that has made more progress in economics, the military, science, technology and politics, than the U.S. In both good and bad, the U.S. is an incomparable State. Globalization or hegemony is a new phase of the U.S. as an imperial having global power, including economic power and power over, information such as the internet. After the Cold War, the U.S. was the winner. Recently this State successfully brought freedom and democracy for peace. The U.S. seems to pull the rest of the world to follow its system. Unfortunately, the U.S. is trapped in imperializing other States. It represented the Jew-Christian ethic that created the capitalist system in economics and secularism system in politics. Anti-Americanism (along with anti-Europeanism) is a broad based phenomenon that cuts across Arab and Muslim societies. It is driven not only by blind hatred of religious zealotry of extremists but also by frustration and anger with U.S. foreign policy among the mainstream in the Muslim world. The West's espousal of self-determina-tion, democratization and human rights is often seen as a hypocritical "double standard" when compared to its policies, what is actually does – for instance, imposing sanctions upon Pakistan for its development of nuclear weapons while failing to press Israel and India on their nuclear development.

The moral is so evident in America's helping Kosovo is seen by many Muslims totally absent in the U.S. policy of the Muslim community refers to the misconception and misinterpretation of the jihad as the Quran's command. Jihad (to strive or struggle) is sometimes referred to as the Sixth Pillar of Islam.

The Quranic teaching of jihad have been of essential significance of Muslim self-understanding, piety, mobilization, expansion, and defence. Jihad as struggle pertains to the difficulty and complexity of living a good life; struggling against the evil in oneself-to be virtuous and moral, making a serious effort to do good works and to help to reform society. Depending on the circumstances which one lives, it also can mean fighting injustice and oppression, spreading and defending Islam, and creating a just society through preaching, teaching, and if necessary, armed struggle or holy war. The two broad meanings of jihad, non-violent and violent, are contrasted in a well-known Prophetic tradition. It's said that when Muhammad returned from battle he told his followers: "We return from the lesser jihad (warfare) to the greater jihad".

The greater jihad is the more difficult and more important struggle against one's ego, selfness, greed, and evil. Jihad is a concept with multiple meanings, used and abused throughout Islamic history. Although jihad has always been an important part of the Islamic tradition, in recent years some have maintained that it is a universal religious obligation for all true Muslims to join the jihad to promote Islamic reform or revolution. Some look around them and see a world dominated by corrupt authoritarian regimes and a wealthy elite minority concerned solely with its own economic prosperity and awash in Western culture and values. Western governments are perceived as propping up oppressive regimes and exploiting the region's human and natural resources, robbing Muslims of their culture and their option to be governed according to their own choice and to live in a more just society.

Better understanding and a comprehensive study of Islamic teaching in respect of relations between Islam and the West, both by Muslims and the others (Westerners) will eliminate the misconception of a jihad in one side; and misconception of Islam and the Muslims in the other one. Understanding Islam and Muslim peoples will be one of eliminating terrorism. But the most importance is how Muslims all over the world have a good understanding of how the Prophet explained what really jihad is. Jihad is not "holy war", but "struggle" and "effort". This is a very important religious principle. The term jihad reminds all Muslims that Islam as a religion (al-din) is never something achieved or finished. The revelation is given, but those who follow it have to make an effort, day by day, year after year, to put it into practice in a flawed and tragic world.

Islam Post 9/11

Within hours of the planes hurtling into the World Trade Center of New York and Pentagon on 9/11, Americans were crying out in anguish: "Why do they hate us"? The question was echoed throughout Europe, since no doubt the attack was directed not just at America, but at the whole of Western civilization. However, the tragic events of 9/11 and the fear and paranoia they have generated have set Muslims back. America before 9/11 was on the verge of accepting Islam as one of it own, but after the attack of 911 it has paused to once again reassess Islam and Muslims. What happened on 9/11 and afterward has had significant and mostly negative consequences for the Muslim communities in Europe, and has set back the process of mutual accommodation between Muslims and European populations and the integration of both Islam and Muslims into Europe's social, cultural and political landscape.

In the aftermath of 9/11, people of goodwill on both sides of the divide between the Judeo-Christian and Muslim worlds were filled with deep anxieties. For Westerners, it seemed that a dreadful clash of civilizations had become imminent and unavoidable. For Muslims, it was clear that serious injury had been done to the most powerful nation on earth – a wound that could only call for terrible retaliation. Many Jews and Christians seized on the belief that something feral and evil in the faith of Muhammad had made 9/11 inevitable.

Many Muslims feared that a new "crusade" against Islam would ensue, expressing deeply ingrained impulses in the West. Indonesia has the biggest Muslim population in the world. Some Western educated or Western civilized leaders (Prime Ministers or Presidents) regarded Indonesia as a heaven and paradise for terrorists.

They saw Baasyir as an example of the Indonesian terrorist and that this was proven by some of the Islamic doctrines taught at Pondok Pesantren Ngruki where Baasyir typically teaches his students. The popular words of wisdom among the Santri that says "be alive honourable or die as a martyr" are regarded by Westerners as the doctrine of Islamic extremism and terrorism.

Meanwhile, the well-known words of wisdom among Indonesian Muslims are just a motivation of achievement and teach the students how to live in dignity. This prejudice was supported by the fact that some actors involved in suicide bombings were the alumni of Pesantren or Islamic institutions. Suicide bombing was introduced as a new type of warfare in the Palestinian-Israeli conflict as a response to the brutal aggression by the Israelis.

On February 25, 1994, Dr. Baruch Goldstein, a Jewish settler who emigrated to Israel from the United States, walked into the Mosque of the Patriach in Hebron and opened fire, killing twenty-nine Muslim worshipers during their Friday congregational prayer. In response, Hamas (Islamic Resistance Movement) introduced suicide bombing promising swift revenge for the Hebron massacre.

The Hamas militia, the Qassem Brigade, undertook operations within Israel itself, in Galilee, Jerusalem, and Tel Aviv. In Israel-Palestine, the use of suicide bombing increased exponentially during the second (al-Aqsha) intifada (uprising), which began in September 2000? The most horrific example of suicide bombings or attacks was seen in the attacks of 911. Traditionally, Muslims are unconditionally forbidden to commit suicide, because only God has the right to take the life he has granted. There is only one verse that appears relevant to suicide in the Holy Quran, Q.

The Validity of the Approach

The purpose of study of culture in relation to human rights education and implementation is not "to legitimize such values on the basis of cultural continuity from the past as part of a specific way of life or culture." To regard such a study of culture as purely a legitimization exercise is to reduce it to a selection exercise, i.e. selecting quotes from important texts regarded as basic sources of a particular religion or any other cultural source.

This may be extended to selections from favorable episodes from history. Such an exercise belongs mostly to the propaganda sphere. The promotion and protection of human rights by way of implementation requires much more than propaganda.

Legal formulations of human rights (international as well as local) only constitute an initial stage in the achievement of these rights. The gap between law and its implementation needs to be bridged if human rights formulations are not to remain mere illusions. Bridging this gap is an exercise in social transformation and such transformation can only take place within a living cultural context, which needs to be addressed. The essence of the pursuit of human rights is to establish the dignity of the human being as the most central concern of society. This end cannot be pursued without at the same time making efforts to understand the indignities that are meted out to human beings in that society and the cultural forms by which such indignities are constantly reinforced. For such a purpose, what is required is not selective use of quotes from religious texts or other sources of culture. For example, to select quotes from Buddhist texts which are supportive of freedom of thought and expression or on the rights of women may be an interesting exercise but hardly enough to meet the needs for achieving a proper implementation of these rights. An example of the study of culture from a human rights perspective is the work of Dr. B.R. Ambedkar on the issue of untouchability and his promotion of the notions of equality and fraternity in the cultural context of Hindu India.

The fear that cultural studies may lead to complications is hardly a serious objection. All attempts to move from ignorance to understanding creates complications and this is especially so in such issues as implementation of human rights norms and standards. The search for uncomplicated means of modernization is not a new one. It is shared by leaders from differing political perspectives. Pol Pot believed in wiping out the past as a fundamental tenet of his modernization philosophy and experimented with it ruthlessly within the four years he was in power. This was his way of doing away with the cultural complications involved in dealing with local culture. A less sincere attempt in this direction was the cultural revolution of Chairman Mao.

The political perspective of avoiding cultural complications has been articulated most clearly in Singapore by Lee Kuan Yew and in Malaysia by Mahathir. It was particularly stressed that possible ethnic confrontations need to be avoided to achieve rapid modernization. The end result was either to restrict freedom of expression and human rights altogether as in the case of Singapore or to a very great degree as in the case of Malaysia. It is quite natural that for a country like Sri Lanka, which is bedeviled by ethnic violence, to admire a seemingly less complicated model of development. What is implied in such a proposition, however, is to accept an authoritarian model of development as a way out of ethnic conflict. In fact minority parties and many liberal intellectuals preferred a strong Head of State capable of settling ethnic issues as against a democratic government which was perceived as too weak to deal with the views of the majority on the ethnic issue.

In fact, authoritarianism of some sort was seen in Sri Lanka as a short cut to modernization from the late sixties. The "limited dictatorship", as advocated by Felix Dias Bandaranayake is well known. The attempt at a full authoritarianism was attempted by J.R. Jayawardene and Ranasinghe Premadasa, the first and second executive Presidents of Sri Lanka. Such authoritarianism was seen as an imperative for economic modernization of the country and received support from the powerful economic lobbies in the country and outside. Many intellectuals gave theoretical and moral support to this political venture.

This authoritarian model was less complicated in that it believed in the use of violence against dissenters and was expected to be able to carry out modernization rapidly. The resulting displacement of democracy is well documented. The ethnic issue grew into civil war and the country, instead of achieving modernization, descended to unprecedented chaos. This very chaos in turn can create a desire for simple methods of getting over such chaos and achieving some form of prosperity as some countries have achieved in Southeast Asia. However, the experience of the last two decades has distanced most people from the belief that such a result could be achieved through authoritarianism.

Modernization in the West was accompanied by a fundamental transformation of culture achieved through religious reformation. Perhaps this process contributed to the evolution of democracy and its accompanying modernization. Thus modernization in the West included the replacement of the feudal culture with a democratic culture. Such transformation was not an automatic process following economic modernization but a conscious process achieved by the critical examination of the cultural foundations of the feudal society in different countries. The feudal lords as well as the feudal clerics came under scrutiny as a part of this transformation.

In a country like Sri Lanka, is it possible to protect and promote human rights without a thorough scrutiny of society and culture? If one answers this affirmatively, then it is quite understandable to divorce human rights issues from issues relating to culture. However, the experience in Sri Lanka shows that despite increase in the number of legal enactments on human rights and quite a lot of programs for education on such rights, the country's human rights problems are increasing. There have not been significant improvements either in the civil or the economic rights spheres. Any serious attempt at promotion and protection of human rights must be accompanied by an effort to understand the root causes for the existence of such a situation.

A short examination of some of the basic human rights problems may be useful at this stage. Equality remains a basic issue that the Sri Lankan psyche does not easily accept despite the Constitutional recognition of the concept as a fundamental aspect of the legal system. Sri Lanka has a very deeply rooted caste system both among the Sinhalese as well as among the Tamils. To regard the Sinhala Buddhists who constitute over 69.30% of the population, as a homogenous community, is to overlook the deeply-rooted caste system that exists among the Buddhists even more than in non-Buddhist Sinhala communities. In India, Buddhism rose as a social movement that radically rejected and replaced the caste-entrenched Hinduism. Buddha went so far as to exhort the rejection of Hindu sacred texts (Shastras) as a part of radical rejection of caste.

Centuries afterwards it took a ruthless Hindu counter-revolution to oust Buddhism from India and to re-enforce a rigid caste system. However, when Buddhism was introduced to Sri Lanka and was accepted by the Royalty of the time it incorporated unto itself the existing caste hierarchy of the country. Later, even the organization of Sanga attained a caste character. This continues to the present. Thus in Sri Lanka Buddhism - the world's most egalitarian philosophy popularly regarded as a religion - lost its capacity to contain the concept of equality within its body of thought.

The opposite of original teaching - the caste system- was accommodated within itself. As a result, a deep religious barrier exists in the country reproducing discriminatory practices among the Sinhala Buddhists themselves. In provinces such as Kandy, Ratnapura and Matara, where the population is overwhelmingly Sinhala Buddhist caste-based discrimination exists to appalling degree. It is the caste character of Sinhalese that prevents the acceptance of the Tamils on an equal basis. A race that does not accept equality among themselves is not likely to accept equality with other races. Buddhism as is practiced in Sri Lanka has been psychically transformed to accept and justify caste and is unable to generate social energy to accept racial equality.

While some intellectuals have tried to create the notion called Sinhala Buddhism, as an important component on the contribution to anti-Tamil racism, they have failed to raise the issue of caste which deeply divides the Sinhalese. Lack of familiarity with equality as a human experience among the majority community itself is more responsible for the present ethnic crisis than any other factor. Caste discrimination exists in the Tamil community too. The caste system of Tamils in Sri Lanka is even more rigid than the Sinhala caste system. There have been many Tamil movements fighting for such rights attending to Kovils (Hindu Temples).

At the early phase of militant organizations of Tamils in the middle part of this century, their violence was directed towards "higher" castes of the Tamils themselves (this was so in southern rebellions of the South in 1971 and afterwards also). Perhaps the continuing violence in Tamil communities has leveled down caste barriers among the Tamils living in these areas. The study of cultural factors relating to lack of familiarity of the concept of equality in Sri Lankan culture can contribute greatly to understanding the present situation of the country and will help towards finding ways to cultivate a culture of equality.

A doctrinal basis for this exists in Buddhism as taught by Buddha, though the actual Buddhism as found in Sri Lanka has assimilated local caste prejudices. Another important human rights problem in the country is the general tolerance of violence. The use of torture by the police is endemic. Psychological forms of torture are so common that no one even cares to challenge them in a court of law. As far as law goes, the Constitution of Sri Lanka has incorporated the provisions of the International Covenant of Civil and Political Rights against torture and cruel and inhuman punishment. The Supreme Court of Sri Lanka has given several laudable judgments protecting these rights as absolute rights which know no limit.

However, torture and inhuman treatment remain quite an accepted cultural habit, so that anyone who has some connection with the police gets its support to punish their less influential opponents. During the times of instability, use of such violence reaches unimaginable proportions. In the South, such occasions were the periods around 1971 and 1988-1993. And in the Tamil areas it has continued from early 1980 up to date. The extra-judicial killings have now become quite a part of the stuff the Sri Lankan psyche has learned to put up with. There were a considerable number of such deaths in 1971 in the South and between 1988-92 the conservative estimate of such deaths is twelve thousand (NGOs have claimed the number to be sixty thousand.)

The bodies were exhibited on the roads and were thrown into rivers. The attempt to prosecute offenders is almost negligible. Even the horrific cases such as the killing of over thirty school children have not ended in the prosecution of all the suspects. While there have been protests, these have not been in proportion to the massive violations. An old psychic habit has asserted itself and there has been the willingness to adjust to the situation as if fearing that the pursuit of justice may lead to further trouble. Among the weaker sections of the population, tolerance of such violence may be a way of expressing their weakness. Among the socially strong it can be a way of asserting their power and authority.

In either case, promotion and protection of human rights implies understanding of such human behavior. Houtart analyzed the statistics of the participants in 1971 and claimed that there was a clear indication of a link between heavily discriminated castes and the participation in rebellion. After the rebellion, when thousands of youth surrendered answering a call of the government for amnesty, interviews were conducted to find the extent of each person's involvement. One question was about the caste of these persons. Belonging to a particular caste was regarded as prima facie evidence of possible participation in the rebellion. In the suppression in 1988-1993, some of the worst police violence was directed towards some "low" castes.

A further important human rights issue is the seeming indifference towards the weakest in society. This is a very important aspect in a country where over 40 percent of the people live below the poverty line. (It must be noted that the category below poverty line in a third world country like Sri Lanka is very different from a similar category in the first world where it is implied that poverty is relative poverty. In a third world context this means lack of basic food, shelter and clothing.) Still, most businesses including those providing professional services rely on the exploitation of the poorest.

In the agricultural sphere which is the largest economic sphere, the traders rely on the purchase of products below the cost price. Many attempts by the state and other agencies to regulate price mechanism have not been resolute enough to be successes. Suicides among peasantry are high. In fact, the suicide rate in the country ranks among the highest in the world. Recent published statistics showed 70,000, suicides from 1983 to 1997, a number higher than the accounted for deaths in ethnic warfare during the same period. Vast numbers of these suicides have taken place among the poorest. Those who have died in the ethnic war on both sides also, for most part, belong to poorest sections of society.

The professionals have a long-standing cultural habit of exploiting the ignorance and the backwardness of the poorest sections of society. A frank relationship where professionals inform their clients of the things that these clients have as a right to know is not yet a part of the local culture. While there is some improvement in the right to information as against the state, there is hardly any improvement in the area of scrutiny of professional behavior. Enforcement of the right to health implies scrutiny of practices of the medical profession: due process rights require an examination of the legal profession. The poor can have the benefit of such scrutiny only if the guardians of rights such as the press and the human rights community take a serious attempt.

The indifference to the poor is related to the caste-based character of the society where "lower caste" by definition are the socially weak. The social consciousness in Sri Lanka has been determined by the land distribution of the feudal society. The landless were dependent on the land owners, usually referred to as "Radalayas". Radalayas were arrogant and trampled on the people with impunity. The impunity of the "upper caste" and people who belonged to a higher status than those known as "Sananya Minissu" (ordinary people) is a deeply imbedded cultural concept. Recently, (June 1997), a senior judge who has been presiding over some serious human rights cases said," independence of judiciary in this country is a myth where even getting a warrant executed is impossible if the suspect does not happen to be a "Haramanis" (small person).

While legally no one is immune from prosecution, in reality, many are. Thus medieval conceptions still continue in the practical application of laws. Radalayas treated "Samanaya Minissu" with contempt and use of violence against such people was a common practice. One example is a criminal case which happened in the seventies in a town in the south called Akurassa. One Radala family occupied positions in town such as posts in town council and the cooperatives. One male youth, who was a son of a woman who worked for this family, joined the local communist party and at one cooperative meeting challenged the Radala master on some points.

Such a question was too much for this man to bear. He stabbed the young man to death with a huge knife and surrendered to the police with the knife in his hand. According to a close relative he never regretted this act. A farmer from Tabutthegama, Anuraddhapura summed up what human rights means to poor people in the country-side: "When the officer-in-charge of the police station shoots our cow and takes it to a party at his home, my mother prepares chillies and sends it through my father to the police officer's house. This is the way my father tells the officer that he bears no grudge for the police officer killing his cow. If the officer feels that there is some ill-will my father may face other problems."

The cruelty that "upper castes" have perpetrated in the past centuries on the "ordinary people" is immense. It may well be the psychic patterns of this behavior that gets repeated during times of disturbances by way of crude killings, humiliating forms of the disposal of bodies, and other forms of violence. Is it not the same psychic pattern that creates in the victims inhuman and cruel forms of revenge? With more people from "low castes" getting educated due to free education, resentment grew in rural "upper" castes and much violence developed on this basis. In the promotion and protection of human rights it is very necessary to study and understand the patterns of violations in the country.

The Sinhala language in its grammatical form still retains a distinction of addressing people on the basis of status. In the colloquial form such distinctions are expressed in even a more harsher manner. Another important area concerns rights to information and freedom of expression. Besides the limitations imposed by the state there are limitations which are culturally imposed. A close scrutiny of patterns of corruption and a pattern of violence is not generally pursued consistently. Even the pressure to expose the extra-judicial killings did not reach anywhere near to similar investigations in Argentina. To hide things under the carpet continues as a cultural habit. The cultural habit is re-imposed by the use of violence against those who break the taboo. This violence is often initiated privately.

Creating a human rights culture involves much more than legalistic approach. As against the Indian Marxists of the pre-independence period who ignored social and cultural aspects Dr. B.R. Ambedkar argued, "History bears out the proposition that political revolutions have always been preceded by social and religious revolutions." The sensitivity the conservative elements show against examination of religion from a religious point of view was demonstrated by the ex-communication of Fr. Tissa Balasuriya, a Sri Lankan priest, for his attempts to look into the rights of women from a theological point of view. The literature relating to this debate is a rich source on the issue of Religion, Culture and Human Rights.

Bibliography

Armstrong, Karen. *Islam: A Short History*. New York: Modern Library, revised ed., 2002.

Ali, Syed Ameer. *The Spirit of Islam: A History of the Evolution and Ideals of Islam,* with *a Life of the Prophet*. London: Chatto & Windus, 1978.

Bloom, Jonathan and Sheila Blair. *Islam: A Thousand Years of Faith and Power*. New Haven, CT: Yale University Press, 2002.

Booth, E. *Aristotelian Aporetic Ontology in Islamic and Christian Thinkers*. Cambridge, 1983.

Bowker, John. *What Muslims Believe*. Oxford, UK: Onewworld, 1999.

Burrell, D. *Freedom and Creation in Three Traditions*. Notre Dame, 1993.

Burrell, D. *Knowing the Unknowable God: Ibn Sina, Maimonides, Aquinas* (Notre Dame: 1986).

Cook, Michael. *The Koran: A Very Short Introduction*. Oxford, UK: Oxford University Press, 2000.

Corbin, H. *History of Islamic Philosophy*, trans. L. Sherrard. London, 1993.

Craig, E. (ed.), *Routledge Encyclopedia of Philosophy*. London, 1998.

Davidson, H.A. *Proofs for Eternity, Creation and the Existence of God in Medieval Islamic and Jewish Philosophy*. Oxford, 1987.

Elias, Jamal J. *Islam.* Upper Saddle River, NJ: Prentice Hall, 1999.

Fakhry, M. *A History of Islamic Philosophy* , 2nd ed. New York, 1983.

Gibb, Hamilton A.R. and J.H. Kramers, eds. *Shorter Encyclopedia of Islam.* Leiden: E.J. Brill, 1997 (reprint ed.).

Hodgson, Marshall G.S. *The Venture of Islam,* 3 Vols. Chicago, IL: University of Chicago Press, 1974.

Keller, Nuh Ha Mim, trans. *Al-Nawawi's Manual of Islam.* Cambridge, UK: The Islamic Texts Society, 1996.

Leaman, O. *An Introduction to Classical Islamic Philosophy.* Cambridge, 2002.

Marmura , M.E. (ed.), *Islamic Theology and Philosophy.* Albany, 1984.

Nasr, Seyyed Hossein. *The Heart of Islam: Enduring Values for Humanity.* San Francisco, CA, Harper San Francisco, 2002.

Newby, Gordon D. *A Concise Encyclopedia of Islam.* Oxford, UK, Oneworld, 2002.

Peters, F.E. *A Reader on Classical Islam.* Princeton, NJ: Princeton University Press, 1994.

Qadir , C.A. *Philosophy and Science in the Islamic World.* London, 1990.

Renard, John, ed. *Windows on the House of Islam: Muslim Sources on Spirituality.* Berkeley, CA: University of California Press, 1998.

Renard, John. *Seven Doors to Islam: Spirituality and the Religious Life of Muslims.* Berkeley, CA: University of California Press, 1996.

Ruthven, Malise. *Islam in the World*. New York: Oxford University Press, 2nd ed., 2000.

Schimmel, Annemarie. *Islam: An Introduction.* Albany, NY: State University of New York Press, 1992.

Schuon, Frithjof. *Islam and the Perennial Philosophy.* London: World of Islam Festival Publ. Co., 1976.

Sharif, M.M. *A History of Muslim Philosophy,* 2 vols. (Wiesbaden: 1963-6).

Stern, S.M. *Medieval Arabic and Hebrew Thought* , ed. F. Zimmermann, London, 1983.

Stern, S.M., Hourani, H. and Brown, V. (eds.), *Islamic Philosophy and the Classical Tradition.* Oxford, 1972.

Waines, David. *An Introduction to Islam.* Cambridge, UK: Cambridge University Press, 1995.

Watt, M.W. Islamic Philosophy and Theology. Edinburgh, 1962, revised ed. 1985.

Watt, William Montgomery. *The Formative Period of Islamic Thought.* Oxford, UK: Oneworld,1998.

Watt, William Montgomery. *What is Islam?* London: Longman, 1970.

Williams, John Alden, ed. *The Word of Islam.* Austin, TX: University of Texas Press, 1994.

Wolfson, H.A. *Studies in the History of Philosophy and Religion* , ed. I. Twersky, G.H. Williams, in 2 vols. Cambridge, MA, 1973, 1977.

Wolfson, H.A. *The Philosophy of the Kalam.* Cambridge, MA, 1976.

Ziai, H. "Islamic Philosophy," in *The Oxford Companion to Philosophy,* ed. T. Honderich. Oxford , 1955.

Index